Little Children, Big Needs

Little Children, Big Needs

*Parents Discuss Raising Young Children
With Exceptional Needs*

Don Weinhouse, Ph.D., *and*
Marilyn Morse Weinhouse, M.A.

University Press of Colorado

Copyright © 1994 by the University Press of Colorado

Published by the University Press of Colorado
P.O. Box 849, Niwot, Colorado 80544

The University Press of Colorado is a cooperative publishing enter-
prise supported, in part, by Adams State College, Colorado State University, Fort Lewis College, Mesa State College, Metropolitan State
College of Denver, University of Colorado, University of Northern
Colorado, University of Southern Colorado, and Western State College of Colorado.

Library of Congress Cataloging-in-Publication Data

Weinhouse, Don, 1947–
    Little children, big needs: parents discuss raising young children
  with exceptional needs / Don Weinhouse and Marilyn Morse Weinhouse.
        p.   cm.
    ISBN 0-87081-324-2 (alk. paper); ISBN 0-87081-338-2 (pbk., alk.
  paper)
    1. Parents of handicapped children — United States — Psychol-
  ogy. 2. Handicapped children — Services for — United States. I.
  Weinhouse, Marilyn Morse, 1950– . II. Title.
  HQ759.913.W44 1993
  649'.151 — dc20   93-48760
                                                              CIP

The paper used in this publication meets the minimum requirements
of the American National Standard for Information Sciences—Perma-
nence of Paper for Printed Library Materials. ANSI Z39.48–1984

∞

10 9 8 7 6 5 4 3

This book is dedicated to the fifty families whose stories are told in the following pages. Our deepest thanks for sharing your experiences so that others might learn and grow. May the many challenges you have lived with and are yet to face bring strength and richness to your lives, and may your children blossom into everything they can be.

Contents

Contents

Preface

The quotations and stories in this book were derived from interviews with the parents of fifty children representing a wide range of disabilities. These disabilities include cerebral palsy, Down's syndrome, health impairments, developmental delays, emotional disturbances, autism, hearing and visual impairments, speech and language delays, possible learning disabilities, hydrocephalus, microcephalus, spina bifida, and at-risk prematurity. At the time of the interviews, the average age of the children was 3½ years, with a range from 2 months to 6½ years.

We conducted the interviews in the children's homes, all of which are located in Wisconsin. At the time we spoke to the parents, thirty-eight of the fifty marriages were still intact, and from those thirty-eight couples, twenty-two fathers participated in the interviews. We started out from a basic questionnaire, then allowed the discussion to branch off into other topics, recording everything on audiotape that we later transcribed into more than 900 pages of text.

We have made an effort to allow the parents to speak for themselves, with a minimum of interpretation or explanation. Although some generalizations may be drawn from the experiences they describe, this text is not presented as a research study. The quotations are from people discussing their own experiences and feelings. Other parents may have had similar experiences and feelings, but readers should beware of overgeneralizing.

This book is not meant to be a comprehensive review of the subject. It is meant to provide readers with some insights into the lives of fifty families who are doing the best they can.

Don Weinhouse
Marilyn Morse Weinhouse

Little Children, Big Needs

1

In the Beginning: Pregnancy, Birth, and Early Infancy

Pregnancy is usually a time of excitement and abundant expectations, a time when family and friends prepare for the arrival of a healthy, beautiful baby who will bring more love and joy into their lives.

The first environment this new life has is the mother's womb. Many pregnant women make great efforts to become suitable "homes" for their growing fetuses. They try to minimize pressures and anxieties, refrain from taking on new responsibilities, be as peaceful and relaxed as possible, eat a balanced and nutritious diet, and avoid habits such as smoking, drinking, and drugs that might interfere with healthy fetal development. Although not all women follow through with all of these resolutions, the vast majority enter this period with good intentions.

And then comes the birth. The expectation is that the few — with luck very few — hours of pain will culminate in the emergence of a healthy, whole child, who will be placed on the mother's tummy, held, caressed, loved, and soon thereafter accompany the proud mother and father home.

One of the many ironies of life is that this pregnancy-birth process does not always progress as expected. Although most infants are born healthy, without any identifiable diseases or disabilities, some enter life challenged with significant exceptional needs — as little children with big needs. What happens when a birth is accompanied by complications or difficulties, and the newborn child requires immediate and perhaps ongoing medical attention or other interventions?

Question:
Why me? I did everything my doctors and the books told me to do. Why did this happen to me?

Answer:

Most parents of children with disabilities never know for sure what caused their child's special needs.

Professionals can sometimes pinpoint the cause of a disability, but far more often than not the cause remains forever unknown or at least uncertain. Quite often there is no one, specific cause but a combination of factors that leads to certain conditions — a combination of a child's genetic makeup and the environment, including the mother's womb.

This frustrating truth leads many parents on a quest to find *the* reason to explain their child's exceptional needs; they hope that if the single reason is found, a "cure" will be available or, at the very least, that the wondering, self-doubt, and suspicions will end. When the cause is unknown, many parents become engulfed in a web of uncertainty and self-doubt that evokes memories of past events and analyses of any and all out-of-the-ordinary occurrences that may have taken place during their child's early development.

Ruth, a single mother raising three children, typifies this pattern in her search for an explanation for why her third child is developing so slowly. Christian is a cheerful, attractive, social little 2½-year-old with severe limitations in vision and hearing (doctors and other professionals have not settled on a diagnosis or classification but at various times have referred to Christian as developmentally delayed, multiply handicapped, blind-deaf, and mentally retarded).

Ruth: When I was almost nine months pregnant with him, my girl-friend took me grocery shopping. I was walking down an aisle and I slipped on a wet spot on the floor. I went flying — wham! — and landed right smack on my bottom. My rear end was a little sore, but I felt fine. After resting for a few minutes, we left the store. Except for a sore knee — from the fall — I felt fine.

When I got home everybody kept saying, "Call the doctor, just tell him about it." I didn't want to make a big deal out of it, but I did. The doctor heard the story and yelled, "Girl, you get down to the hospital right now. I want to see you there in thirty minutes!" So I went down and they took an X-ray and checked me out. My knee was a little sprained, but they said the baby was fine.

> I had false labor two days after that. I had never had false labor with the other two pregnancies. I have asked since if that fall could have had anything to do with Christian's being so slow in learning and doing everything, but they [the doctors] always say no. I don't know, though. I think about it a lot. It always comes back to me because it's, like, one of the only things I can point at and say, "Hey, maybe that's the reason. Maybe it was the fall."
>
> It doesn't seem right to have a child with all the problems that he has and not know why. If I just knew why, I think I could accept it better and just put all of these thoughts aside, but I keep thinking about it and wondering. I ask myself everyday, and everyday I end up with "Why me?" I don't know if it was the fall or God's will or the delivery. I just know that something went wrong somewhere.

The frustration of not knowing why is often overwhelming. The ability to relate causes with effects makes life seem more rational, more orderly. It allows individuals to feel more powerful and in control. When causes can't be identified to account for events, the world tends to appear less organized, understandable, and controllable. One person we spoke to summarized the majority opinion on the subject of searching for causes:

> After a certain point, after you've eliminated all the medical conditions and possibilities that might have quick fixes, the circumstances where a cure or a medicine or some kind of procedure is specific for what your kid has, it's sort of crazy to keep searching and wondering what caused it. You really have to get past that and get on with life.

Question:
We had testing done when I was pregnant, so we knew our child was going to have some special needs, but we didn't know what to do about it. When you know your child isn't going to be normal, how do you decide what to do?

Answer:
This is a moral, personal decision that parents must make. The key ingredients are (1) gathering as much information as you can, and (2) sharing thoughts and concerns with your partner.

Medical technology has advanced to the point where a number of biochemical, chromosomal, and spinal abnormalities can be identified in the early stages of pregnancy; however, technology cannot tell parents what to do with that information. Do they allow the pregnancy to continue, knowing that their child may be retarded or crippled? Do they opt for an abortion, ending the life of a tiny person who might possibly have had only mild disabilities? Hopefully, these decisions will be based on as much reliable information as can possibly be gathered, as well as open communication of thoughts and feelings among family members.

Rusty's story provides an interesting perspective from which to view this much-discussed issue. Rusty is a cute, playful, funny 5½-year-old child who has a variety of severely disabling conditions. His parents, Patty and Ben, are presently separated, but they agreed to be interviewed together. Rusty has just moved to a residential group home, where he will live until Patty and Ben decide how to reorganize their lives.

Patty: Rusty's got a profound hearing loss, seizures, mental retardation — to what degree we don't know — he's hydrocephalic [a condition in which spinal fluid seeps into the brain and causes varying degrees and types of damage], shunted [a tube must drain excess fluid from the brain], and has cerebral palsy.

The pregnancy went fine up until the fifth month, when I had an ultrasound test — they actually look inside you with this ultrasound machine thing and take pictures of the fetus. You can even watch and see the tiny little baby moving around inside of you. Then it was discovered that he had hydrocephalus.

You've really got to learn a lot fast when something like this happens, or you're just letting the doctors make the decisions for you. So we started reading and calling around and trying to pick up as much information as we could from the start. My obstetrician made recommendations, but we also put a lot of effort into figuring out what was going on and finding specialists to consult.

We went down to City Hospital and consulted with this one doctor who came real highly recommended. He's a specialist in intrauterine shunts [the procedure is carried out on the fetus's brain while the baby is still in the womb].

The first shunt that was put in relieved the pressure off the brain and seemed to be working OK. Two weeks later I went for another ultrasound and they found that the shunt wasn't working, so they put in another one, and while they were doing that they discovered that there had been a brain bleed, probably from the first shunt. It was like his head or his brain was hemorrhaging inside. We went back two weeks later to have another ultrasound and learned that the second shunt wasn't functioning. His head was growing again. I guess you know that if you don't shunt them and get that extra fluid out, the head gets bigger and bigger and creates more and more brain damage. You can actually see it when you look at the ultrasound pictures. You can see the head grown all out of proportion. So then three weeks later they did a test and found out that the first shunt that they placed had fallen out and the second one had clotted from the blood.

Through all of this we're just wondering, "My God, what is this kid going to be like? What's going to be left in his brain that hasn't been damaged?" You see, there was no way of knowing exactly how much damage there would be, but they were pretty sure that it was going to be major.

You just don't know, though. We've met lots of parents of kids with hydrocephalus who were told their kids were going to be severely retarded, but the kids turned out with only minor, mild stuff. The same thing goes for Down's syndrome. We've met lots of those parents, too, and many were told before their child was born that they'd be severely retarded, and the parents should have an abortion or put the kid in an institution after they're born, but then their kids turned out to be only mildly retarded, with lots going for them.

If I would have found out about the hydrocephalus within abortion limits I would probably have had an abortion, but I was one week over the time limit for a standard type, so we didn't really consider it.

Ben: You can't really say that you would have had one. We would have had to talk about it quite a bit. We might have. We've discussed this a lot over the past few years, and it's pretty interesting. While this was all going on, with the shunts and brain bleeds and hospitals and stuff, we did a great job of doing our homework, you know, learning all about hydrocephalus and all the medical stuff, but we never really discussed our feelings or fears all that much. We both thought about abortion but never really discussed it. I think if we had brought the issue out in the open rather than hold our fears and thoughts in as much as we had, it might have happened. I don't know.

Patty: Maybe, but I don't think so. But you're right. We both thought about it but didn't communicate it much to each other. I think parents who are going through something like this need to talk about their fears and ideas and feelings as much as they can because sometimes, when you hold stuff in, you block off a lot of your options, a lot of your choices.

Ben: Anyway, even though we were over the limit for a standard abortion, one of the doctors at the hospital was perfectly willing to kill "it" — he called Rusty "it" — upon delivery. Even if he was born alive, even if we let it go full term, he was perfectly willing to kill him — "terminate the pregnancy." He could "terminate the pregnancy" for us. I couldn't believe it when he said that. He's saying, "terminate the pregnancy," and I got this echolike thing in my head saying, "Kill my baby, kill my baby, kill my baby . . ."

Patty: I think one reason we reacted so negatively then was because we were both blocking off those thoughts — not expressing them — because the idea was too painful, too terrible. If we had talked more, shared more, it wouldn't have been so shocking to hear him bring it up.

         Sorry to repeat myself, but it's real important for parents to know that you really need to get all the information you can to help you make decisions, and then you need to discuss it. You need to sit down together and discuss the choices and your feelings — bounce it off each other. If you don't do that you might end up not having choices, or making decisions that you might not have, because you kept something inside too long.

Although most people allow their minds the freedom to envision different, unpleasant events and life choices and become only mildly or moderately upset with the pictures, the same thoughts or pictures suggested by someone else may be far more distressing. One may casually use the phrase *terminating the pregnancy* and imagine a clean, neat, rather minor medical procedure; however, the receiver of the communication may hear "kill my baby" and see a far more disturbing, unpleasant picture and experience the deep, moving loss of a loved one.

Once again, the decision about what to do with information must be made by the parents. The final decision is a moral one and open to individual choice, yet the steps leading to the decision are clear and require parents to gain as much information as possible from a variety of sources and then share their thoughts, feelings, and fears — communicate.

Question:
It seems like there are a lot of people in my family who have had problem pregnancies and something wrong with their kids. Can problems run in families?

Answer:
Yes. Although most difficulties that arise during pregnancy, as well as special needs that occur in early childhood, are not repeated within families, it is not uncommon for a woman who has one problem pregnancy to have another, and in some families subtle and not-so-subtle environmental and/or genetic factors exist that lead to exceptional needs' being repeated, child after child.

The good news is that most difficulties that arise during pregnancy, as well as special needs that occur in early childhood, do not recur within families; the bad news is that such repetition can happen. Most notably, severe hearing impairments often are genetic; a number of emotional disorders, such as manic-depressive (bipolar syndrome), have been linked to inherited chemical imbalances; learning disabilities tend to run in families, particularly in males; premature births (which in themselves are not a disability but put children at risk of suffering related disabilities) can be the result of poor prenatal care; and children born into poverty to a mother who is mentally retarded have a higher likelihood of being mildly mentally retarded.

Ellen, a single mom with three children under the age of 5, all of whom receive special education services for a variety of mild to moderate delays (cognitive/thinking, speech and language, large and small muscle coordination, psychological), tells about her children and pregnancies:

Ellen: I have three kids. There's Sara — she's 18 months old and has speech and language delays, can't roll over, and can't stand up or walk yet. She wears special orthopedic shoes because her feet turn out. There's Jackie — she's 3½ and has crossed eyes and is delayed in speech and language. And there's John, my biggest problem. He's 4½. His speech and language are real low, real poor, and he's got real behavior and emotional problems. His father abused him from the time he started walking and getting around. John gets really violent sometimes, and I just can't control him or take my eyes off him for a minute.

I had a hard time carrying all three of them. I was high-risk pregnancy on all three, like I had lots of different kinds of troubles that could have caused problems for their developing.

That's the way it is in my family. It seems that lots of us have had hard times carrying babies, and lots of my cousins and relatives have turned out with problems — usually not serious, like John, but different kinds of problems, mostly with speech and language and in school — learning and stuff.

My doctors said a lot of my problems with the births were because I didn't take care of myself and I did too much, but it seems like even when I did what they'd tell me to do I'd still have problems, so I figured, "What's the difference?"

All pregnant women need to pay particular attention to their health and well-being prior to and during pregnancy; however, when a woman has a history such as Ellen's — a history of difficult pregnancies and parenting children with disabilities — it is critical that they make every effort to change their diet and lifestyle, as well as seek professional medical care, as early as possible. Although certain problems may be unavoidable, many can be averted or minimized with lifestyle changes and proper medical care. It is also critical that parents who are at increased risk of delivering prematurely or having a child with any type of disability (e.g., parents who themselves are retarded, drug or alcohol dependent, learning disabled, anorexic, and so on) be aware of their own risk factors and any possible alternatives and interventions that are available.

Much of the foundation for the person we are to become is built prior to our leaving the delivery room. Our genetic makeup and prenatal (from conception to the beginning of labor) and perinatal (during the birth process) experiences play a critical role in determining whether we will someday be star athletes or chronic invalids, scholars or profoundly retarded individuals, psychologically intact beings or autistic-schizophrenics. Although experiences that occur postnatally (after birth) are also important, they usually do not possess the potential for quite such dramatic effects. This cause-effect relationship is clearly demonstrated by statistics that reveal that genetics and prenatal and perinatal experiences are the primary causes of severe and profound disabilities, whereas later life experiences, such as being raised in an unstimulating environment, poor nutrition, abuse, and neglect, most often have less serious effects and are the primary causes of mild and moderate disabilities.

The significant contribution of experiences prior to birth is effectively summed up by a neonatal intensive care nurse:

Nurse: It really bothers me when people talk about or refer to "zero," like zero to 1, or zero to 3 years old. I mean, *zero* implies nothing; it implies the beginning, the start. I meet children when they are "zero," but, believe me, they are not "zeros." They are incredibly developed, complex, functioning life forms.

I prefer the term *birth*, birth to 1 year old or birth to 3 years old. Birth is a point or time in life but by no means the beginning or start of life. Using *birth* rather than *zero* gives more credit to what has already occurred, to the fabulously rich and dynamic process of fertilization, growth, and development prior to that first independent breath of air.

Do me a favor, please: next time you hear someone refer to infancy as zero to x months or years, please correct them or remind them that infancy is not the beginning and that newborns are not "zeros."

Pregnancy and early infancy are such critical periods that proper medical attention and lifestyle adaptations are a must, especially for mothers with individual or family histories of difficult pregnancies, births, or exceptional needs.

Question:

My marriage and life are a mess, and now I'm pregnant. I want to get out of my marriage, but I'm afraid to make any big changes now. What should I do?

Answer:

Assuming that you've tried everything in your power to make the relationship work, it's strongly recommended that you consult with trusted friends and family members and construct a plan before you end the relationship.

The answer to this question depends on two critical ingredients: (1) Have you done everything possible to make the relationship work? and (2) Is it reasonable to expect things to be better if you do end the relationship?

Many partners are ready to separate or divorce at the first sign of trouble. Have you and your husband discussed your problems and tried to work things out? Have you considered or pursued marriage counseling? If the answers to these questions are no, you may want to think about putting some more effort into making it work. If the answers are yes and the situation is still unacceptable, it may be time to move to the second step.

Although pregnant women should make every attempt to avoid placing themselves into stressful situations — such as ending a relationship — sometimes decisions like this cannot be avoided. If you can create a reasonable, somewhat positive visual image of yourself proceeding through the pregnancy, birth, and infancy of your child without your partner, then this may be your best choice. One first step would be to discuss the issue with trusted friends and family members. Another important step is to make a plan before committing yourself to a decision.

Both of these steps are well illustrated in the following biography. Brenda was overjoyed to learn that she had become pregnant. She already had one son, and the thought of a second child made her feel "like things were going to turn around for me, like it was gonna make everything right." She had no reason to suspect that her second child would be born prematurely with a number of life-threatening medical conditions.

Brenda: My husband and I didn't get along. I thought he'd be happy when he heard I was pregnant. Like, maybe it would make a difference, maybe it would help. Boy, was I wrong. He was pissed. Things went from bad to worse. And believe me, they started off pretty bad.

You think of pregnant women getting treated real well, like in the movies, where the husband runs out in his pajamas to buy the wife chop suey and strawberries. What a joke! All I got was yelled at, threatened, and pushed around. It was like I did this terrible thing to him, like I deserved to be treated bad because I messed up and got pregnant. He was so angry and mean.

There was a lot stress and a lot of tension and a lot of bad things going on, and I didn't take good enough care of myself. There was just a lot of mental abuse and physical abuse. I'd try to talk to him about my feelings, but he'd just get mean and angry.

He wouldn't talk about it or go to counseling or do anything to improve the situation. He just thought everything was fine, like this was the way life and marriage were suppose to be. Ha!

Anyway, I was really messed up. I know I didn't eat right, like skipping lots of meals, eating junk and stuff. I didn't sleep right either. We had a lot of late nights, and I know I didn't get the rest I was supposed to. I didn't cut down on my smoking like I was supposed to; in fact, I think I increased because of the stress. The bigger I got and the more tired I got, the more I just hung out and ate junk, smoked, and argued. You'd think being pregnant would help you clean up your act, but with me, my bad habits seemed to just get worse. I sort of got nervous and just let myself go.

Sometimes I think I was trying to hurt myself. I mean my self-respect was so low that I just wanted to hurt myself. I know it was my fault, my doing it to myself, but my husband was part to blame, too. He'd just put me down every chance he had and hurt me and make me feel bad. Looking back, I should've gotten out of there — just left him — but I didn't have the confidence to do it. It just didn't seem like a reasonable choice.

I had Jimmy in the first week of my sixth month. As soon as he was born they rushed him to intensive care. He was only 12 inches and all scrunched up — a tiny little thing, no bigger than a football.

Jimmy spent ninety-nine days in the neonatal intensive care unit (NICU), ninety-nine days that would have been better spent in his mother's womb. Brenda broke many of the "rules" for a healthy pregnancy and had her son three months prematurely. Now he is just over 2 years old and has had a variety of different surgeries. Although his development is delayed in all areas, he is progressing steadily.

Was Jimmy born early because of Brenda's smoking, poor nutrition, and stress? She'll never know for sure, but it's quite possible. Research has clearly demonstrated that all these factors increase the likelihood of premature birth. But there is no way of knowing if Jimmy would have been born full term if Brenda had taken better care of herself. Statistics are useful in predicting possible outcomes in large populations; however, they cannot reliably explain individual cases.

Brenda: Looking back on it, I know I should have gotten out of the marriage sooner, probably as soon as I knew I was pregnant. I had this silly hope that it would all work out and that my husband would change and start treating me better and want the baby. But down deep I knew it was just a fantasy.

Jimmy may have had all these problems anyway, but I think that a pregnant woman — no, make that any woman — shouldn't allow herself to be treated badly. It's a tough decision to break up, but I think it's better to do it sooner — at least separate or something — rather than to let yourself get as low as I got.

I had friends and my brother who kept saying they'd help me get out, but I didn't listen. They had it all planned out for me, too, like the "great escape," but I just couldn't imagine being pregnant and having a baby without a husband — old-fashioned, I guess. No matter how bad it got and how much my friends and brother pushed me to get out, I just couldn't do it, couldn't see it as a real choice. If I had it to do over again, though, I'd have gotten out of there. I'd have moved in with my brother, like he asked me to, or with one of my friends. I had the chance, but I didn't take it. As it turned out, my husband and I split up shortly after anyway, so it's pretty clear that I made the wrong choice.

This story was not meant to imply that a pregnant women involved in a bad or abusive marriage or relationship is likely to have a child born prematurely, with medical complications: the message is that living under conditions such as these can be very stressful, and stress is not a recommended addition to a healthy pregnancy.

Question:
They've taken my baby to the NICU and I feel so alone and afraid. What should I do?

Answer:
Make every possible, reasonable effort to spend as much time as you can and to make physical contact with your child and find someone to talk to about your feelings and fears — right away!

Parents most often recommend two approaches to this critical event: (1) make every effort to spend as much time with your baby as you can, and be both aggressive and reasonable with the medical staff, who may at times appear to thwart your efforts to hold and spend time with your newborn, and (2) talk about your feelings: with friends, family, other parents in the hospital, and the staff.

Draw a picture in your mind: You're in the delivery or birthing room and a baby has just been born. The baby is handed to the parents, who engulf their little one in a shower of love. Tears of joy stream from their faces as each touch, sight, and sound bonds them closer together.

Although this bonding actually began, in a subtle way, many months or years prior to this time, perhaps as far back as when the mother and father first thought of having a child together, these first sensations act as catalysts, drawing love and caring from and between child and parents.

Now imagine this same mother and father, but this time picture them alone. Their baby has been born with a life-threatening condition that requires immediate, intensive medical intervention. The hospital staff has rushed the infant off and left the parents behind. Rather than feeling the warm, smooth body of their newborn, they are left to feel their tears and loss; the sight of their baby's face is replaced with that of blank hospital walls; and the sound of crying, that sound that had been awaited for many months, is replaced by the slow, irritating tick of a clock.

DeeDee, the mother of a 6-year-old who is now developing quite normally, with the exception of what may be a learning disability, has strong feelings on the subject of what parents should do when their child is taken to an NICU:

DeeDee: I never got to hold him or nothing. I got to touch him through the isolette, but it took weeks of patience before they finally let me hold him. Then it was for just a few minutes at a time. They had him so medicated that he seemed like he was hardly even alive. He was having a lot of seizures [abnormal brain activity, which in extreme cases can cause brain damage] and was totally sedated because they wanted to limit any damage that might occur, sort of like let his brain rest. He had all these tubes in him — for feeding and medications and everything like that. Once they had some of the tubes out of him, that's when I could first start holding him. Then they had all they could do to keep me away from him. I just kept going back and holding him. I couldn't get enough. It was like all I wanted to do was hold him and love him. I was afraid that if I put him down, if I let him go, he'd die. That would be it.

I found out later, after this was all past, that a lot of the NICU moms get to spend a lot more time with their babies than I did and get to hold them more. You just need to let people know how you feel and what you want. I tend to be the type of person that holds my ideas and feelings in and lets others sort of boss me around. I guess I did that when they took Kevin away. Well, I know now that I should have expressed myself more and let them know what I wanted, what I needed.

I'm in counseling now and dealing with a lot of different stuff — feelings and emotions — and I realize that I held in a lot those first few weeks that I should have expressed. I just bottled up my fears and stuff after they took Kevin away, didn't talk to anyone about it, and let it build up. That's not a good idea.

The messages here are clear, and they are repeated by most parents of infants who are rushed to the NICU: make every effort to spend time with your baby, and hold and touch the infant as much as you possibly can (the NICU staff may not encourage this — out of concern for your baby's physical health — so you may need to find a balance between your own expression of needs and assertiveness and their reluctance). Find sensitive and caring people to talk to about your feelings.

Jim's first sight of his daughter, Cindy (who suffered from a number of life-threatening conditions and would later be diagnosed as having cerebral palsy), was not what a father hopes or plans to see. In his words, "She was brown and lethargic and hardly moved at all." Rene, Jim's wife, remembers the fear and confusion more than Cindy's color or condition. They both recall that the first hour after Cindy's birth was the most tortured and painful experience of their lives.

Rene: As soon as she was born, the doctor went into action. She wasn't breathing, so he took a syringe kind of thing and suctioned her nose and mouth and tried to get her going on her own. I kept asking, "What's wrong? What's wrong?" . . . Then they took her away. She was gone. I'm in the room with a nurse, and Cindy and the doctor are gone. I don't know what's going on. Jim's gone, the baby's gone, the doctor's gone, and I'm lying there, going crazy. I was ranting and raving all over the place, "Get me out of here! I have to go see my baby!"

Jim: Within a couple of hours a priest had given Cindy her last rites and they had taken her to another hospital to the emergency neonatal care center. I stayed with Rene.

Rene: That was probably the worst part — I mean, she's already had her last rites and I haven't even held her or looked in her eyes yet.

It all happened so fast! One minute I'm excited and thinking about how the baby's going to look when she pops her head out; I'm planning all these things in my mind, like holding her and feeling all this relief and love and how we're going to call everyone with the good news — and the next minute they're giving her the last rites and they've taken her away.

After she made it through the first few hours, they didn't think she'd live three weeks. The nurses and doctors tried to stop me from following Cindy to the other hospital, but they couldn't hold me back for long. I demanded to be transferred, demanded an ambulance take me over there. They kept saying, "Oh no, oh no, you aren't ready for that yet." But they couldn't stop me. You really need to let them know what you want because the medical personnel tend to treat you like a

little kid who doesn't even get a vote — whose opinion
doesn't count.

Once I got to the NICU I had to really let them know that
being with Cindy and holding her was important to me, because they sort of had the attitude that they were going to save
her and give her everything she needed. Well, fine: "You save
her, but I'm in this, too, and God forbid, if she doesn't make it,
at least I'm going to be her mom as much as I can, for as long
as I can."

I could hardly believe it was me talking, because I'm rarely
the forceful, assertive type, but I *became* forceful when they
took my baby away. I don't know; maybe it's being a mom or
being in an emergency situation, but that's not the way I
normally am. Something, like, came over me.

Some may say that Rene should have listened to the medical staff who
advised her not to follow her baby to the second hospital and that she
needed to rest and wait awhile. Most of the parents who responded to
this question, as well as the authors, disagree. They and we believe that
most mothers are able to make reasonable and rational decisions
throughout this process, and in the majority of cases, medical professionals should listen to and respect their requests.

Question:
I've heard how important the first few weeks of life are in forming
the relationship between parents and their child. I'm worried that all the
medical problems we had in the beginning are going to damage that
relationship forever. Is that true?

Answer:
No, that's not true. It's a challenging and difficult way to start, but it
need not "damage" your relationship. Some parents believe it can even
be an enhancing or strengthening part of their relationship with their
child.

Numerous studies have reviewed the significance of the first few
hours, days, and weeks of parent-child relationships and have discussed
the potentially damaging effects of circumstances such as those just described in the previous section. But in truth no two people interpret or
react to a crisis in exactly the same way. Although most childbirth classes

recommend that for ideal bonding to occur, an infant should be placed on the mother's stomach immediately after birth and fathers should be as involved as possible, as soon as possible, the absence of these recommended practices by no means implies a faulty or damaged relationship. In fact, some parents regard their child's life-and-death struggle as a cementing experience, one that draws them closer to one another.

Cindy and Tom are two such parents. Their first three children were born without complications. Simon, their fourth and last, began life a bit differently.

Tom: When Simon was first born, he was on the critical list, and all I did was pray to God that he wouldn't die. I prayed and prayed that my baby would live. We knew he had Down's syndrome and might have some medical problems, but that didn't change my love for him. Actually, it might have made it that much more. The whole time he was borderline [in critical condition], when he was in trouble, I was right there with him. I don't mean holding him or in the room with him, I mean connected. I loved him from the start, and any problems he had just made me want to be there for him that much more. I didn't want this little guy to suffer; I wanted him to pull through. I was wishing and praying that I could take his suffering and pain, that I could have it instead of him. Sure, it would have been great to have held a normal, healthy baby and not have all these problems, but it wasn't that way. I had Simon, and I was going to love him no matter what. I just wanted him to live, so he could be whatever he could be.

Cindy: When he was born, he had a problem getting oxygen, . . . and they had him in the intensive care nursery. They were really concerned about that and the potential for heart problems and all these things that often occur with Down's syndrome. So it was kind of scary. I was real scared! He was born at around nine o'clock at night, and at midnight they're telling me he's in intensive care and he might have to go to Children's Hospital.

You know, during those first few hours I promised myself that if he made it through, if he lived, I'd love him with everything I had. I didn't care that much about the Down's syndrome. I just wanted my baby.

Both Cindy and Tom stated throughout the interview that the fear of losing Simon during the first few hours and days made them feel much closer to him, made them appreciate all that he could do rather than focus on his delays and things he could not do. Even though they couldn't hold him, they were emotionally and spiritually beside him during the entire ordeal. They believe that this time of trial and uncertainty created as deep and lasting a bond as would have occurred from the initial holding and caressing they missed.

Question:
For some parents these early problems may help form an even closer bond with their baby, but it can have negative effects, can't it?

Answer:
Yes, it can.

And it often does. As is the case in most difficult life experiences, individuals respond in their own unique fashion. Similar events can leave one family devastated, whereas another family may pull together and be strengthened.

Compared to Tom and Cindy, Chuck and Jan reacted quite differently to the premature birth of their first child, Corrine (now almost 4 years old):

Chuck: It really was tough. I had a very difficult time handling it at the beginning. I couldn't — I mean I wouldn't — even go in the nursery for the first four or five days. My mind was a whirl-wind of thoughts and possibilities; I was a real mess.

I think that what I was anticipating was that she wasn't going to make it. You see, it was really touch and go in the beginning, and she could have died at any time. I think it was going through my head that it would be easier if I was less involved, that if I spent much time with her, I wouldn't be able to handle losing her. I guess I was trying to cut off my feelings for her, cut her off. I really didn't think I could deal with getting to know her and then having her die. If I didn't see her, didn't get close to her, then losing her wouldn't be so hard. I'm sort of ashamed of it, but I think that's really what was going on.

We love Corrine, of course, but all the stress and pressure of those first months can't be ignored. It was obviously a different experience than it was with Abby [Corrine's younger sister].

You had to learn everything about how to deal with her. You don't handle a preemie [premature baby] like you do a regular, full-sized baby. They don't communicate the same way; I mean, it's harder to figure them out. You add that to not being able to hold her so much, and to the stress, and then to her being blind [this diagnosis came later], and you have to figure it's different. I don't know; maybe during those first couple or three years I was a bit more mechanical or business-like with Corrine than I might have been — not quite as loving and natural. You don't really know how it would have been without all the complications, so it's just guesswork.

As far as how it affected our relationship today, our bond, we'll never know for sure, but you figure it must have had some effects, and probably not in a positive direction. I'm not the type of person that keeps looking back thinking, "If I had done this, then this might be different." You just have to take what you've got and make the best of it. I mean, if I spent a lot of time wondering how things could be, or might have been, I'd have very little energy to deal with what is.

Jan: Sometimes I think about it, about how things might have been, and I think maybe it made me a little harder, maybe a little colder. Like Chuck said, he sort of pulled away to protect himself. Maybe like that. I don't know. We were going through so much in the beginning there that it wasn't "normal" — whatever "normal" is — but it's hard to say exactly what it all means or how things might have been.

I know that after that first experience, having Corrine, I really appreciated it when Abby was born without complications. It was wonderful. We got to hold her, play with her, and do all those things we missed the first time around. I don't know that we love one more than the other or not, or how all that time in the hospital and all the stress affected Corrine or our relationship, but I do know that we shared a lot more joy and touching with Abby during those early stages. I guess it must mean something. Her birth was so much easier. I mean, the pressures weren't there like they were with Corrine, so we had a lot more to give.

Jan and Chuck don't really know what effects Corrine's early difficulties have had on their relationship with her, but they are relatively certain that all the early complications, fears, and stresses made them less able to share their love and develop a close and caring bond during the first months of her life. It is only common sense that when the relief, joy, excitement, and wonder of a healthy, typical birth is replaced with the sorrow, depression, and anxiety associated with early health impairments, the process that bonds parents and children will somehow be altered. For some, that alteration will no doubt be negative, but for others a stronger and more loving bond may well be formed.

Question:
We're being asked to make critical, life-and-death decisions constantly and quickly. How do you know if you're making the right decision?

Answer:
You usually don't. You gather all the information and advice you can and then put it all together the best you can and decide.

Parents were divided on this issue, about one-third preferring to go with the old adage that the doctor knows best, allowing the doctor's advice to lead the way — not wanting too much data about all the various choices. The other two-thirds stated that they wanted more information and wanted to be the final decision makers.

The vast majority of parents recommend that those involved in life-and-death decisions make every effort to maintain a clear perspective on the present and not let uncertainties about the past and fears of the future interfere with their ability to respond and make new decisions. As one father put it, "You really need to take a deep breath, try to clear out all that's past and may come, and make a decision. If you hold onto those doubts — which there will always be — or hold onto your fears, you won't be able to do what you have to do, which is make a decision, now."

Many parents of typical infants, toddlers, and preschoolers feel helpless against the numerous infections that attack their young children. These families fight on-again, off-again battles with different strains of bacteria, usually placing their hope and trust in one of a variety of antibiotics. This is a normal and expected part of family life, but when the infected child is fourteen weeks premature, weighs 2 pounds, and is receiving antibiotics through a central line, the everyday becomes critical, life and death hanging in the balance.

Carmen, the mother of a 6-year-old girl with only minor delays in speech, language, and motor coordination, was faced with many life-and-death decisions during her daughter's first three months of life. Her recommendations are that parents read, study, and ask questions:

Carmen: I read everything I could get my hands on and constantly asked people — doctors, nurses, therapists — what they thought. I'd use friends and family to bounce ideas off of, sort of like sounding boards: "Here's what I think; what do you think?" When a question or decision would come up, or if I knew one was coming up, I'd hit the phones, calling professionals and family and friends for their opinions, and I'd hit the library and read, read, read. I was lucky because the hospital we were at had a medical school and a great library, so I'd go down there all the time and read up on stuff. The librarians and students were real helpful, so they'd find articles for me and I could read them and gather my own information.

You never know for sure if you're doing the right thing, but my theory was that I wanted to make my decisions based on knowledge rather than just take the advice of one doctor.

Question:
They told me that I could go home, but my baby needs to stay in the hospital. How can I leave my baby behind?

Answer:
It's hard, but you just have to do it. Your life has to remain in some type of order or you won't have that much to give your newborn.

You just have to do it! When a newborn is too small to come home or medically too fragile to leave a hospital, there comes a point where most parents need to get on with other life responsibilities. Other children, a home, a job or career, and personal care must all be attended to if parents are to remain fully functioning and able to keep their lives intact. Yet some parents become so overwhelmed by the needs of their newborn that they disregard other parts of their life. This can be destructive to parent and baby alike.

Returning to Brenda's childbirth experience reveals a glimpse of what it's like to leave the baby behind.

Brenda: I stayed in the hospital only five days [after learning that her premature son, Jimmy, was going to require an extended stay in the NICU]. It was very, very hard to leave him there. When I left after having A.J. [her first child], I took him with me. I didn't just walk away and leave my baby, desert him. But now I knew A.J. needed me at home. Still, it was a tug-of-war inside of me.

When he was born he was 1 pound and 7 ounces, then he went down to 1 pound and 2 ounces. I wanted to be with him all the time, but it wasn't possible. I had another child and a home and other responsibilities. I had a regular life, too. I couldn't be there all the time, but I couldn't get him out of my mind either. Part of me stayed there, with him, even when I left. I tried to keep up my other responsibilities, but my mind, my concentration wasn't with me. I kept thinking about Jimmy and how little he was and how he was alone, without his mom, in that hospital.

It seemed to me at the time, during those ninety-nine days visiting the NICU, like the only thing that was really real was what was happening with Jimmy at the hospital. It was like when I'd be out doing other stuff, out of the hospital, it was all kind of a fantasy or imaginary, like I was in a haze or cloud or something. I guess because inside I was really at the hospital, and even though my body would leave to go home and do things, my insides never left that NICU.

It's sort of a no-win situation. I mean, you can't stay at the hospital the whole time — you'd crack up — but when you aren't there, you spend most of your time emotionally hooked in there anyway. You have to get out, though, and at least try to keep your life in order: pay bills, take care of the kids, do the housework, cook, all that stuff. You just have to do your best.

Jan, another mother of a premature baby, wanted to save as many of her maternal leave and sick days as possible until her daughter, Corrine, was released from the NICU. Since Corrine was being well cared for in the hospital, it seemed that going back to work would be a good way to save a few days; however, leaving the baby behind was harder than she had imagined.

Jan: After Corrine was born, it was obvious that she was going to have to stay in the hospital for some time, so I figured I'd go back to work and then take off when she was ready to come home. I tried to continue my regular schedule pretty much as it was before. I was working full time, taking care of the house, doing all the regular stuff I had always done, and also, after work each day, I'd leave school [Jan is a teacher] and drive to the hospital — it was two hours round-trip — spend time with Corrine, and then turn around and come back home and prepare for the next day, back to school.

You'd never know when you were going to get a phone call, when the phone would ring and something had to be done. We'd get phone calls asking for permission to do all sorts of things, from little things to serious medical procedures, like really heavy decisions. We had to make a lot of decisions right there, over the phone. That was real hard. Every time there was a call you got nervous, like, "What's it going to be this time?"

Do you know how hard it is to deal with something like that and then have to go right back to work?! It's hard, believe me. I work in a school, so I had children I had to face. I'd get off the phone, and I'd want to rush down to the hospital, just to be there, but I couldn't. I'd have to go back to my students.

There was no letup. Work was still work, with all the same things that needed to be done, the same responsibilities. Home was still home, with cleaning and cooking and mail and everything else. Then, on top of all this, you add going back and forth to the hospital and all the medical problems and the anxiety of not knowing.

I think I tried to do too much. I didn't realize how hard it would be to go back to work, with Corrine still in the hospital. Looking back, I probably shouldn't have tried to do so much; maybe we should have gotten more help in the house, or I should have taken some more time off or something. You can't really stay with them in the hospital all the time — it's just not reasonable to drop everything else; anyway, there's not all that much you could do there. But you can't just return to life as it

was before, because that can just be overwhelming. I think
what's best is to go home to a somewhat limited routine — cut
out whatever you can. That way you can sort of keep up your
regular life but still have part of you left over for all the
traveling back and forth and all the stress and decisions and
stuff.

In these words Jan summarizes the ideal approach to leaving your baby
behind. You have to keep your regular life and responsibilities going, but
if you try to do it all, it will probably be too much. Work on temporarily
eliminating or postponing nonessential elements so that you reserve time
and energy for the responsibilities and emotional drains associated with
not having your baby at home and having to deal with the NICU. Don't
try to resume life as usual, and don't try to spend all your time in the
NICU: find a compromise!

Question:
What can you do to get ready for your child's release from the
hospital, from the NICU?

Answer:
Lots of things, but primarily learn all you can and get your supports
in place.

The basic answer here is that you can do a lot to prepare. When asked
this question, parents responded in many different ways:

- Spend a lot of time at the NICU.
- Make sure you're confident with all the medical procedures.
- Get to know the local emergency services, and let them know
  what's happening.
- Have all your supports lined up — a parent support group, your
  local pediatrician, child care help, a neighbor to call in case of an
  emergency, financial assistance, etc.
- Cook meals and store them in the freezer.
- Get some in-home hobbies or activities ready.
- Make a schedule of responsibilities for each partner.

Once Corrine was ready to come home, Jan and Chuck were more
than ready to welcome her. They were tired of driving back and forth to

the hospital; weary of endless, detailed technical consultations with a variety of specialists; constantly fearful of that midnight phone call; and, more than anything else, anxious to begin their home life together, as a family:

Jan: Right before Christmas she had met all of the goals — she had met the minimum requirements to leave the NICU. She was up to the weight — see, they have to be at least 5 pounds or right around 5 pounds. They have to have gone without apneas [breathing stops] and bradycardias [slowed heart rate], and be sucking, to be able to eat. She was OK on all of that. But just to be safe, she came home with a monitor, to keep check on her vital signs. It would set off an alarm if her breathing stopped or if her heart rate got too slow.

        They weren't sure whether or not she needed the monitor, but they didn't want to take any chances. That was OK, though, because after spending all that time in the hospital, we became pretty familiar with the equipment, and it does give you a feeling of security. It was a real scene, all those alarms going off and changing the leads and the wires. When I look back at those first few weeks home, I'm real glad that we had time to prepare for it. The NICU had given us time to get ready. All the stuff we had to do just seemed like everyday chores, not like a real big thing. And by that time 5 pounds seemed like a great big, healthy baby, whereas before we probably would've been scared to just pick up such a small thing.

        Before she came home, I stopped working and got everything ready, everything in place. I tried to anticipate all the things that would come up during those first few weeks together in the house and be prepared — things like getting her room ready, notifying the emergency agencies, talking to her pediatrician, interviewing people who might help around the house with things, getting some activities going to keep me busy at home — I just tried to have as much ready as possible. When she came home, I came home and stayed home: I stopped working. It was important to me to be home with her and to have some good times together, to have fun with her when she was real little.

Adults are responsible for the lives of their children. Yet few mothers or fathers enter parenthood with training in handling life-threatening medical emergencies; in fact, many or most new parents return from the hospital barely able to change a diaper and bathe or feed their newborn. Jan and Chuck found themselves with responsibilities far beyond their preconceived perceptions of their own abilities, yet they took charge, gathered needed knowledge and resources, and learned to care for their daughter. Although the time Corrine spent in the NICU was difficult for Jan and Chuck, it gave them both the time and the motivation to better prepare themselves. They — especially Jan — probably tried to do too much, but they were wise to learn all they could about how to care for their daughter and to anticipate what their needs would be once Corrine came home so they could prepare the environment to meet as many of those needs as possible.

Brenda, whose son Jimmy spent ninety-nine days in the NICU, learned that in order for him to leave the hospital, she would have to prepare herself. During her dozens of visits to the hospital and hours and hours of interaction with medical personnel, she began to develop the competencies and confidence that she would need once Jimmy was home.

Brenda: I remember I had to go for CPR and monitor training before he could come home. It was real hard, thinking that he could die any minute, that he could just stop breathing or his heart could stop. A couple of times he did quit breathing. You could see the color just drain from his face. There he was, in my arms, and he'd just stopped breathing, and the color would start leaving his face. If I hadn't been trained on what to do I would've freaked out, but as it turned out, I was trained and I handled it real well. I would tap him on the feet or smack him on the feet, you know, tickle him — anything — because he'd just, he'd forget to breathe.

Holding him, feeding him, bathing him, everything, it was all different from A.J. [Brenda's older son]. Jimmy was so tiny, so fragile. When I look back at what I knew for my first boy, I wonder how he ever made it. Like I knew nothing, like I was just lucky that he was strong and everything went right. That just wouldn't work for Jimmy, though. You just can't treat a 2-pound baby the same as a 9-pound baby.

If most parents who enter the world of the neonatal intensive care nursery are untrained, uncertain, and petrified, few leave without an enhanced sense of personal knowledge, skill, and confidence.

Tips for Parents

- Talk to each other, share thoughts, fears, hopes, etc.
- Cut back on responsibilities and stresses as much as possible during pregnancy.
- Seek medical guidance at the first signs of pregnancy.
- Make every attempt to hold and be with your newborn, even if they take the baby to the NICU.
- Gain as much information as you can from as many sources as possible so you can be an informed decision maker.
- If your child requires an extended stay in an NICU, make every effort to limit your out-of-hospital routine to essentials and prepare for the baby's homecoming.

Tips for Professionals

- Be cautious in your choice of words; consider how others may perceive your ideas before you express them.
- Be aware of individual family histories, beliefs, and practices that may impact pregnancy and early development.
- Provide parents with resources and information so they can participate in decision making.

Conclusion

As this chapter has revealed, newborns are not zeros. An infant's first independent breath is by no means the beginning of the baby's life but a sign of having survived the greatest challenge he or she will ever face. If that first breath is taken by an infant free from genetic differences or weaknesses, one who has endured a typical prenatal and perinatal experience, chances are quite good that the years to come will not lead to exceptional educational needs or disabilities, and if they do, they will be mild. If, however, a child's genetic makeup is atypical or the period between conception and birth has been marred by difficulties or any type of abuse or neglect, the newborn will be at risk, and considerable energy and expense may be required to achieve levels of functioning most parents take for granted.

Pregnancy and birth are a joyous and natural process for most, but for some they are first steps on the road to exceptional needs.

2

First Concerns and Reactions

The families introduced in Chapter 1 became aware very early in their children's lives that they might have exceptional needs; however, the majority of disabilities are not identified until later in life. In general, more serious problems are diagnosed early, less serious ones later. This is especially true in the conditions of mild retardation and learning disabilities, which are usually discovered only after a child enters kindergarten or first grade.

Prior to receiving a formal diagnosis, most parents of children with disabilities spend weeks, months, or sometimes even years wondering whether their child is "normal" or if their behaviors are signs of developmental "differences" or "disabilities." No two parents react in exactly the same way to early concerns or to a formal diagnosis.

Question:
How can I tell the difference between a real problem in my child's development and something that just seems different but he'll grow out of?

Answer:
In many cases you can't tell the difference, but a useful rule of thumb is, "If in doubt, check it out." Rather than wait and see, most parents and professionals recommend early action, which includes careful observations of your child and the gathering of information.

This book focuses on children whose special needs are recognized prior to kindergarten, yet an overwhelming number of those who will eventually receive some type of special services blend in with other children fairly well during the infant, toddler, and preschool years.

Parents and professionals may have concerns, questions, fears, or doubts, but more than 90 percent of children under the age of 6 are close enough to "normal" so as not to cause alarm. "Wait and see" is one of the most frequently heard sentences in reference to mild and sometimes even moderate delays.

Many parents, however, are not willing to wait and see. They watch, read, compare, question, and search out answers. The earlier the delays are identified and services provided, the better prepared the family will be to deal with situations as they arise and, with most disabilities, the greater will be the eventual achievement level of the child. Three general areas of development that parents observe most keenly during the early years are large motor development, disposition, and speech and language.

The mother of a 2-year-old who was significantly delayed in motor coordination had suspicions about her daughter's development months before any formal testing was requested. Her description of the difficulty she had convincing her pediatrician, friends, and family that something needed to be done is a common story.

Mother: She was a very normal, healthy newborn baby. I didn't start becoming concerned until she was 6 or 7 months old and still not moving around much — she wasn't trying to roll over or creep or crawl, and couldn't sit up. By the time she was 1 year old, I said, "Hey, something is wrong here." I was getting pretty nervous. The pediatrician kept saying that everything was fine and I shouldn't worry. He suggested that we "wait and see." I just felt like something wasn't right. Everyone was saying, "She's OK; she's just developing slower. Don't worry; she'll be just fine." I hoped and prayed they were right, but I knew they weren't. Well, at about 15 months they finally believed me, and we were referred for testing. They took her right in at the ARC [Association for Retarded Citizens] and started her in therapies and teaching her stuff.

This mother had a good idea of what the normal motor development sequence was supposed to be. She saw what other children the same age as her daughter could do and was concerned. Despite her concern, more than nine months passed before action was taken and special services were sought. Although nine months may seem like a short while, it is over half a lifetime for a 15-month-old.

Another area of development many parents watch carefully is temperament, which may include activity level, ease of handling, disposition, and mood. Common adjectives used to describe children are hyperactive-lazy, happy-grumpy, easy-difficult, flexible-stubborn — all of which tell something about how the child relates to the world, about his or her temperament.

Parents often hope for a quiet, easygoing infant, especially parents who have had or known extremely active or difficult babies, yet it is sometimes this very same silence or passiveness that triggers first concerns. The father of a 5-year-old boy diagnosed as speech and language delayed and mentally retarded, with "autistic-like" behaviors, describes his early concerns:

Father: We didn't notice much difference until he was about 9 months old. He just wasn't doing much. He just sat there, and he wasn't talking at all. He didn't even crawl. I suppose when he was even younger, like a little baby, we wondered because he was always so quiet. All he would do was sleep and eat. We liked it for awhile. You know, you always like a "good baby," but you want to hear something, you want to see something. People would always say, "You're so lucky; I wish my baby was so good." At first that made us feel better, but we became more and more concerned. These other kids would be all over the place. I guess that would be hard, but you want to see it sometimes. He just wasn't like the other kids, just very different.

        He looked like your normal baby, so it was hard to admit that something might be wrong. He looked just fine, but you could just see he wasn't doing the stuff he was supposed to.

It was this child's disposition that led his parents to seek help. Both father and mother watched other children and knew what their child was supposed to be doing. They watched, compared, and grew increasingly concerned.

A third area that commonly alerts parents to atypical development is delays in speech and language development. Cooing and chortling as a young infant, babbling at 6 months, the first word by 1 year, two-word phrases at 2 years — expectations abound as parents witness the amazing unfolding of language. When this unfolding does not occur according to the averages on statistical charts, many parents begin to get nervous. Knowing that many typical, "normal" children develop faster or slower than the charts indicate can relieve anxiety only for a short time. If they don't see steady development at approximately the same rate as in other children, parents want to know why.

The mother of a 1½-year-old boy who had just been diagnosed as having both a mild to moderate hearing impairment and speech and language delays was worried about her son's lack of verbalizations. This concern was prompted by something she read in a book:

Mother: When he turned a year old I was looking at this book that goes through different stages and tells about how babies develop. The book said that at around 6 months old or so he was supposed to say at least "mama" or "dada" — you know, at least one thing that sounded like a word. Well, he still doesn't do that. He's 18 months old and he doesn't say any words or make any sounds that resemble real words. He wasn't, and still isn't, doing any of the stuff he's supposed to be doing for his age.

This parent took immediate action and contacted the speech and hearing clinic at her local university. Her child received testing and referrals and soon after was fitted for a hearing aid and began receiving speech and language training from a certified professional.

Although children with delayed speech and language skills most often catch up and develop according to expectations, the delays are sometimes symptoms of other, more significant exceptional needs, such as hearing impairments, learning disabilities, mental retardation, and speech or language disorders. It is wise to watch, listen, and keep track of a child's development and seek resources if and when concerns arise. This can be done without anxiously comparing a child to developmental charts and becoming overly concerned about slight deviations or differences. It is best to find a reasonable balance between patience and assertiveness, concern and acceptance, waiting for development to occur and pushing to encourage progress.

Question:
My spouse won't admit that there's something different about our child. What should I do?

Answer:
You usually can't make someone face the facts. Once you've expressed your opinions and concerns, and your partner seems to be denying what

appears to you to be reality, you should give your spouse time to consider what's going on while you continue to gather information and resources and, if necessary, pursue testing.

Most expectant parents plan on having children who are at least as healthy, smart, cute, and wonderful as other children they have known. In truth, many future mothers and fathers probably think, or at least hope, that their child will be far above the masses; they have fantasies of parenting a one-in-a-million, beyond-all-expectations extraordinary human being. An occasional fear or nightmare is common ("What if . . .?" or, "Our baby could be born . . ."), but in the majority of pregnancies, parents do not expect problems or abnormalities.

Once a child is born, this same tendency continues. Mothers and fathers want to see their children as "normal." It is therefore not surprising that when evidence begins to build that a child's development may not fit expected molds, parents are likely to interpret that evidence in a way that retains the child's "normalcy" and allows for retention of previously conceived expectations and fantasies. For some, this distortion or misinterpretation of information is only a manifestation of a cautious nature, but for others, it may be a serious denial of reality, an unreadiness or inability to accept what is.

In either case, denial is a common stage in the process of identifying and dealing with the diagnosis of exceptional needs in young children. Within limits (to be discussed in this and later sections) it is a stage that allows the time to gather information, search out resources, redefine expectations, and look within. Although denial may take many forms and serve a variety of different purposes, its basic function remains constant: to help prepare individuals for what is to come. Denial provides individuals with extra time to gain strength and resources to deal with something they are at that moment unable to handle in a more direct fashion.

The following dialog illustrates how one father used denial to prepare for the eventual acceptance of his daughter Polly's disability.

Ric: I'm a rather easygoing person by nature. I usually don't like to worry about things unless there's a real good reason. You know, like there are enough problems around without making up new ones. So when Bev [Ric's wife] started comparing our older girl, Sonya, and Polly's development and looking for problems, I just said, "Whoa, hold it!"

It was like she was going out of her way looking to find something wrong, which is absolutely just not my style. I kept saying, "Well, they're two different kids." We've never officially had our older one tested, but we suspect that she's gifted, so trying to measure the baby to a gifted child won't work. You can't say, "The older one did this at six months; she did this at a year; she was doing this by now." I wasn't going by that because I figured it was just looking for trouble, looking for problems.

Polly couldn't gain weight; as a matter of fact, she kept losing weight. She was way too young to go on solids, and it was a very frustrating time for Bev. As it turned out later, the real reason was because she had a weak sucking reflex, which is a sign of cerebral palsy, but we didn't see that. I kept trying to interpret all the facts in such a way to make it a simple, easy, no-big-problem kind of thing. For quite a while I thought she was allergic to milk — that maybe that was all there was to it. Then I was convinced that her problem was that she was taking in enough food but just not getting anything out of it, not digesting it properly — a simple problem having to do with digestion. So I started collecting stool samples and bringing them in to be tested. The doctor didn't really ask for them, but I did it. Like on a hunch or something. I wanted it to turn out to be something really simple, real easy, so I tried to find a solution without looking really clearly at the facts.

I guess I was suspecting that something was wrong but not on any order of magnitude, not a big problem. Bev suspected much earlier that it was something more severe. I suspected it was just something small and simple, or just a stage that she was going through.

Bev kept saying, "Let's get some testing done; let's take her to a specialist; let's do something!" But I just tried to downplay it and get her mind off it — you know, change the subject or get her to wait a while and see what happened. If it hadn't been for Bev, it would have been a much longer period of time before Polly saw a specialist, before I would have suspected that there was a condition that required a specialist.

Bev: I knew before I went to see the specialist for testing that there was something wrong. I would talk to Ric about it and say,

"Ric, there is something wrong. We've got to do something."
He'd go, "Oh, for heaven's sake, knock it off, you worrywart.
It'll pass. Don't worry about it." Then I'd go into the bedroom, close the door, and cry and be real nervous and upset,
but he was convinced it was nothing and that she'd grow out
of it. He just couldn't see what was going on — he was
blocking out a lot of stuff that seemed real obvious to me.

When the doctors told us it was cerebral palsy, Ric didn't
accept it right away like I did. He thought they were off base.
He finally came around and believed them, but even then it
took him a long time to really accept all the ramifications, to
admit that she wasn't going to be normal or close to normal.

Professionals generally agree that in providing services to young
children with exceptional needs, the earlier a need is identified and
services provided the better. Ric's denial delayed this process. The critical
question here is, "How long can you wait? How long can someone allow
a partner's denial to slow down the process?"

Our answer is "not long." We believe that a parent should begin
gathering data and resources as soon as a concern arises and should
consider formal testing if and when those uncertainties continue to exist.
Waiting until a partner is convinced that testing needs to be done can
waste valuable time. The mother of a 6-year-old diagnosed as autistic
summarizes this perspective and the opinion of many parents:

Mother: You just can't wait around for your husband or wife to see
            things like you do. In some cases you'd be waiting around
            forever. Like my husband: he wouldn't go to a doctor if he was
            dying. If he had — and he has had them — a serious cut or
            infection, do you think he'll go to a doctor or to emergency?
            No way! So I'm going to wait for this man to make a decision
            about whether my child has emotional problems that need
            help?! Do you think I'm crazy?!

            I just took my boy in and started the ball rolling [by getting
            testing and counseling]. My husband thought I was crazy for
            making such a big deal out of it, but that's life. Ryan was
            diagnosed as autistic three years ago, and do you think my
            husband has come around yet? Nope. He still thinks that it's
            going to turn out OK — that it's a temporary, developmental
            type of thing — and that all the stuff I'm doing isn't that

necessary. He says that when he's with Ryan, when he's in charge — which is about twenty to thirty minutes a week — things are never as bad as I describe them.

So how are you going to deal with someone who sees things like this? I'll tell you how: you just take charge. You go and do it — get the testing done, get the services, do your best. You keep him informed, but you don't let him stop you!

The decision about what to do with your child (gather information, search out resources, and pursue testing) is much easier than the issue of confronting a spouse's denial. In most cases the best approach here is to keep your partner informed about what you're doing and why and allow him or her to digest and accept it at his or her own speed. With luck, your partner will come around and join you in your efforts to meet your child's needs; however, you can't force or make people see or believe something that they aren't ready to deal with.

Question:
How do you tell your family and friends?

Answer:
The best policy here is honesty. There may be a temptation to "not upset them" or "tell them the truth later," but sharing information as it becomes available and as you're ready to talk about it usually works out best.

After learning that their child has a disability or exceptional need, many parents wonder what and how much they should tell others and what sort of reaction the news will bring.

First, remember that you don't have to call everyone right away. Although sharing information in this way may be an individual or family tradition, after a shock like this, few people are in a state of mind to handle a lot of talking and explaining. Second, it's best to stick to the facts, especially over the phone. There may be a temptation to leave out "minor details," such as mentioning that your child has Down's syndrome or spina bifida, or that your newborn baby weighs only 3 pounds, but this is a mistake that just leads to problems and hurt feelings later.

These concerns ran through the mind of the mother quoted below as she struggled with the decision about how to share the news of her newborn daughter's spina bifida and hydrocephalus.

Mother: The hardest part, I think, was telling our family. This was the first grandchild on either side. My husband's first reaction was to just call everyone and say everything was fine. He didn't want to worry them and felt that he didn't have all the information yet. I couldn't decide what to do and kept changing my mind, but finally disagreed with him and decided it would be best just to share the facts. I was worried that if we didn't tell them the truth, they'd all tell other family members and friends and then, later on, we'd seem like liars, and so would they. So we agreed to tell it like it was, to share what we knew but not to rush out and do it. Neither of us could handle calling anyone right off, so we decided to wait a few hours or until we were in the mood — you know, wait until we were up for it. As you might guess, our closest friends and family called the hospital and asked, so we didn't have to take the first step. Those who we didn't call for a couple or a few days understood why we waited — most of them had heard through the grapevine anyway and were sensitive enough not to call us. The ones we did call we just basically gave the facts, and when we didn't know something, we just told them that. My husband later said he thought that was the best way. He said that at the time he just wasn't thinking real clearly.

The father of a 3-year-old boy recently diagnosed as legally deaf believes that timing is critical in sharing information with friends and family:

Father: We found out — I mean we got the final word, because we've been expecting this for months — but we got the final word that he was deaf about two months ago. There are still some family and friends that we haven't told. We called our parents when we found out, and my wife's sister, but that's it. As it comes up, while we're talking with people, we'll tell them, but we didn't call everyone we know. It's not that we're hiding it or anything, but we figure that those who need to know will find out, and we don't have to get on the phone with the whole world.

In summary, when you share information with friends and family, *don't lie*. Tell the truth, but remember that you don't have to jump right on the phone with every new bit of information. Take your time, catch your breath, talk to your spouse, and when you're ready, share what you know with those you feel like talking with. Remember also, that there is no rule that says everyone you know needs to be called within a certain time. Those who really love and care about you will find out soon enough.

Question:

Family and friends tell us that everything will be OK, but we know it won't be. How do you deal with people who try to convince you not to worry?

Answer:

You learn pretty quickly who's good to talk to about certain things and who isn't. Don't keep banging your head against a wall — if you know that every time you talk to certain people about your concerns it ends up being a bad experience, don't discuss that topic with them.

Not only are parents often able to deny realities they aren't ready to deal with, but family and friends also may encourage the process. We have all heard the well-intentioned friend or relative say, "Don't worry. It'll turn out OK." Although this may at times be a helpful suggestion, at other times it may slow the process of acceptance and block the exploration of feelings and ideas.

The mother of a 2-year-old girl who is approximately one year behind in all developmental areas talks about how she handled family members who couldn't accept the situation:

Mother: It wasn't so much our denial, but, like, some of our relatives would deny it — still do deny it. They say, "No, no way. Nothing's wrong." That kind of makes us angry because we're telling them, "Yes, this is how it is." They say, "Oh no, no way; go and see someone else." It's real confusing! You want to believe them. You really want what they're saying to be true, but you know it isn't. You know you've got to accept it, that she needs help and all, and get to work doing something, but it just makes it harder. It makes it harder to believe it, harder to get down and do something, to start the process and keep it going.

I've gotten to the point where I just won't discuss it with my sisters or with my mother-in-law. There are lots of other things for us to talk about, so I figure why put myself through the wringer every time I'm with these people? If the subject comes up, I just slide around it and move on.

I've got lots of other relatives and friends I can talk to about this, so they're the ones I bounce my ideas off of. When you get into a situation like this, with a real-life crisis, you've got to start figuring out who can help you in what areas, who your good influences and bad influences are.

Most parents agreed with this mother — agreed that you sometimes reach a point where you just avoid the topic with certain people — yet many stated that it's very important to make an effort to let them know how their nonacceptance is affecting you. Give them clear messages that you feel confused and upset when they react in certain ways. Only when you've honestly given your best shot at this method should you consider avoiding the subject altogether.

Question:

Once I realized that my child really did have a disability, I felt like I was on an emotional roller coaster. I still feel that way sometimes. What can I do to get back some stability?

Answer:

For many parents, the diagnosis of an exceptional need in their child is comparable to the death of that child — their "normal" child no longer exists. Recovering from this newly discovered truth usually takes time, introspection, and the formulation of a new set of expectations and goals.

It usually takes time — at least weeks, usually months, and some-times years — for parents to regain stability after learning that the child they had expected and hoped for does not exist and that in his or her place is a child with a disability. Parents first need to acknowledge their feelings and experience their grief. They then must let go of the fantasy child they had hoped to have, drop their original set of expectations. These steps should lead the way to accepting the child with a disability for who and what the child is and can be.

The process just described can include a multitude of emotions: denial, grief, anger, frustration, hurt, depression, acceptance, love. These feelings may last anywhere from a short time to forever; they may ebb and flow, intensify and diminish, depending on various circumstances;

and they affect spouses differently at different times. Following is a description of how the process began for Bev and Ric (the father who refused to acknowledge the problem) after their daughter Polly's cerebral palsy was diagnosed.

Bev: After the diagnosis of CP [cerebral palsy] was made, we came home and were pretty upset.

Ric: For the first few days, I was a mess. My head was just completely scrambled eggs. You go through a process of trying to sort out your thoughts and everything and you just keep going in a circle. You come back to right where you started from. You don't get anything resolved. You don't get anything answered. Sure, you've gone through — or, rather, you *feel* you've gone through — a thinking process, but you've got no answers, like, "Where do we go next? What do we do? Where do we start?" So I would say for a few days I was just complete scrambled eggs.

Bev: I think you go through this pretty much like when someone you love is dying or dies. You go through like a grieving process almost. First, you're like, "Well maybe [the doctor's] wrong. Maybe it's a mistake. Maybe we should get another opinion." We went through all that.

Ric: Yeah, the thing was that her mother and my mother both died of terminal cancer and some of the processes, the thought processes, are really the same. The denial process is real similar, like, "We're going to beat this thing. It isn't so bad."

Bev: I think over the past couple of years I've gone through every emotion there is ten times. The emotions come and go, and sometimes I'll be fine for awhile, and then something will set me off. Something will make me angry or hurt or fearful or maybe, once in a while, I'll get lucky and go through a period of being really up and optimistic and accepting the situation.

It's strange, too, that Ric and I rarely have the same feelings at the same time. One week I might be angry, and he's feeling depressed, and then, a few days or weeks later, I might feel pretty up and accepting, and he might be angry.

Ric:

Overall, though, it's smoothing out for both of us. As time goes on the emotion swings are less dramatic, and I think our experience of having felt all these feelings before is kicking in a bit and making it easier.

Then, too, it's getting easier because as time goes on we're less attached to that old picture of what we originally thought Polly would be, and we're learning to love and appreciate her more and more for who she is and what she *can* do.

Bev: What do they say? "Time heals all wounds." I think it's true, and it's happening with us.

Sometimes it helps to hear the same answer in different ways. The father of a 5-year-old identified at birth as having Down's syndrome has experienced many of the same emotions as Bev and Ric. He has similar recommendations.

Father: You really need to get in touch with your feelings and deal with them because if you don't, they won't go away — they just stay hidden, right below the surface, and pester you and bug you until you deal with them.

I did that when my boy was younger — I didn't deal with my feelings. He has Down's, which makes the chances of being a real good athlete very close to zero. I had been a real good athlete in school and still love sports and had always had this picture of playing a lot of ball with my kid. I wouldn't let go of that. I remember working with him all those hours, trying to get him to stand up and walk, thinking that with enough work he could be the first kid with Down's to play on his high school's baseball team. I just wasn't dealing with reality. I was hung up on this picture, this image of another kid, an ideal kid. It was good that I put in all that time, that I'm putting in all that time working with him. But before I wasn't really doing it for him as much as for my fantasy of who I wanted him to be, while now I'm more in touch with who he is and who he can realistically be.

So, basically, I recommend that parents do all the things that I didn't do: deal with your feelings; talk about it; get into counseling, either alone or with your spouse or with the whole family; love your kid for who he is, not who you want him to

be; look at the goals and expectations you had before you
found out about the disability and discard the parts that are
unreasonable, and start making more reasonable ones.

Question:
I've just learned that my child has Down's syndrome. What should I
do first?

Answer:
Get in touch with other parents of children with Down's syndrome
and meet them and their children.

Probably the least subtle, most obvious first concern occurs when a
child is born with visible differences. Such is the case with Down's
syndrome, which is typically identified within the first month of life.

Parents of children with Down's syndrome relate that the most
critical thing to do after learning about your child's condition is to talk
with other parents of kids with Down's and meet some kids who have it
and are doing well.

Upon learning that their newborn infant, Betty, had Down's, Leslie
and Jeff were able to benefit from a parent who had been there. As soon
as Betty's condition was identified, the hospital contacted Vera, who had
also given birth to a daughter with Down's syndrome in the same
hospital just one year earlier:

Leslie: I'll never forget when Vera came to my room. I mean, it's like
           my fairy godmother must have sent her. I had all these ques-
           tions that I was holding in, afraid or too shy to ask, but she
           knew what they were without me saying a word. She knew the
           questions and had lots of ideas on the answers. Talk about
           resources — that woman was an encyclopedia. She brought up
           a whole stack of books and articles. Every time I would walk
           down the hallway in the hospital, nurses were reading those
           books. I mean, I couldn't even read them because the nurses
           were, which kind of made me feel good, that at least they
           wanted to know more about it. And to meet her daughter,
           Karen, and see that a child could have Down's but still be so
           cute and be able to do so many things, that really helped.

           When Vera had her daughter up here, nobody came and
           talked to her. The nurses didn't know how to handle her or

anything. She says that she wouldn't wish that on anyone. That's why she always goes now to meet parents who have Down's babies.

She taught me more than any of the medical staff or social workers. She helped me see that things could work out, that Betty could be a lovable, valuable person and that it wasn't my fault — I didn't cause it. I'll never forget how she helped me.

Parents helping parents — it's a critical link in the chain of resources (this topic is continued in Chapter 8). Vera, the helper Leslie just described, provides another perspective on parents as resources for other parents and explains how she was able to convince one hospital to link parents together:

Vera: After my daughter, Karen, was born with Down's, and I think after I sort of got my act together, I went to the OB department and said, "Look, you can't have just this one pamphlet here that's twenty years old. You've got to link new parents with other parents, get them information, find them services. . . . Don't send a social worker in to see a new parent. They don't want to talk to them. I didn't want to talk to a social worker. At that time you want to talk to somebody who really knows what you're going through. I don't think anybody but another parent can do that. If there is a bad experience with the doctor — you know, like the way he tells them (and there are good and bad doctors out there) — then it's especially important to have more caring people around, people who really know what it means."

Sometimes people — like friends, relatives, the nursing staff — will completely avoid you because they don't know what to say or they're afraid of saying the wrong thing. I think that saying the "wrong" thing is better than saying nothing at all. So I really tried to make improvements there, so that right from the beginning there's some kind of outreach or some-body that the parents can call to say, "Look, where do we go from here?"

Doctors, I think, tend to get a little too medical or a little too blunt sometimes, and with social workers you never know. Some are real good, but even the good ones aren't as helpful as other parents.

It's also important for them to meet some kids and grown-ups who have Down's. You see, most people have this image of someone with Down's being severely retarded and mentally disturbed. When they actually meet some kids and grown-ups with Down's and realize that most of them walk, talk, have a real life, are loving and funny, then it's easier for them; it helps them clean that old, out-of-date picture from their minds.

One morning I talked to this father [Jeff, Leslie's husband, from the preceding story]. The mother was asleep and they had just told the father that his child was Down's. He didn't have anybody to talk to, so I went up there. He just had like a million questions. I mean, I don't know if it was all nerves or what, but he kept talking and talking, and he kept saying, "Now is this a stupid question?" I said, "There are no stupid questions. If you feel it's important, then it's important. I've never heard a stupid question from a new parent of a child with Down's syndrome."

"There are no stupid questions," as Vera states. But at times it does seem that parents are afraid of appearing stupid by asking too many questions; at other times their reluctance may be a learned response. Some professionals, some people, seem to have time to talk with you, almost regardless of when or how you approach them; others are usually in a hurry. Perhaps part of the explanation for parents' reluctance to ask questions has to do with patience. Do they perceive the professional with whom they are dealing as a patient person, as a person who will take the time to answer their questions, take the time to go over all the facts, explain them, and work through the decision-making process together? Parents who have just learned that their child has Down's syndrome need to talk to someone who is knowledgeable about the condition and has the patience to listen and respond to a million questions, most of which are being formed only as they're being spoken.

Tips for Parents

- Seek information and advice as soon as concerns arise.
- Follow your instincts: if one professional tells you to wait and see, and you're still concerned, seek a second opinion.

- Discuss your concerns and feelings with your spouse, friends, and close relatives — don't hold in your feelings.
- If certain friends, acquaintances, or relatives constantly give you a hard time or bad advice about your child, simply avoid that topic when speaking with them.
- Share information about your child only when you feel ready; avoid the temptation to make things appear better than they are.

Tips for Professionals

- Avoid the wait-and-see approach; if in doubt, check it out — or refer parents elsewhere.
- Be prepared for those parents who respond to your diagnoses with anger and denial, and learn techniques to deal with these aspects of the grieving process.
- Share what you know as you learn it, but avoid trying to influence parents with your personal values and opinions.
- To work effectively with these parents you must be patient and sensitive.

Conclusion

Many parents, as well as their families, friends, and helping professionals, adopt a wait-and-see posture in response to early concerns. Anxiety is often more common than action. Although this approach does allow parents time to clarify their concerns and prepare themselves to deal with what may eventually become a disturbing diagnosis, in most cases it's better to seek professional advice earlier rather than later. Parents who have concerns need to follow their intuition and seek out answers, regardless of the doubts or denial of friends and family.

It is also recommended that you avoid the opposite temptations of (1) sharing all new data right away with all friends and family and (2) not revealing information to friends and family because "all the facts aren't in" or because it may be too painful to them or you. Share that information you are ready to share, you want to share, with those you wish to share with. Whenever possible, avoid getting into details with people you expect to respond in a way that will discourage you, and make every effort to discuss issues with those who will help you deal with questions and concerns in a positive and caring way. Quite often one of the very best resources for parents in this situation is other parents who have similar concerns and have made progress in dealing with their concerns.

3

Services for Young Children

Individuals often remain unaware that certain services exist until a need for those services arises. You may have lived in the same area for your entire life — walked, jogged, ridden a bicycle, and driven a car down the same street 1,000 times — but never noticed a certain store or sign. However, once you need the services provided by that store or sign, you notice it each time you pass. So it is with services of all types for young children with exceptional needs. One father aptly describes the situation:

Father: I never had any idea that so much was out there. My first two kids didn't need any of that stuff, so I never knew about it; but when my daughter was born, we sure found out in a hurry. I mean, you've got different kinds of doctors with specialties you never heard of; you've got occupational therapists, physical therapists, speech and language specialists, early intervention programs and teachers, equipment, all kinds of equipment. It's like a whole world out there, a whole little world of special education, and I never knew it was there. You go through thirty years of your life reading about this stuff, you know, bumping into it here and there, like in newspapers, TV, radio, and just on the street, but you never really notice it, like it doesn't register, until you need it.

Various early childhood special education services have been in existence for years, but recent legislation, funding, and public awareness have dramatically increased the number of programs for children birth through 5 years old. Although the types of programs, quality, and cost may vary from state to state, county to county, and town to town, services *are* available. Some of these, and parents' reactions to them, are discussed in this chapter.

Question:
What sort of educational and therapy services are there for children under 3 years old?

Answer:
This varies from place to place; however, services are available all over the country, and in most states they are guaranteed by law, much like public school services.

The types of special services available for children ages birth to 3 years old vary greatly. Programs may be centered in the homes, with professionals mainly providing education and consultation for parents and some direct services for children; they may be housed in centers or schools, where teachers and therapists assume more of the responsibility for giving therapy and instruction and less responsibility for parent education and consultation; or they may blend both a home- and center-based approach and offer a combination of services. More important than the model or type of service provided is that the child and family receive the benefits of a program that will best serve their needs. No two children, no two families are exactly alike. Programs must therefore have some flexibility so that they best benefit each child and family.

Two critical factors in the delivery of these services to young children are timing and intensity. In most cases the earlier services begin the better, and the more intensive and often services are provided the better.

In Chapter 1 Bev and Ric discussed some of the difficulties they experienced before Polly, now 3½ years old, was born, and Ric revealed how hard it was for him to accept that something might be wrong with his daughter (she has CP). The following passage continues their story, describing how they learned about special education services and the process by which they became involved in trying to best meet Polly's needs.

Bev: We were referred to United Cerebral Palsy [UCP] by our family doctor. At that time UCP didn't have an infant stimulation program, so they referred us to the Association for Retarded Citizens [ARC], who had a program that handled all kinds of handicapped children. Whatever the handicap was, they had therapists there.

Polly started in the program when she was 7 months old. That first year I took her to therapy four times a week and sat there and watched. When I came home I'd do the therapies myself and then try to teach Ric.

You name it, they had it — all these specialists, all this equipment. They really knew what they were doing. They'd give her this kind of therapy and that kind of therapy, work with her on this skill and that skill. It was just amazing to me how they got to it so fast. I mean, one minute I'm sitting home with my baby and only Ric and I know what's going on, and the next minute we're involved with all these people — caring, educated, trained people — who are doing all this for us, and for free!

ARC was incredibly supportive, even as far as Sonya, our older daughter [age 8]. When Sonya first started to understand and realize that her sister was not like other kids' siblings, she had a little bit of difficulty. She'd cry about it and get angry and upset and say it wasn't fair. ARC even dealt with that. They gave us books for her to read, ideas of things to do, and recommended people for us to talk to. They were real supportive with that kind of thing and how to deal with it in the home and how to help other children in the home accept it. They were great.

ARC did all it could to incorporate Bev and Ric as critical elements in Polly's educational program. Ric recalls how they helped relieve him of some of the guilt and insecurity he had been feeling since Polly's CP had been diagnosed:

Ric: The people there, the teachers and therapists, really saved me. I had been feeling real low, kind of depressed, ever since we got the diagnosis, because I sort of felt that I had slowed things down with all my hesitations and denial and stuff. Well, they kept telling us what a good job we were doing and how good it was that we had started with her early. They really encouraged us and made us feel like we were doing it right, and that if we worked hard and kept it up, what we were doing was going to make a real difference in her life.

One critical ingredient in early and intensive services is incorporating parents' resources, priorities, and concerns into their children's programs. ARC realized that for their services to make a real difference, they would have to involve Polly's parents and encourage them to follow through with interventions.

Question:
Where can I find out what services are available in our area for children birth to 3 and their families?

Answer:
Begin with your pediatrician, or if you are fortunate enough to know any parents who have children with similar special need, ask them. These resources should get you off to a good start.

Most often the best place to begin a search for services is with your pediatrician. He or she can refer you to the local (city or county) agency that is responsible for assisting children and families who have needs similar to yours. Your pediatrician may also have pamphlets that describe your child's condition, including listings of state and national agencies that may provide information and assistance.

Early in your search you may come into contact with other parents of children with similar disabilities. These parents are most often a gold mine of practical information and resources. Their perspective — fellow consumers of services — can often lead you through the maze of programs, people, and red tape much more quickly and efficiently than can any other source.

Some states have initiated what is referred to as a single point or portal of entry. This means that there is one contact agency whose responsibility it is to assist individuals in learning about *all* resources available to them throughout the state. To find out if this system is in place in your state, ask your pediatrician or call the local or state office of the Department of Social Services or Human Services or Education.

The following two stories — one describing a parent who had an easy time learning about the system, and the other describing the experiences of a parent who ran into some roadblocks — will more clearly illustrate how this process works.

Maria, the mother of 2½-year-old Carmen, who has a significant speech and language delay and a mild-moderate, bilateral (involving both ears) hearing loss, was very fortunate in her search for services:

Maria: I feel very lucky because everything just sort of fell into our laps. Our pediatrician said that Carmen's speech and language was a little delayed. He contacted the ARC and the speech and hearing clinic at the local university, and within a couple of weeks all the observing and testing was done for free. They found out that she had a mild to moderate hearing loss and was about a year or year and a half behind in speech and language. Right away they [ARC] got her into their program, and we got into a program at the university to help us learn how to work with her better. The social worker at ARC then helped us find a way to get money to pay for two hearing aids, helped us get Carmen into a wonderful day care center, got us involved with a group of other parents who have kids with hearing impairments, and even made arrangements for her to enter a special summer program that the school district will be running this summer for preschoolers. All this just sort of happened.

Maria's experience was not as typical as we would wish, but some agencies, areas, and states do make services this easy to access.

The other extreme in finding services is described by Ruth, whose 2½-year-old son, Christian, is still not receiving all that is available in their area to help him deal with the challenges of his cerebral palsy.

Ruth: I'll tell ya, they don't make it easy on parents. I mean, all these programs are out there, but try and find them all. And then, once you find them, try and get into them. You have to be a lawyer to figure out some of the forms they give you. Really.

It's kind of depressing because nobody knows the whole picture. I mean, this person knows about this program, and that person knows about that program.

Then, too, you don't always get the same answer. Like with AFDC [Aid for Families With Dependent Children], and Social Security, and Family Support, with them and all the rest of the programs I never take one no for an answer. I've learned that people, the people who work at those places, each have their own interpretations of things. It's not as cut-and-dried as they lead you to think. With each of those three I just mentioned, I was told that I didn't qualify — "No way," they said. But I'm in all three now. When I'd call or meet with someone and they said I didn't qualify, I'd just say, "OK, thanks for your time" and hang up the phone or leave the office. I make sure to get their name, too. Then later that day, or maybe the next day, I call or make an appointment with someone else and try again. You wouldn't believe how many times it works, and the second person says that you qualify.

The agencies hate it when you do that, but ask any parent and they'll tell ya that if you don't do it you're just asking to get pushed around. Parents is the best way to find out what's really going on. If I want to know what's available or how to get something, I'll always call other parents first. See, they know all the ins and outs; they know who to see and what to say.

Most parents experience something in between the two extremes described by Maria and Ruth; however, parents should heed Ruth's advice. Don't take one no for the answer; double- and triple-check any information you receive. And perhaps most importantly, keep in mind that there is probably more out there than you are aware of, no matter how well informed you are. Keep your eyes and ears open.

Question:
What sort of educational and therapy services are there for children after the age of 3?

Answer:
All states guarantee a wide variety of special education services to children ages 3 and above.

In all states and territories of the United States, special education is guaranteed by law for those ages 3 and above who qualify. Although some differences in entrance qualifications, service delivery methods, and quality and intensity of services exist, great strides have been made since the early 1970s to create a more consistent and effective system of special education.

Begin by calling your local elementary school or the office of the director of special education in your school district. If you have a concern about your child's development, your school district must honor that concern and provide you with a complete evaluation free of charge. They must also offer to meet with you to discuss the evaluation, and with you — you are supposed to be an equal participant in any decisions that are made — determine whether or not your child qualifies for services and, if so, what the goals and objectives of those services will be. (These goals and objectives are part of a larger document, called an individualized education program, or IEP, that outlines a child's special education program.)

At this point the most critical variable determining what services your child will receive is the list of goals and objectives you and the school district personnel decide upon. Parents who negotiate a more comprehensive list of goals and objectives generally receive more services.

Most experts recommend that this process be divided into two separate meetings, one to determine eligibility and another to establish goals, objectives, and other parts of the IEP. But very often the meeting that is held to determine your child's eligibility for services will lead right into a discussion of program goals, objectives, and the IEP (assuming that your child does qualify).

Following is a list of recommendations that will help ensure that your child receives the best services available and that you navigate this system with as little stress as possible:

- So that all of your concerns are adequately dealt with and all information is gathered, ask to participate in the decisions about what areas are to be evaluated/tested.
- Ask for copies of all assessment reports prior to the meeting that will determine your child's eligibility. That way, you will have time to consider evaluation/test results, discuss them with family and knowledgeable friends and resources, and list your questions.
- In advance of the meeting, so that you are less overwhelmed by what may be a large group of professionals, each of whom has thoughts on your child's educational program and information to share with you, write down your questions and ideas, discuss them with a friend or someone who can help you express yourself, and attend the meeting with that person.
- So that you have plenty of time to consider all the facts and issues, don't sign or agree to anything you don't completely understand and support.

Now, with this background in mind, your original question — "What sort of educational and therapy services are there for children after the age of 3?" — can be answered. An excellent answer is provided by the father of a 6-year-old who is two to two and a half years delayed in most areas of development, and speaks and understands language at the level of a 2-year-old.

Father: When we went in to write Ronnie's first IEP, when he just
            turned 3, we really didn't know what was available in the
            district, so we just sort of let them lead the way and we said
            OK. He was placed in a program they called "preschool handi-
            capped." He went to school with ten other kids with all sorts
            of disabilities, for four mornings a week, and saw a speech and
            language pathologist once a week for twenty minutes. We
            were real pleased with the program and loved the teachers.
            Then we found out, talking to other parents, that some kids
            were getting a heck of a lot more as far as special services.
            Some of the kids in his class — now these are kids no worse off
            than Ronnie — were getting occupational therapy, physical
            therapy, three times as much speech and language therapy as
            he was getting, and the list goes on and on. There was a little
            girl in his class who had CP, who I'll admit was a lot worse off
            than Ronnie and couldn't talk at all, who had a little mini-com-
            puter supplied to her and an augmentative communication
            system [a small, computerized speech-synthesizing instru-
            ment]. Oh, yeah, and she had a specialist who came to the class
            twice a month to train the teacher and her on the communica-
            tion system.

            So the next year, when it came time to rewrite Ronnie's IEP
            [IEPs must be evaluated at least once a year], we discussed all
            Ronnie's needs and all the services that were available. They
            were real nice about it, and he got a lot more services that year.
            It makes you wonder, though, about why we had to ask. If we
            hadn't asked, I don't think they would have offered all that up,
            and I don't think that's right. It sort of discriminates against
            people who put faith in the system and figure that they'll just
            naturally get what they deserve.

All imaginable services are available everywhere in the country.
Unfortunately, the law requires only that services "benefit" children with
exceptional needs and leaves open to negotiation what a child requires to
"benefit." Following the four recommendations listed earlier in this section should help parents achieve as much benefit as can reasonably be
expected from a system — the nation's schools — suffering from severe
financial difficulties.

Question:
After my child starts receiving services, what will be expected of me?

Answer:
Expectations differ from program to program; for most programs to succeed, however, parents must be supportive and follow up with activities at home.

Even though many young children spend the better part of their waking hours away from home, most parents remain their children's primary teachers and models. Furthermore, one of the most significant determinants of a child's developmental progress is the functional level (intelligence, understanding of childrearing techniques, problem-solving abilities, etc.) of his or her primary care giver, which is usually the mother. It is therefore critical that professionals concerned with the developmental needs of young children consider home and family settings, making every effort to help parents identify their resources and strengths and prioritize and satisfy those needs that relate to raising their children.

The importance and value of including parents in early intervention services is clearly illustrated in the story of Sally May. Sally May was an 18-year-old, unmarried high school dropout when her first child, Barry, was born. She was sitting alone in her hospital room when the doctor walked in, informed her that her son had Down's syndrome, and asked her if she wanted to keep him or give him up (have him sent to an institution or placed in a foster home). Sally May, with the guidance of her mother, decided to bring Barry home (she was living in her mother's house at the time) and do the best she could.

Sally May: My doctor called Social Services and told them about Barry. A man came and saw me while I was still in the hospital. He gave me a lot of pamphlets and a lot of books about it [Down's syndrome] because I didn't know nothing. Then, before I even left the hospital, the doctor and the Social Services guy got together and talked to the local infant preschool program.

When Barry was 4 weeks old, they [teachers and therapists from the infant preschool program] started coming to our house. He was just 4 weeks old! They started leg exercises and were showing me what to do with him and stuff. They came about once or twice a week. When they came they would show me how to handle him, ways to sit him up and lie him down, all sorts of stuff. They tried to show me ways to help him that I could do during our everyday stuff, like not a lot of extra homework stuff, but just like, "Hold him this way; feed him like this; when he's lying down make sure about this and that." There was a lot of things to remember. Then they gave me other things to do, therapies and such, whenever I had time and energy. I really didn't know nothing about being a mom, especially about all those therapies and such. They taught me stuff I never knew. My mom never knew it neither, because my mom would sit in on the little sessions so that she would know more about it, too, and so she could help out.

After a couple of months with the therapist and teacher, then a speech and language teacher started working with us, too. She came to see how his sounds were coming — cooing and stuff — and how coordinated his tongue and throat and sucking were. She gave me lots of ideas, too, like to keep talking to him and stuff — to always be talking and telling him what I was doing. It sounded strange to me at first — talking to a baby who can't even understand a word — but I did it, and now I see where it was real important, because if you don't talk to a baby, how are they going to learn to talk?! She only came, like, maybe once or twice a month, because there wasn't much to tell at such a young age. Otherwise it was just the home teacher [an early childhood specialist who travels from home to home, working with children and families] and sometimes the therapist. The home teacher would come in twice a week, work with him, show me what to do so I could work better with him, and sometimes she would leave stuff, like toys and books and equipment, at my home, and I'd work with him all week.

Even experienced parents can benefit from the services of an early intervention team. The mother of a 6-year-old boy blind since birth reflects on the assistance she has received over the years:

Mother: We have four kids, two with special needs, and have worked with lots of teachers, therapists, and doctors over the past few years. Some have been real helpful and some a little less, but they've all made us think about what we're doing and, in their way, helped us do a better job.

Sometimes they make you feel a little guilty — like if they think you should be doing a lot more with your kids, kind of trying to lay guilt trips out. But most of them have been real supportive and tried to encourage us and give us ideas that we can fit in with our regular lives.

In most cases professionals will attempt to reinforce those things that parents are already doing well, at the same time providing occasional suggestions for ways to incorporate therapies and teaching into everyday activities and interactions. Professionals who ask parents to perform specific therapies ("homework") should make these requests with sensitivity to parents' schedules and the expression, on the part of parents, of a desire to participate in such activities.

Question:
They say that my child is mildly retarded. How much can she learn? What are her limits?

Answer:
No one can really tell you. Knowing that your child has a certain level of mental retardation tells you primarily how fast, rather than how much, she can learn.

Mild (IQ range of 55–70) and moderate (IQ range of 40–55) mental retardation, despite frequent misconceptions, are conditions better characterized by a slowed *rate* of learning rather than a limited *capacity* for learning. When given the proper environment and stimulation, children with mental retardation can learn far more than might be expected.

Amanda, the mother of a 4-year-old girl with microcephalus and a number of delays, expressed the importance of this issue of rate vs. capacity in the following way: "Little by little, step by step, it comes. It's slower, and it takes a lot more time and work and energy, but it comes." Amanda and her husband, Claude, relate how they have approached the education of their fourth of five children, Heather:

Amanda: We don't know a lot about her level of retardation except that she doesn't talk much — she doesn't verbalize very well — and she's been slower in most everything, especially fine motor [coordinating smaller muscles, such as fingers] and gross motor [coordinating larger muscles, such as legs and arms].

She's been down to University Hospital, and basically all they said was, "We'll see what she'll do." They wouldn't commit themselves as to how far she would go. The only thing they said was the name for the condition is microcephalic, which means that her brain isn't growing as much as it should. But there's a lot of different causes, and they don't know which cause was hers, and they don't know the prospects — like how smart or slow she'll be or how much she'll learn.

When she had her 4-month-old baby checkup, they said she wasn't as responsive as a baby would normally be. At 9 months they noticed her head wasn't growing. They began charting her and testing her and stuff, and we did all we could at home to work with her and teach her. They recommended things like mobiles in the crib, touching different parts of her body with different "feely" kind of things — like soft and rough and wet, and slimy, all sorts of "feely" stuff — lots of music and talking to her, playing with toys and getting her to reach for them and try to move to them, stuff like that. They said it could only help, so we did it just to be sure, like to cover our bases.

A few months later, she was about 17 months old then, she started with the infant program run by the county. They really went out of their way to listen to how we were doing with Heather. I mean, they wanted to hear about all the things we did with her and how we were responding to her, and about how we were handling it, her being so slow like she was. They said that with mental retardation there was always a lot that could be done early on in life — that putting in some extra effort while she was young would make a big difference as far as what level she'd achieve. They helped us come up with a bunch of things we could do at home that might be helpful. I really liked that because a lot of the things we came up with I could just do in the regular schedule, without making special preparations or spending a lot of time and such. But you could see they were good ideas to help Heather — just good, practical ideas to do, like sitting her up on the counter and talking to her while I was gettin' meals ready; leaving her on the floor more, to practice moving around, instead of in her playpen or high chair; buying certain kinds of toys and putting them all around her — those sorts of things.

I really liked the attitude of the people who worked with us. It was like, "You'll get back what you put in." We got the feeling that whatever we did with her was going to make her smarter and more capable. It wasn't like, "Oh well, she's retarded, not much to work on, case closed." It's true, too. We've done a lot of reading since this whole thing started, and it's amazing how much more these kids will learn if you focus in on the details and make sure they get things, learn things. It's sort of like when someone's retarded, there's almost always more potential there than you ever get to. Lots of times part of the problem with retardation is that they don't or can't or won't go out and learn as much on their own. Someone, like teachers and parents, has to keep closer tabs on what they know and don't know and set things up so they can learn what they have to.

So be prepared for your child's learning to come slower, but don't start putting a lot of limits on how far he'll be able to go or how much she'll be able to learn. You'll need more patience and your child will need a lot more guidance and practice, but your child *will* learn.

Question:
My child is just an infant. What could they possibly "teach" her?

Answer:
Lots!

The first few months of life set the stage for all learning that is to follow. Babies need to experience and experiment with their senses of taste, smell, touch, hearing, and vision, and with their movement. It is through these senses and actions that they gain an understanding of the world around them. What we think of as cognition, or intelligence, is dependent upon a strong motor and perceptual base. Activities designed to strengthen motor and perceptual skills will help prepare a child for later cognitive and intellectual learning.

Amanda, the mother quoted in the last question, continues to describe working with her daughter Heather's microcephalus and mental
retardation, stressing the critical importance of starting early in life:

Amanda: The teachers and therapists always made sure that we knew
          why they were doing things so that we could relate the thera-
          pies to everyday activities. Sometimes they'd bring materials,
          like feely-touchy things and rattles and toys, for us to use at
          home. One of them called them "IQ builders." She said that a
          little child's play was their form of work, and it was building
          their coordination and senses and thinking skills just as sure as
          reading and studying would for an older child or grown-up. It
          only makes sense when you think about it. It's like lifting
          weights to make your muscles bigger, except with babies
          they're touching and tasting and listening and playing with
          toys instead of weights, and instead of building big biceps,
          they're developing their coordination and working on their
          senses and teaching themselves how to think and problem
          solve.
              We figured that the more we got her moving and playing
          and actively using her brain to figure things out, the smarter
          she'd be. When she was real young, like before she even
          turned a year old, they were working on all sorts of things
          with her. They did a lot of stuff to make her more aware of her
          body and balance and touch — all her senses, really. Things
          like rolling her up in a blanket and rolling her around, playing
          in the water, touching sand and cornstarch and flour and rice
          and stuff; sitting in rocking chairs and on little horses, swings,
          all that stuff; listening to different sounds on tape recorders.
          They'd work on paying attention, too, looking at books and
          pictures and dolls and puppets, and listening to songs and
          rhymes and stories — lots of using her eyes and ears. There
          was always something going on.
              They'd do lots of things with speech and language, too. You
          know, we worked and worked trying to get her to say any-
          thing. She didn't verbalize much except to sort of make a
          grunting-shouting noise and laugh. She hardly cooed or bab-
          bled at all, except a little bit once in a while, and then it would
          disappear and she wouldn't say anymore for days — sort of on
          and off without making any kinds of sounds. So we didn't

know if she was going backwards or forwards or what was happening. The teachers did lots of techniques and taught us lots of techniques to help with that, too — to make her use sounds more. Things like us responding more when she'd make the smallest effort to make any sound, and making her ask for stuff — she didn't actually use words, but making her at least grunt, you know, use some sounds to express herself. There were just lots of different techniques that we had never thought about.

I think the programs were real good for her. I was always hoping she'd outgrow them and she wouldn't need them, though, because I didn't want anything to be wrong with her. But I think they were good for her because the people were consistent and they did the same things everyday, and they did it step fashion: one step at a time. They knew what you had to do first and then what came next. Before we started with all this, we didn't know how to do that, but now we do. They knew little by little how to get kids to where you wanted them to go.

Kids like Heather have a tendency to just keep doing the same thing over and over again — sort of like once they learn something they tend to stick with it and not want to stop. Well, the teachers and therapists taught us how to change the toys and the environment around so as to encourage her to stretch herself a bit more. We didn't teach her so much as we did just set up situations for her to learn.

Adrian [Heather's younger brother], he sees something once, he can do it. He sees a toy, plays with it for a minute, and then he's an expert. He just does it — no training, no analysis, he just does it. With her you have to first get her interested in it, and then maybe coach her and show her. Eventually she may get it but maybe not. Sometimes she picks things up real nonchalantly, and you wonder, "How did she do that?" Something else, though, it just doesn't sink in; she just doesn't come around, so you have to set things up so she can practice that skill so she can learn it.

Infancy is the time of life dedicated to learning about the senses and body; it's a time to experiment and explore sensations that enter through the mouth, nose, skin, body movements, ears, and eyes. Typical infants tend to take fullest advantage of this period and during their limited periods of wakefulness devote nearly 100 percent of their energies to experimentation and exploration. Children born with disabilities, including developmental disabilities (mental retardation), however, often are less self-motivated and require that their environments be altered somewhat to encourage their experimentation and exploration. For these young children to become the most they can be, parents and professionals must go beyond simply providing a rich environment and then observing the child learn; they must at times manipulate the environment, paying special attention to reinforcing desired behaviors, encouraging children whose self-motivation may not be enough to push them to new learning.

Question:
I've heard that there's some inconsistency in services around the country. Is that true?

Answer:
True. Not only are there inconsistencies around the country but sometimes even within a given agency or school district or county.

Federal and state laws attempt to bring order and consistency to services, but many other factors make this an often elusive goal. These factors include the heavy financial burden special services place on local school districts and agencies, differing values among communities, professional burnout, pay discrepancies between school districts (usually the sponsors of programs for children 3 and older) and community agencies (most often the sponsors of programs for children from birth to 3 years old), short supply of professionals (critical personnel shortages exist in many specialties), and greater demand than ever before (due primarily to medical advances in saving babies born prematurely and increased use of drugs in pregnant women). Each of these factors contributes to the feeling one mother expressed: "You've got to appreciate it [services] when you've got it."

Gordon, the father of Jed, a 5-year-old with severe emotional difficulties, discusses his experiences trying to find services for his child:

Gordon: Where we moved from there was nothing, zero. It was like we were supposed to do it all on our own. We started having serious concerns when Jed was about 2½ or 3 years old. You could tell he was different. He was a real handful and very emotional. You'd never know what was going to come next. Our house was usually a wreck, and so were we. Marsha [Gordon's wife] was afraid to take him out by herself. She wouldn't leave the house with him unless I came. For almost a year she never took him out by herself.

Well, I called the local school district, and they referred me to the county. Someone came to our house, but they didn't even go through an evaluation or anything. The lady said that if he did qualify — which she didn't think he would — the classroom was an hour and a quarter bus ride, each way. That would mean two and a half hours a day, on a bus, to attend a class that only met for two and a half hours. We thought it was crazy. Anyway, the class was basically for autistic children, and Jed probably wasn't severe enough. She recommended that we look for private family counseling. Anyway, soon after that I was transferred here.

What a difference! We got here and called the local school district and found out that there were lots of programs for kids like Jed. We weren't here for more than a few weeks before he was enrolled five days a week in a special classroom, right here at our neighborhood school.

He's got about six or seven kids in his class, and there are two teachers — I guess one's an aide. He sees a speech teacher twice a week and a counselor. He's been in the program for only a few months and we're already seeing changes. They've got him on a real strict routine at school and have given us a lot of ideas to follow up with at home. Basically, it's just a set schedule with contracts and charts and agreements for different kinds of behaviors. We do it at home, too. Our house sort of runs like the army — I mean *by the book* — but it's really working, so we can't complain. My wife can even handle him out of the house now, which I think is pretty incredible.

I can't figure out how services could be so different from one place to another. I'm keeping my fingers crossed, though, because I know it may not last forever.

Cindy, the mother of Simon, who is almost 3 years old and has Down's syndrome, expresses her disappointment in the system's inconsistencies:

Cindy: Everything's getting cut back. I just think that maybe it's
            because they don't have enough money. I've been watching
            the local program here for almost three years. Each year they
            have more and more children and it's gotten tighter and
            tighter. I've seen the EEN [exceptional educational needs]
            teacher get very tired. She doesn't have the time to do the
            planning that she used to. She just has so many children to
            watch and take care of and all kinds of different programs to
            coordinate with and evaluations and meetings. The system is
            just running her ragged!

                When Simon first went to the program, they had a little
            notebook that they'd send to us almost every day. They'd
            write a little note about what he'd done. Now it's two or three
            months and they don't write anything about what he's doing,
            so I know they're busy. If I didn't know how good it could be
            — how it used to be — it wouldn't be so frustrating!

Cindy is upset because she knows the type of job Simon's teacher has
done in the past and is capable of doing, but the increased number of
students created a situation that would not allow her to perform at her
best. The burden of more students detracted from, at very least, the level
of communication between teacher and parents. This change had a significant effect on Cindy's attitude toward Simon's teacher and educational program.

Sometimes a certain position is so difficult to fill that it either remains
vacant and services are not provided at all, or a steady stream of part-time
and temporary personnel flows through. This situation is exemplified in
the following description of a mother's frustration in trying to find
physical and occupational therapy services for her 2½-year-old, recovering from a stroke:

Mother: Things were going well for awhile, but then the OT [occupa-
            tional therapist] got a higher-paying job somewhere else. It
            took months to find a replacement for her — they said it was
            hard to find someone qualified to work with young children
            who would work for what the agency could afford to pay.
            Finally they hired another lady, but she had never worked
            with kids at all, and as it turned out, she only stayed a few
            weeks anyway.

While all this was going on, the PT [physical therapist] had a baby, and they couldn't find anyone to replace her while she was on maternity [leave]. After her maternity was over, she decided not to return. There we were, losing valuable time, with no therapies whatsoever. Our insurance wouldn't pay for private [therapy]. . . . It was really a big mess!

Through this whole time there was no one there [at the infant center] who could really help us that much. They, I mean the teachers and director, were having a hard time, too, and, well, it's like we were sort of getting the message, "Don't hassle me; I've got all I can take."

When the supply of helping professionals is not great enough to meet the demand of children requiring services, one of three outcomes can be expected: (1) a rise in supply (more professionals entering the marketplace), (2) a fall in demand (fewer children qualifying for and/or receiving services), or (3) dissatisfaction (supply lagging behind demand). At the present time the supply of helping professionals is rising very slowly, the demand for services is growing rapidly, and dissatisfaction is not uncommon.

The most likely explanation why the supply of helping professionals is not meeting the demand of special needs lies in the balance between stress and financial rewards (pay). The stress involved in working with young children with disabilities and their families is quite great; the pay is not.

Question:
What can I do to ensure that my child receives good services and that those services continue?

Answer:
Find out as much as you can about your child's condition, search out all available services, and get involved. Being successful in these endeavors will require reading, going to conferences, talking with other parents, attending meetings, joining parent organizations, and becoming politically active.

Parents have traditionally been the most active group in securing services for children with exceptional needs. Had it not been for their efforts, landmark public laws such as PL 94-142 and PL 99-457 may never have been passed, and the condition of special education in the United States would no doubt be many years behind what it is today. To ensure that what has been gained is not lost and that further advances continue to enrich the lives of children and families challenged by exceptional needs, parents need to continue their active support of existing programs and lobby for new programs and increased funding. They need to express themselves loudly and clearly about how programs can benefit their children and their children can benefit society, and about programs they like and those they don't like.

In order to advocate in this way, parents need to understand their children's conditions and be aware of services that are available. To be a strong advocate or lobbyist requires knowledge and understanding. Parents must therefore read and learn about their child's disability, attend conferences, join support groups, and network. Through activities such as these they will become more knowledgeable about the condition of special education and be more able to suggest how it might be improved; they will prepare themselves for the numerous letters they will have to write, phone calls they will have to make, and questions they will have to answer.

Jim knows well how the process works. For the past thirty years he has been an active advocate for children and adults with various types of developmental disabilities.

Jim: I remember back to the late sixties and early seventies, when
            we were starting to push for programs and laws. It seemed like
            it was a lot easier to get parents involved. Where I lived there
            was a group of about twenty-five or thirty of us that met
            regularly, shared information, wrote letters, called members of
            the legislature and Congress, carried signs at rallies — we
            were real involved, real busy. Now it seems that parents are a
            lot more complacent. I think you could call it spoiled, maybe.
            Everything was handed to them: programs, funding, due
            process, IEPs, mainstreaming. . . . I don't think that some of
            them even understand that all this had to be fought for. They
            just take it all for granted. Well, believe me, because I know:
            the government can take this away anytime.

            We still need to keep it together. We, parents of kids and
            adults with special needs, need to keep on top of what's going
            on in special education and in the legislature, or we could just
            end up with a real crisis.

Charissa, the mother of a 6-year-old boy, Reggie, who has been diagnosed as having attention deficit disorder (ADD) with hyperactivity and may have a learning disability, is well aware that parents need to know about their child's condition and available resources and become politically involved.

Charissa: I had the hardest time getting any services for Reggie. They [the school district] told me he didn't qualify because he wasn't far enough behind where he was supposed to be for his age. I told them that he had ADD, was hyperactive, and probably had a learning disability, too — it sort of runs in his dad's family, and Reggie has some of the early signs — but they stuck to their guns and refused to admit him.

I studied and learned as much as I could about ADD and hyperactivity and learning disabilities and got real involved with a statewide group that is pressuring our state and the federal governments to make services more available to these kids before they start failing in school. I learned an awful lot in the process and made a lot of contacts.

As you might guess, the next time — it was a year later — that I tried to get some help from the local schools, I was much better prepared. This advocacy group I'm in made Reggie into sort of a test case for the state, so we brought in a lot of information and experts and our own test results. Guess what? Reggie got into the program I wanted, and now we're getting lots of different services from the schools.

It was hard work, but I think it was worth it. I couldn't just sit back and let him fail like I knew he was going to — let him get two or three years behind and all frustrated and then get help.

A few months after this interview took place, the federal government established new guidelines that will make it much easier for children such as Reggie to receive services. Not all parents can fight the system as

Charissa did, but all parents can learn more about their child's disabilities and available resources and can actively pursue programs and funding that will help brighten their child's future.

Tips for Parents

- Always double- and perhaps even triple-check with different people before resigning yourself to the idea that certain services are unattainable.
- Remember the four recommendations to make the most of the special education referral process:
  1. Ask to participate in the decisions about what areas are to be evaluated/tested.
  2. Ask for copies of all assessment reports prior to the meeting that will determine your child's eligibility.
  3. In advance of the meeting, write down your questions and ideas, discuss them with a friend or someone who can help you express yourself, and attend the meeting with that person.
  4. Don't sign or agree to anything you don't completely understand and support.
- Do as much as you can while your child is young — the earlier the better.
- Keep up-to-date on your child's condition and programs and, if at all possible, let people in power know your opinions.

Tips for Professionals

- Make every attempt to supply parents with as much information and as many resources as possible.
- Don't say no if the real answer is maybe or probably not or I'm not sure.
- Avoid making parents feel guilty about not doing their "homework" with their children.
- Whenever possible, reinforce what parents are already doing with their children rather than giving new ideas; when you do supply

new ideas, try to fit them into daily routines rather than making requests that will take time from parents' already busy schedules.

Conclusion

Once parents have accepted that their child is in need of early intervention services, they must seek out all available resources and see to it that services are provided as early, competently, and intensively as possible. Most disabilities have innate tendencies to become more serious and more limiting when not remediated; however, when proper intervention occurs, limiting effects are diminished and individuals are more able to maximize their potentials.

This maximization of potential is further encouraged when competent, compassionate, and caring professionals include parents as co-therapists and co-teachers. When professionals, parents, and children with disabilities work together, the likelihood that they will meet their goals and objectives is dramatically increased.

4

Parents Appreciate Professionals Who . . .

Parents look for and appreciate many qualities in professionals. When asked the question, "Besides competence, what do you expect from professionals who help you with your child's special needs?" parents gave responses ranging from frivolities such as free coffee in the office and balloons for the kids, to practical considerations such as reasonable costs and flexible hours, to heartfelt pleas to save lives and bring sanity back into homes and relationships.

Despite the diversity of responses, five general requests were mentioned time and again:

1. Treat us like human beings.
2. Be honest with us.
3. Lead us to resources.
4. Be patient.
5. Encourage us.

Although we have made an attempt to turn these five topics into separate sections, in truth the overlap is considerable. It is difficult to treat people like human beings without being honest; lead them to resources without being patient; or provide encouragement without treating them like human beings, being honest, leading them to resources, and being patient.

Question:
My child is going to require many different services over the next few years. We're fortunate because there are lots of professionals to choose from in our area. The problem is that I don't want to jump around — I'd like to continue with the same people for years, if possible. What do other parents of kids with exceptional needs look for in a helping professional?

Answer:

Besides professional competence, parents look for many qualities, but one that is often repeated and always near the top of the list is "someone who treats me like a human being."

The first thought that comes to mind for many parents when asked what they expect from professionals is, as one mother expressed it, "to be treated like a person, treated with respect. I like it when I get the feeling that what I believe and want matters and that I'm more than just a case number or appointment or another session or examination." More simply stated, people want to be treated like human beings. Many of the parents interviewed shared the belief that they would prefer working with someone they could talk to, someone they felt really cared, even if that person was a bit less talented or brilliant than another, less communicative and less caring professional.

Frustrated by a lack of personal contact or connectedness with their family doctor, the parents of 2-year-old Seth, Daniel and Claire, searched for someone who could help them deal with their son's many medical needs and at the same time treat them with respect and make a difference in their lives:

Claire: We weren't feeling too good about our family doctor and heard about a new doctor who had just moved to town. He didn't have many patients yet, but everyone said he was a real caring and sensitive person.

Daniel: He'll call here at times just to talk and see how we're doing. Maybe later he'll get too big and start being less personal like the rest of them, but it sure feels great now — it keeps us satisfied.

He was always real friendly with our boy, Seth, too, and he looked at Seth like he was a real person, not just another sick body. He played with him, and you could just tell that he cared.

Claire: He's the first person we go to when we have a problem or we need something for Seth. He directs us where to go. With other doctors we'd sometimes get the feeling that they were counting the minutes, counting the seconds. This guy does it all and doesn't even need to be asked or pushed. It's like he cares enough about Seth to want to know about everything else that's going on, like about therapies and other appointments [with other medical specialists]. He's like the ringmaster. I inform him about what's going on, and he'll say, "OK, now why don't you go ahead and call this person" or, " I'll get in touch with that person."

The time Seth had his eye surgery, two days later, out of the blue, our doctor called: "How did Seth make it through the surgery?" He's just thinking about his patients, and he really cares.

"He really cares!" Once you've spent some time in the search for services and begun wondering, "How come I've got to be a raving maniac to get anything from anyone?" you learn to appreciate it when you find someone who really cares.

Robert and Mary, the parents of 4-year-old Ben, had already lost one child during the birthing process and were quite apprehensive about their second pregnancy. Having been involved in the first loss, their pediatrician was well aware of the anxiety both parents were feeling. With tears in her eyes, Mary recalls the following interaction with her pediatrician:

Mary: As soon as Ben was born, they found them [lumps under the skin], just in the small of the back. He had, like, five of them. Well, they could also feel a couple in his arms and a couple here or there. One afternoon my doctor walked in, and I said, "Did you get the biopsy results back yet?" He looked at me and said, "The cells are abnormal." I just looked at him. I said, "It's cancer, isn't it?" and he started crying. He left the room. He didn't even answer me. I mean, because he had been with us for our first one — he knew we lost our first one — and now with our second one having cancer, he was probably in shock.

A few minutes later he came back and spent a long time with us, not as a doctor or as an expert but just as a human being, a loving, sensitive human being. He really cared. You could see it in his face and hear it in his voice; you could feel it just being with him.

He was just a wonderful support person. Anytime you needed encouragement, he didn't, like, try to be the big boss type and all serious and professional. He was real, a real person, and he just made us feel like he cared and like we were important and our feelings were important.

This concern can be communicated in many different ways. Marsha, a mother who has spent considerable amounts of time over the years dealing with many different helping professionals, searching for assistance in dealing with her 5½-year-old son who has serious emotional difficulties, says:

Marsha: The way they [professionals] say hello is important to me. I mean, if they are too busy to even say hi, to smile and shake your hand, what does that say? To me it says, "Let's hurry up and get this done. I'm a busy person."

Some of the professionals who have worked with Jed [her son] are so warm and concerned. You just look at them and you know they care. There's this one teacher who makes me feel good every time I see her. She looks right into my eyes and I feel like she's really with me. I don't know how to say it, how to describe it exactly. It just seems that even without talking or saying anything, I'm sharing with her and she's sharing with me. She's not like some others I've worked with, always looking at papers and charts and books; she looks right at me.

Because helping professionals so often find themselves in emotional, stressful, sometimes even life-threatening situations, these interpersonal skills are of critical importance. A parent's primary need frequently is not professional expertise but someone to talk to; during those encounters, good eye contact, patience, and concern are far more valuable than three or four graduate degrees.

Professionals have the potential to make a significant impact on the families they work with. Barb remembers most vividly many weeks of visiting her infant daughter, Kris, as she lay in an NICU with a life-threatening heart condition:

Kris: The people there are so real, so down-to-earth, so honest — I guess working on a children's ward you have to be like that. They sort of become part of your family; well, they become your life when you're living there and all these other families are living there. They sit in the lounge and have coffee with you or just sort of hang out. In the middle of the night if you need somebody to talk to, they're there. If they lose a child, they walk around the halls crying. They're real people. I'm not saying it was just nurses. It was some technicians and medical students, too. The ones that are there constantly with you and watch the kids get better or watch them get worse. This one nurse in particular really thought that my husband and I should leave together sometime, and he volunteered to stay after his shift and sit in our room so that we could go out to eat and just be together, away from the hospital. I'll always remember that. Sometimes it doesn't take all that much extra effort to make a difference and make people feel good.

You need to connect with people like that sometimes. I mean, when it's all business, all charts, therapies, cc's, medications, decisions, all that life-and-death stuff, it's just too much. When the people you see all the time are just business and nothing personal, it's too much. Can you imagine? Without the personal part, I couldn't take it.

More: people functioning under stressful conditions require more attention, more time, more individualized care, and more sensitivity from professionals. The more serious and involved the case, the child, the situation, the more a parent needs. Parents of kids with special needs must search out professionals who will relate to them as human beings and, based upon that person-to-person relationship, provide them with the "more" that they need.

Question:
I like it when the professionals keep me informed about what's going on, but sometimes it's too much. Sometimes I even feel like I'd rather not be told anything. Should professionals share everything with us or just what we "need" to know?

Answer:
Most parents prefer honesty; they prefer being offered information and then having the opportunity to make their own decision about whether or not they want to hear or read more.

There are many different approaches to honesty, and for each approach there may be hundreds of different reactions. Some people just want "the facts"; others want the truth only if it isn't too painful; still others may want the truth but only in small bits and pieces, provided at just the right rate to keep them informed without being too upsetting. What may seem like an honest communication to one may seem unduly harsh or cold to another. One person's reaction to a professional's explanation may be, "I wish she would get to the point," whereas another may think, "What's the hurry? I have so many questions!" It's clear that you can't please all of the people all of the time.

And yet certain approaches to revealing information seem more commonly accepted and appreciated than others. Readers are reminded that there is no set formula for how much honesty an individual can take. Each situation, each human being, is different.

Mother: My baby was no more than an hour old and the doctor comes in and tells us she's got hydrocephalus and spina bifida. She starts telling us about all the possibilities, like being crippled and retarded and stuff. I mean, we were shocked.

Father: I couldn't believe it. I mean, the baby came out looking real good, and then all this.

Mother: It was like getting hit in the head with a brick. It was like, "Oh, my God!"

Father: But she [the surgeon] was there, like real straight and steady, letting us know everything. She told us about all the things she could do and what the chances were, like what could happen. There were a lot of decisions to make, and she wanted us to make them. It wasn't like our daughter was going to be like this or that. It was all a matter of chances, percentages — maybe this, maybe that. She didn't know for sure how our baby was going to be. She might be retarded, but she might be a genius, too. The surgeon just told us the chances.

Mother: I'm glad, too, because since then I've talked to lots of parents who weren't told. They were told, "You should do this" and "We should do that." They were just bossed around and not given choices.

Father: Yeah. Parents have the right to know everything. We're the ones who are going to live with the kid, going to spend our lives with her, so we should be the ones to decide.

In order to take control of the decision-making process, parents need to have as much information as there is as soon as possible. It is the responsibility of helping professionals to share relevant data as it becomes available; however, this free flow of information doesn't always occur. It's not at all uncommon for professionals to mask their thoughts and feelings with the statement, "Let's wait and see." Although this platitude may well mean that enough data has not yet been collected and that it's too early to make any judgments, it sometimes means, "I have a suspicion that something is not right, but . . .":

"I don't want to alarm or upset you."

"I'm not going to share what I think because there isn't that much we could do anyway."

"I'm really busy, and I don't have the time to look more deeply right now."

"Let's wait and see" may at times be appropriate advice, but at other times it's dishonest, a cover-up, and can delay interventions that may best be started right away. Raphael, the 2½-year-old child discussed in the following dialog, is presently functioning at or above his age level in all areas; however, if his pediatrician had not honestly shared his concerns or if Raphael's parents, Frank and Sue, had followed the wait-and-see advice of family and friends, he might not now be experiencing the same levels of success.

Sue: Raphael was a slow talker. We didn't really pick up on it except to notice that he wasn't saying much. He did a lot of pointing and saying "ah, ah," sort of like a grunt. When we took him in to see the pediatrician for a regular 18-month checkup, the doctor asked me what Raphael was saying for words. At that time he was only saying "ball," "mama," "dada," and "Alf," because he likes the television program "Alf." That was basically it. The pediatrician told us that by the book, a child should be saying a lot more words and even be starting on some two-word phrases at 18 months. I just was floored. So he said, "Let's have him evaluated." I said, "Sure, fine." So he gave me the name of the local center.

            I called them, and they came and evaluated him and said that even though Raphael was 18 months old, he was only at about the 12-month level in speech and language. We talked about it and figured out it might be because he was just spoiled and got everything handed to him without having to talk. So we enrolled him in the program a couple of weeks later and since then he's done great.

There were a lot of people, friends and relatives, that said, "Oh, let him go at his own speed," but we thought it couldn't hurt getting the extra help. No one at his preschool, not the teachers or the director, thought there was anything to be concerned about. I mean, they never mentioned anything, and then when we had him evaluated, they looked at us sort of like "Why? What's the problem?" After Raphael got started in the speech program, then the preschool teacher and director said, "You know, we suspected that. We were going to mention it to you." What were they waiting for, Christmas?! That sort of upset me, that they waited to tell me. I'd prefer a little good old-fashioned honesty myself.

There's no way he would have made the growth he did if we had just waited and hadn't gotten the help. I mean, if that doctor hadn't been straight with us, if he had just been like the rest and said, "Oh, let's give it six months or a year, you know, wait and see" — if that had happened, I'm sure Raphael would still be behind, maybe even further behind, and we'd have a big problem.

Recall a theme from Chapter 2: "If in doubt, check it out!" Think of all the time, money, anguish, and lost potential that could be saved if the advice "Wait and see" were to fall out of fashion and "If in doubt, check it out" were to become the standard.

For this new standard to become a reality, some professionals will have to become more honest. They will need to risk making more incorrect "possible" diagnoses, take the chance of making parents a bit more nervous and concerned, and invest the time to gather enough information to make educated guesses rather than postponing recommendations until nature has taken its course for a few more days or weeks or months.

Parents need to know what the possibilities are. They need to have as much advance warning as possible if atypical development is suspected. They have a right to ask that this information be shared with them in a way and at the pace in which they can best deal with it.

Question:

I think there are a lot of resources out there that I'm not getting to. Besides the standard agencies and parent support groups, how do you find out what's out there?

Answer:

Agencies and parent support groups are a good place to start. After that it's a matter of asking around. The professionals you are already working with should have a number of good referrals.

Ask the professionals you are presently working with (pediatricians, day care directors, teachers, and counselors); these people should have a good idea of what's out there and be able to direct you toward what you need. Actually, you shouldn't even have to ask: competent helping professionals should make recommendations as soon as they become concerned.

Following is a description of how this process can work. Unfortunately, what is about to be described is not as commonplace as it might be but a portrait of excellence that surpasses most experiences. The parent of a 5-year-old preschooler who was demonstrating unusual, often aggressive behavior tells about a conference with her child's day care director:

Mother: She [the day care director] asked me to come by and see her. Well, we started talking and got onto the subject of Tammy's behavior. We both agreed that it was bad and getting worse, but I didn't really have a clue where to go from there. Then she [the director] pulls out this big thick notebook. . . . She opens it up and it's got all these sections, like pediatricians, dentists, psychologists, baby-sitters, financial needs, family services. . . . In each section she's got little notes and papers from other parents, like parents from the center, telling about the people and places in the book. It was incredible!

So we look at the book and talk about where I might go and what I could do to get help. It was neat because I could read all about different programs and get ideas. I got the names and numbers of a couple of agencies and a couple of psychologists, and I figured we were about done when the lady [the director] takes me over to her library and asks me if there's anything specific I'd like to read about, to get more information about. Well, then I got all these articles and books that helped me with problems I'd been having with Tammy.

I mean, talk about having it together; this lady was prepared! I really appreciated all she did for me.

Besides other professionals or agencies or readings, another valuable resource for parents can be other parents. Sharon, the mother of 5-year-old Evan, the child with autism who was introduced in an earlier chapter, discusses a resource she wishes had been available to her but wasn't:

Sharon: It would be so neat if agencies would have a list of people who have children with exceptional needs and are willing to help other people. I would have somebody there right away. If a diagnosis was made, I would say, "OK, this is what's wrong. Now I want you to know that someone will be visiting you — a mother who has just gone through this — and she will be coming tomorrow or the next day to talk to you. If you have any questions, you can ask her." I think something like that would be good. Something where you could have somebody to share this with initially. I don't think most mothers and fathers, husbands and wives can absorb so much at once. They need help.

I think it's best having somebody come right into the house — I would say, within the first few days — and say, "OK, my son/my daughter is autistic, too. I know what you're feeling." If they would even just sit there and talk to the new parents that had just found out about their child — the ones that had just found out wouldn't even have to talk — just having somebody else talk to them and say, "This is what happened to me. This is how I felt. I went through this. I cried for two weeks. I still don't know which way is up. We had financial problems. We had trouble with finding baby-sitters. My kid does this and it still drives me nuts." To just talk to them and maybe answer their questions. To know that you are not the only one and to know that there are a lot worse cases. That would be great!

It's a lot harder to call someone and ask for help than it is to answer the phone and say, "OK, sure you can come over." A lot of parents just stay home and tough it out themselves. They'd like to talk to someone else who's been through it, but they're shy or scared to call, to take the first step.

A good start in the process of searching out resources is this book. Look at the resources listed at the back. Beyond that, the first two places to go are to professionals you know and trust and to other consumers of services. Talk to people who utilize the type of services you are looking for; learn about their experiences; get names and phone numbers and make connections with people in similar situations. As one father so colorfully summarized this search for services, "Think of yourself as a prospector looking for gold. You have to keep digging and digging. Whether you don't find anything or you find a huge lode, odds are there's a lot more somewhere close by. You just got to keep searching, keep digging."

Question:

I'm an impatient person and I'm worried that raising a child who learns really slowly is going to drive me crazy. What can I do to develop my patience?

Answer:

Although there are many psychological and spiritual techniques to help develop patience, a common recommendation made by parents is to surround yourself with patient professionals and model on and learn from them.

Patience — not being hasty or impetuous, gathering all necessary information before acting — is a valuable characteristic in dealing with people. Yet when schedules are full and many jobs are waiting to be completed, parents and professionals may not always take the time they would like to. Many individuals feel compelled to rush, even though they haven't put forth their best effort. This may be acceptable, perhaps even standard, practice in certain fields of endeavor; it is far less acceptable, however, when helping others. Those whose responsibility or job it is to help others are expected to take the time.

Many parents report that they have learned a lot from observing professionals who work with their children. Professionals who model patience and the ability to see and appreciate growth and change, no matter how small, set a wonderful example for parents. This patience is beautifully described by Bill and Marge as they tell about the first time they met the occupational therapist for their son, Ken, a 3½-year-old with a neurological disorder, deafness in one ear, paralysis on one side of his face, visual problems, and delays in all areas of development.

Marge: It sort of gets depressing when you don't see a lot of change. You wonder if they're ever going to learn. Ken started out pretty slow. I mean, he just wasn't going through the stages, the learning and changing and stuff, like our older one had. Then the occupational therapist started coming out to the house.

Bill: When she started, she didn't know what Ken could or couldn't do. She sat for half an hour or forty-five minutes that first day just seeing if he could tap two things together. Tapping toys together. She would take toys and tap, tap, tap, and then put them in Ken's hands and wait. That just amazed me. I didn't know there was any human being that would sit there for forty-five minutes and do that same thing. She was just an unbelievable person.

And I'll be, by the end of that session, she had him doing it: he was tapping two toys together. She had us work a lot on things like that. She put in a lot of hours with Ken; so did we. She'd sit there and wait for him to do things himself. She'd just sit and wait. Every time he'd put out any effort, any effort at all, she'd compliment him and make him feel good. I mean, she sure could wait. Me, I'd want to do it for him if he didn't do something, but she'd just watch, and somehow, sure enough, if that little guy wouldn't surprise us and make an effort.

Marge: Now, two and a half years later, when I took him to school for his evaluation, his OT [a different OT] says he's not that far behind in working with his hands. He can cut with a scissors and do lots of other stuff, so in that field, where we worked with and we knew what we were doing, he's come a long way.

Bill: So now there's a nice little light at the end of tunnel. She helped us see that he could learn. So that was a good, encouraging sign. I don't know if we could have been so patient and worked so hard if she hadn't shown us originally, back then, that he could do it. I really appreciate that.

Another parent, the father of a 3-year-old son with severe delays, had difficulty seeing any improvement because his child's development was so slow that it seemed nonexistent. He was aided in becoming more patient by a teacher, very patient herself, who charted and reported developmental milestones:

Father: There was a while there when I got real depressed. It just seemed like we were going nowhere. For two years he had been in an infant program and he had gotten older, but darned if I saw much change in what he could do. Oh sure, there were some changes, but, my *God*, they were so slow.

Then he entered the school here [the boy went from the county-run infant intervention program to the local school district's early childhood special education program for 3- through 5-year-olds] and things started happening. Well, I don't know how much was really a change in him or a change in the school or just a change in us.

Anyway, his teacher started doing all of these charts about what he could do and what he was learning to do, and she'd check him all the time. You could look at these charts and stuff and see that he was learning, see that things were changing. They'd be things that I'd probably not have noticed if they hadn't been measured like that. She did some at school and we did some at home. She showed us what patience really was. I mean, she'd do stuff like watch him for thirty minutes straight, and she'd do this a lot, and she'd count how many times he hit his head — he liked to sort of slam his fists into his forehead, with the knuckle part, sort of like a nervous habit. She'd count how many times he did that and try to get him to do it less. It helped us, me at least, to be more patient and see that things were changing. I'd start looking for little changes, and when I saw them we'd talk about them and we'd all feel good.

She'd [the child's teacher] make us feel good about it every time we'd put out an effort and not give up. She'd, like, say stuff and congratulate us and stuff and try and get us to keep working and keep doing what we were doing, because it was really helping, really doing good.

Patience, mixed with encouragement, helped this father avoid the despair that often accompanies slow growth.

Many believe that in order to develop patience like this — as well as many other skills — it's necessary to have a model, to see the behavior in action. Some people can learn well from books, others from being told what to do; however, many people need to have a model they can watch, listen to, and get feedback from in order to learn and change. The message here is that we, parents and professionals, should make every possible effort to surround ourselves with good models; to watch, listen to, and have the opportunity to exchange ideas with individuals who do what they do very well.

Question:
Some of the professionals we work with leave me feeling really good and competent and successful, but some don't. Am I being insecure or childish because I like to be told I'm doing a good job?

Answer:
Most people want and need to be complimented and told that they're doing a good job. This encouragement is especially important for parents who are trying to raise children with exceptional needs.

Encouragement, often called reinforcement, can help provide parents with support in the difficult task of not giving up. Although some individuals have the amazing capacity to continue their efforts with little or no outside acknowledgment, many are boosted by some sort of positive recognition for their efforts. This positive recognition can be very powerful when its source is a respected professional.

Brenda, whose son Jimmy spent his first three months in an NICU (as discussed in Chapters 1 and 2), received an abundance of encouragement from the staff at her hospital, encouragement that helped her continue:

Brenda: Oh, the nurses that I was telling you about that were in intensive care, they also run the early intervention clinic up there at County Hospital, and I've made some good friends through there, too. A lot of encouragement — they gave me a lot of praise so that when I walked away from there, I'd think, "Hey, I'm doing a good job. I'm doing it."

Sometimes I thought that I would never be able to do it. Before I had Jimmy, it's like I would see other people with children who had problems, and it was like, "How can they, how can they do that? How do they manage?" It's hard enough with normal, healthy children. Anyway, I did do it and it was real hard, but it was worth it.

There are so many things to remember, important, life-and-death things. At first I was really scared, like, "Me, do that? No way, uh-uh!" But they taught me and let me know when I did stuff right. They never made me feel dumb or slow. They, like, showed me I could take care of him, I could do it. And I could, and I am!

Question:
It seems it would be rare to find a helping professional who was technically competent and also had all of the right personal qualities. Are there examples of people who are really like this?

Answer:
Yes! Fortunately, finding professionals who meet these standards is not as rare as you might think. The realization of excellence in the helping professions can and does occur.

In the course of a lifetime most individuals have the opportunity to come into contact with at least one helping professional who has achieved a state of all-around excellence, someone who not only is superbly competent but also exhibits the qualities described in this chapter. In each of the helping professions, a vast array of silent saints, scattered here and there around the nation and world, are quietly doing the best they possibly can to make life a bit better for those fortunate individuals with whom they come into contact. This section will briefly spotlight three of these individuals and attempt to illustrate how one person can make a difference.

The first story begins with the ten weeks' premature birth of Julia (who is 2 years old). Julia's parents, Gayle and Dennis, were in absolute shock once the facts became evident.

Gayle: Starting from the beginning, she was ten weeks premature, a footling breech [entering the birth canal feet first], so they took her by C-section. She only weighed 2 pounds and 8 ounces at birth, very tiny, with a lot of respiratory distress and cardiac arrest immediately. She started out with hyaline membrane disease, which is a lung abnormality that causes respiratory distress. Her respiratory system was entirely too tiny. She was in the hospital three months in intensive care. Two weeks after she was born, she got a really bad infection — they still don't know from what. Within a matter of six hours, it looked like we were going to lose her.

After three months of hospitalization, Julia came home. The stress involved with attending to her many medical needs around the clock pushed Gayle and Dennis to their limits. They weren't getting enough sleep, their business was failing, medical bills were piling up, and there was no time to meet their own personal needs or the needs of their relationship. They were on the edge, ready to collapse. Then along came Penny.

Gayle: It just so happened that when we about reached our breaking point, one of the nurses from the intensive care nursery stopped in. She was really a standout as a nurse — sometimes it even seemed that she was the one the doctors looked to for answers — and a wonderful person to boot. She works in the intensive care nursery where Julia spent three months, and Julia was one of her favorites. Well, she came by just to see how we were doing, and when she found out we had no help, she went into action. She started coming over daily for three- or four-hour periods, just to give me a break, just from her heart, just as a friend.

So this young lady decided to take us on as her personal project, to come and give us a break. She still does that today. We are the very best of friends. In fact, she just recently moved to about four blocks from us to be a little bit closer, give us a bigger helping hand. [Gayle breaks down crying a few moments pass.] There isn't a time, day or night, that I can't call this lady and say, "I'm going to drop. I can't keep going anymore. Can I talk you into giving me a break?" And she's here within five minutes. She's like another mother to my daughter, and Julia looks at her in that way. She's fantastic! I don't know how we could have lived this last year without her.

Penny's professional excellence, along with her demonstration of love and concern for this family, may never bring her great financial gain, power, or national prestige; however, in the lives of those she has touched, she is and will always be remembered as a gift, a godsend.

Unfortunately, actions such as this cannot be taught in a textbook or lecture hall, a supervisor cannot demand them, and no single individual could possibly be so dedicated to more than one family at a time.

The second recipient of our realization of excellence "award" is a pediatric neurologist. Following is a mother's description of what may be regarded as the best of practices.

Mother: When you've seen as many doctors as we have, you learn to be ready for anything. I mean, some of them are real good and some just aren't; some treat you like garbage, and others, well, they treat you well.

Like the pediatric neurologist we took Donna to — that was the most impressive appointment I've ever been at. From the moment we made the appointment, it was just right. They were so friendly and concerned and everything. We got to his office, and they greeted us by name and showed us right in. The doctor came in and was warm and friendly. He sat down and talked with us, no rush job, no "get 'em in, get 'em out" feeling. We looked at the test results together, and he explained everything on them to us and checked to make sure we understood.

More than just medically treating her as a professional person, he really cared. He'd call and check on how she was doing and follow up to compare notes with her other doctors.

We worked with him here for two years before he moved away. He's the best. He's so good, in fact, that we still visit him and consult with him, even though he lives 500 miles from here. It's just, well, when you find someone that good, that competent and caring, it's hard to give him up.

competence + caring + time = excellence

Those who have witnessed the above formula in action, who have come into contact with excellence such as this, are often so impressed that the thought of losing the excellence they have become accustomed to is unthinkable.

Our third acknowledgment goes to an entire team, consisting of a birth to 3-year-old home interventionist (educator), a physical therapist, and a speech and language pathologist. The child is a 3-year-old boy, Freddie, whose premature birth and a variety of medical complications led to a number of delays. As Freddie's mother and father, Shirley and Jerry, speak about the services they have been receiving for the past three years, they alternate between laughter and tears. The week of the interview marked the end of one period in their lives and the beginning of a new period. Because Freddie had just turned 3, his education would now become the responsibility of the local school district. He will no longer receive services from the agency he and his family have worked with since birth.

Shirley: We've been real lucky to have the same three people to work with for almost three years. His physical therapist is just like a book. If you've got any problems, go to her. She knows what to do and she knows just which doctors to send you to, who's the best in the field. If she doesn't know, then one of the others [home interventionist or speech and language pathologist] does. We rely on them to help us decide what comes next, where to go.

When we started out, they all came together, out to the house here. Sometimes they'd work with Freddie separately — they'd come on different days — but sometimes we'd all meet together and talk, because one person can sometimes overlook certain things, like his back strength or diaphragm. Did you know that if your diaphragm isn't strong, it's hard to talk, it's hard to get volume out? I sure didn't know that before! If one misses that, the next one sees it and works on it more, and the next one will do something else a little more again.

Jerry: It would be like every other month they would all meet here, at the house, together. They could regroup and say, "Well, this is what I'm working on now, this is what I'm working on now," and then they always would overlap their therapies, so that they would always be working sort of together, like on the same goals. They really had a *big picture* in mind, like this leads to this, and this leads to this. It all worked real well for us.

When parents and professionals work together, when they share, collaborate, and coordinate their services, the resulting product is greater than the sum of their individual efforts. Professionals working in isolation may miss a detail here or there, but when they combine their skills, the likelihood of oversight diminishes. Therapies and interventions carried out separately from one another may very well benefit a child, but coordinating them yields even more growth and development.

Tips for Parents

- Learn as much as possible about helping professionals before beginning to utilize their services.
- Share your information with other parents.
- Honestly express your needs, likes, and dislikes.
- Surround yourself with good models of those traits (e.g., patience, a positive attitude, sensitivity) you desire to develop in yourself.
- Use encouragement and positive reinforcement whenever appropriate, and if you aren't getting enough from others, tell them you'd like to know when you're doing something right or well.
- Excellence is out there; it *does* exist — go and search for it.

Tips for Professionals

- Remember that your job requires more than professional competence.
- Incorporate the following into your professional interactions:
    Treat your clients and patients with caring, sensitivity, and respect — treat them like human beings.
    Be honest.
    Be aware of resources that are available and make that information accessible.
    Be patient.
    Use encouragement and reinforcement whenever possible.
- Surround yourself with good models of those traits just outlined.

Conclusion

Parents hope and expect that professionals who work with their children will demonstrate more than technical skills and competence. They want to be treated like human beings rather than appointments and to be dealt with patiently and honestly. They also want to be led to resources and encouraged in their efforts.

When these personal characteristics are blended with professional competence, a parent-plus-professional partnership is formed. This partnership helps increase parents' perceptions of their own abilities and makes them better able to deal with the many demands and stresses placed on them in raising a child with exceptional needs.

5

Parents Don't Like . . .

Most people would agree that we learn best through success rather than failure and that being provided with models of how something should be done more reliably leads to future mastery than does observing or studying how something should not be done. Nevertheless, this chapter is dedicated to the study of professional behaviors that parents don't like. We do this in the hope that it will help parents gain a clearer picture of what they can and should expect from professionals and confirm their suspicions that something they are experiencing is not the way things have to be.

The parents interviewed for this book were, for the most part, quite positive about their interactions with professionals. Professionals were frequently mentioned as the most significant members of support networks and critical components in the eventual successes of children with exceptional needs. But a number of parents had strong feelings about certain inappropriate approaches and techniques and quite often asked that their experiences be shared so that others might not have to suffer as they had. An in-depth examination of the 900-plus pages of interviews upon which this book is based revealed that many of the most interesting, emotional, and telling quotations described interactions that were nonexemplary — practices that professionals should avoid and that parents should not accept.

Question:
Sometimes the professionals are really pessimistic. Why, and how can I deal with them better or change them?

Answer:
Many other parents have experienced this, too, and many of them recommend either confronting the professionals with clear expressions of

your feelings (often a very difficult thing to do) or, if that doesn't work, finding someone else to work with.

The line between honesty and pessimism is at times a fine one. Most professionals want their clients to have access to the truth, to understand all the various shades of reality and possibility, yet they do not want to rob them of hope. Without hope, without believing that your actions make a difference, it is very difficult to act in a decisive and positive manner.

In Chapter 1 we introduced 5½-year-old Rusty, who has a profound hearing loss, a seizure disorder, cerebral palsy, hydrocephalus, behavioral difficulties, and is mentally retarded — the degree of which is yet to be determined. His parents, Patty and Ben, were upset by the doctor's suggestion that he could arrange it so that Rusty would die during the delivery. Like many of the parents interviewed, they expressed the frustration, hurt, and depression that results when only the negative is emphasized and little encouragement or optimism is provided.

Ben: Well, there were a lot of professionals who told us that Rusty would never be able to roll over, he'd never be able to exhibit any signing [sign language] activity or anything on that order, and he wouldn't understand anything. [Rusty is presently able to roll over, crawl about, walk with the assistance of a walker, sign fifteen to twenty words, and understand and respond to dozens of words and signs.]

I don't know what their objective is. Some of those people — the doctors and nurses and therapists — are so negative when it comes to handicapped kids. They tend to make it sound so much worse. I would think that a few positives would help, but so many of them don't show any.

Patty: I agree. Even when I take Rusty in now to some of his doctors, I can sense their negativity. I think they really prefer working with the healthy, little, cute ones. They give me the feeling that they think Rusty isn't worth as much as their other patients, like he won't account for much anyway. I went in recently and saw one of the doctors we hadn't seen in years, and he was totally amazed at what Rusty was doing. He even said, "Boy oh boy, who would have guessed it?!" That felt good, but I sure wish there had been more positive statements like that when I really needed them, back in the beginning. You know, more optimism, more recognition for what's going well or what the child might become. They thought Rusty was just a vegetable, a blob, and would never amount to anything. Now that they see what he can do they're giving a few more positives, but back then they had nothing good to say, nothing that would give you any hope.

Rusty's doctors could have provided Patty and Ben with the same data, the same information, but in a different way, in a way that provided some encouragement rather than closing off all avenues of hope.

The language in which thoughts are couched is critical. Both the sender and receiver of a communication can be influenced by a slight change in perspective:

The glass is half empty.	vs.	The glass is half full.
Your son has a significant hearing loss.	vs.	Your son has enough hearing to understand language and learn to speak.
Your daughter is functioning at half her mental age and will always be retarded.	vs.	Your daughter has learned many new skills over the past year and will continue to learn and develop.
Those parents aren't handling it well; they are very emotional and upset and haven't learned to accept the truth.	vs.	Those parents are doing the best they can and are working through a lot of feelings.

If some people see thunderstorms lurking behind every cloud, others see the chance of a clear and sunny day in the smallest patch of blue.

When the interpreters of data are respected professionals, and their interpretation is dark and ominous, the effects upon the listener can be quite overwhelming. Professionals need to translate facts to parents in a way they can understand; they don't need constantly to remind parents of the worst possible scenarios, encouraging fear, anxiety, and pessimism.

What's the solution when you *do* face such a pessimistic professional? The father of a 6-year-old girl who is deaf and blind gives some advice:

Father: You just don't take crap like that! I mean, life is hard enough, my daughter's challenges are significant enough that we don't need some unhappy, bitter, negative know-it-all laying their bum trip on us. If they want to be negative, they can go do it to themselves, not to us. I tell them that, too. I started out as a real nice guy and let people say and do things that hurt me, but a couple of years of that was all I could take. Now I'm right up-front. They say or do something I don't like, and I tell them right off. I figure that if we, if the parents don't tell them, then who will? If they don't like it, if they don't change, then we move on to someone else. We find someone else to work with, someone who can help us see the bright side of things.

Most parents who have opted for honestly expressing their hurt and their desire to hear concerns expressed in more optimistic terms recommend being more diplomatic than the father just quoted. The mother of a 5-year-old with attention deficit disorder and hyperactivity expresses her technique:

Mother: When they say something that's hurtful or putting my son or us down, I let them know how I feel. I don't tell them how they should act or what they should say, I just tell them how I feel. I think that's my best way of getting the message across. I don't want to fight with them, I just want them to know what effect their attitudes and words are having. This works pretty well for me because most of the time when I tell someone how I'm feeling, then they become a little more sensitive and are a little more careful of how they phrase things.

Question:
What do you do when a whole team of "professionals" seems negative, yet they are the only "professionals" you can work with?

Answer:
The answer remains the same: express yourself, and if that doesn't work, look elsewhere for services. Only in very rural settings are services so limited that choices do not exist.

When a professional colors an evaluation of a child with pessimistic predictions, parents may find it difficult to become motivated to fight against the odds, and to lead their child to maximize his potential. When an entire team of professionals approach a child's prognosis in this way, the effect on the parents can be devastating.

Just as we mentioned in the last section, parents need to face this situation with an honest expression of their feelings; they need to clearly express "I" messages — tell what they feel. In most cases this emotionally difficult approach will work and parents will receive more balanced, if not optimistic, evaluations and prognoses. When it doesn't work, we recommend that you try again, then report your attempts to supervisors, and finally, if need be, search for other service providers.

Wilma and Howard had been advised by their pediatrician to have their 3½-year-old daughter, Leslie, evaluated by the local school district. Leslie seemed to be developing speech and language skills slowly, her coordination was poor, and she was not yet potty trained. Wilma contacted the local school, signed a number of consent forms, and over the next three months brought her daughter to a variety of locations to be tested by a number of specialists. Two years later, Wilma and Howard remember the process:

Wilma: When I brought her in the first time, they had me talk to the school psychologist. He said they'd "take care of it" and asked me to sign some papers. I didn't really know what "take care of it" meant, but I figured he knew what he was doing, so I just signed the papers.

           Two, two and a half months went by, and I didn't hear a word from anyone about the testing. Then one day a teacher called — I didn't know who she was; I had only met the psychologist — well, this teacher called and said, "We really have to get going on Leslie's referral; we need to finish everything up in the next couple of weeks. I need to see her tomorrow." I mean, they didn't call or anything for two months, and then it's rush, rush, rush. I just said, "OK," but I was pretty upset about it.

Howard: It wasn't just the teacher either. Then they all started calling, right?

Wilma: Right! Then, in the next few days, all these people were calling to see Leslie. Bring her here, bring her there, wait for an hour, come back in an hour. . . . We were going all over the place. Nobody told me straight out what was going on, but I was picking up real negative vibes — like something is really wrong — from all of them. She must have seen four or five different people. There was the psychologist, the teacher, a speech teacher [speech and language pathologist], some kind of therapist that works with hands and coordination and stuff, and the social worker — he was the worst.

Howard: He was something else! He comes in here asking all these questions, and you know he's thinking, "Yuck, look at this house. How can you live in this dump?! These are all her toys? Like, where are the rest of them? No wonder she's slow; just look around." I mean, this guy wasn't coming out and saying stuff like that; it's just, well, his attitude. I don't know, but he sure didn't make me feel real good.

Wilma: Me either. He'd be asking all these questions, like, "What do you do when Leslie won't go to bed?" and "How much TV does she watch?" I'd answer his questions and you could see on his face, like, "Oh, my God! And you guys are parents? Poor kid." Hey, we love Leslie, and we're doing our best. We don't need that!

It wasn't just him, either. All of them, all the people who tested her, seemed real negative and cold. Every time they'd finish a test, they'd go out of their way to tell me all the things she couldn't do that she was supposed to do. Did they ever say what she could do, or what she got right? *No!* Always negative. Always with these grumpy faces and these looks that made you feel like they thought you were to blame.

After all the testing was done, I got this call from the psychologist one day, and he says, "We have to meet this week to explain her program." I'm going, "Hold on! What program? What's going on?" I didn't say that, actually, I'm just thinking, like, "Did I miss something here? What's wrong with my baby?" So he says, "We have to meet by Thursday. Can you come in tomorrow?" I say, "I guess so, but my husband can't." So he says, "OK, come by school at 3:00."

OK, so get ready for this: I get there and there are like a million people sitting at this big table. I figure I must have the wrong day or the wrong room or something, but he comes over and brings me in. They're all there, all the people that had seen Leslie and a bunch more. They start introducing themselves, and I'm wondering, "What's going on here?" They got people from the county, people from the school — all kinds of specialists and supervisors and stuff. I was just floored, just speechless.

Then they start giving reports. They hand me a stack of papers, they say look them over and see if you have any questions, and then — zoom! — they start talking a mile a minute. Everyone is nodding their heads and going, "Uh-huh, uh-huh," like they understand, and I'm lost, completely lost. It's like a joke, right? Like, I felt like they were all speaking a different language, and they understood each other, and then there was me, just sitting there wondering, "What's going on?" I did understand parts of it, like she's retarded, she's 3½ but she's like a 1½- or 2-year-old in some stuff and a 2- or 2½-year-old in some stuff. But I mean, I missed most of it.

One thing I remember, though, is that they were just real negative. I mean it was all, "She can't do this; she can't do that; she should be able to do this; she should be able to do that." Not one nice thing — they didn't say anything good, nothing about what she could do. I mean, it was terrible.

I read the reports after the meeting, and they were real negative, too. To listen to them and to read that junk you'd think my little girl couldn't do anything, zero. You'd think she was just taking up air, for no reason. I mean, look at her: she walks, she talks, she's happy, she's sweet, she plays, she does lots of stuff. You'd never know it listening to them.

Howard: When I got home that night she [Wilma] was a mess. I thought, "Oh no, someone died." She looked like she'd been crying all day. So I said, "What's wrong?" She hands me a stack of papers. Well, I'm not a real good reader, but I looked 'em over and figured out that Leslie was retarded. It was moderate retarded; the papers said her IQ was 50.

Wilma: I just wasn't ready for it. It was like — boom! No warning: she's retarded, case closed. I was just floored!

We hope you, the reader, are shocked by the conduct of this school district and have never before heard such a horror story. Unfortunately, a number of the parents interviewed described experiences similar to Wilma and Howard's. Although few school districts diverge so consistently and so far from minimal standards of acceptable practice and common sense, this is not an isolated case.

Professionals need to focus on blowing wind into the sails of parents who have children with exceptional needs, not taking wind out of their sails. These parents need more guidance in focusing on strengths, more encouragement, more positive reinforcement, more ideas and resources than do parents of children who are developing without disabilities or delays. The last thing they need is to be robbed of hope.

But what can a parent do when in the midst of a situation such as that just described? It's one thing to express your hurt and feelings to an individual but quite another — and a more demanding and intimidating ordeal — to open up in this way to a team of four or six or eight professionals, many of whom you have never before met. The mother of a 5½-year-old girl who is very intelligent, creative, and also has severe, quadriplegic cerebral palsy has this to suggest:

Mother: I start out very civil and proper. I do all the right things — listen, ask questions, paraphrase when I don't understand, give "I" messages to express my feelings. . . . Usually there's no problem. Most professionals are caring human beings. Some may be a little insensitive or burnt-out, but most have their hearts in the right place. But when reason doesn't work, and I feel I'm not being listened to or they're refusing to see what's really going on, I sometimes get frustrated. I use to take the frustration home with me, but I don't anymore. I decided a couple of years back that if something was weighing on me, bothering me, I wasn't going to leave the professional's office or the telephone or the meeting or wherever; I wasn't going to carry it with me. So I just let loose — let it out. My husband thinks I'm too forceful and demanding sometimes, but I think of it as a healthy venting of thoughts and feelings. I just stand up, close my ears, and let everything that's inside come out. Sometimes I get angry, but usually I'm just loud, honest, and theatrical. It seems that some people don't listen to you unless you get their attention like that.

Many parents, especially those in the early stages of learning about their child's disabilities, have difficulty expressing themselves so openly and sharing their innermost thoughts and feelings. But it is a far more commonly employed therapeutic and communicative technique with veteran special education parents. As one mother vividly states, "Sometimes they [professionals] won't listen to you until you really take charge. You sometimes have to just shut them up and let it all out." Although "shutting them up and letting it all out" may not be a commonly recommended form of negotiation, it can at times be psychologically therapeutic, and, as these two parents state, it can work.

Another option is to search for a different service provider or seek mediation from an outside source. When receiving services from a private source, you can either change to another service provider or report the professional to the supervisor, the appropriate professional organization, or the local better business bureau. When services come from a publicly funded agency, such as the Association for Retarded Citizens or a county board, individuals can petition the director or the board of directors or the state division that oversees that agency. In the case of school districts, individuals who have exhausted their patience in dealing directly with the district may ask for mediation from an outside source or, in the worst-case scenario, request a fair hearing, a process in which the state education agency hires a mediator, at the school district's expense, to determine if public laws or educational statutes have been violated. Once again, however, most of these less-than-desirable alternatives can be avoided if parents honestly tell professionals how their attitudes and words are affecting them.

At this point you may be asking yourself, "What could that team of professionals have done differently? How could they have made the process better?" Following are some basic recommendations:

Time: Start the evaluation process early rather than waiting until the deadline is near and then rushing through.

Information: Keep parents informed at each step. Let them know what's going on and why, and what comes next.

Team approach: Instead of having parents run here and there for separate, often overlapping evaluations, attempt to bring professionals together more. Encourage the parents to be a part of the team, to share their information and insights.

Reports: Include skills the child has mastered and those that are emerging, and keep the overall tone and feeling open to new growth and learning. In advance of formal meetings, provide parents with the opportunity to read reports and have issues and decisions that will need to be made explained to them. Be proactive (anticipate and act before problems occur) and aggressive in recommendations that can make a difference.

Meetings: Advise parents to bring a friend or advocate to support them. Allow meetings to move at the parents' rate of understanding rather than be governed by the clock. Use language parents can understand and look to them for cues about when to move on and when to slow down.

Educational programs: Encourage parents to participate in decision making, and place their needs and requests at the top of the list.

Overall: Remember that every negative thought can be stated positively, in a way that leads to hope rather than despair. The opposite of pessimism is optimism, not false hopes — optimism that efforts will yield positive results, that actions can make a difference.

Just because a child has a disability, just because her or his pattern of growth and development is not typical, she or he need not be significantly handicapped. The greatest handicap holding back individuals with special needs and not allowing them to maximize more of their potential is the way others think of and treat them — an important component of how those with disabilities learn to see and think of themselves. Helping professionals who make parents see limitations rather than possibilities, to focus on weaknesses rather than strengths, are themselves part of the problem.

Question:

One of our child's therapists wants to do "her" program without asking what we'd like or if we understand what she's doing. Isn't it reasonable to want to be a part of the program and know what's going on?

Answer:

Yes, you are being reasonable. Actually, most professionals want the understanding, support, and participation of parents. If you want to be more involved, you should express yourself and ask what you can do. If that doesn't work, tell the professional or their supervisor that you aren't pleased.

The following story describes one family's unfortunate first experience with the profession of physical therapy and illustrates how critical parent involvement and support can be. Gretchen was identified as having cerebral palsy when she was almost 2 years old. Her parents, Berta and Hans, most vividly recall the first professional they dealt with on a regular basis, a physical therapist:

Hans: Her therapy was a waste of time, an absolute waste of time. That therapist just barged right into our house, no explanations, no discussions. She just barged in and wanted to just sit and play with Gretchen. We'd ask her about other things, like walking and eating with silverware, you know — things she needed to know — but that therapist just said, "I know what I'm doing and, believe me, this is best for her." Now, listen: doesn't it make sense that if she's got a sister [Gretchen's sister, Heidi, is two years older] and she's got oodles and oodles of toys of every kind, and lots of neighborhood kids around, she doesn't need some high-paid professional to come to the house and play with her?

Finally, I got sick of her. It wasn't just the play thing, it was the way she thought she knew it all, and like she wouldn't even try to explain it to us because she didn't think we could understand what she was doing or why she was doing it. I finally said, "I don't want you back here anymore. Stop coming. Just stop; don't come back." So we got rid of her. We haven't let any of her kind [occupational or physical therapists] into the house since. None of 'em.

Berta: There were so many practical things she needed work on, like walking, going up and down steps, stepping over things, and holding a spoon — things she couldn't do that she needed to learn. I would think that those are the basic, the very basic and everyday activities of a child, and those are the things that a kid has to contend with in daily life. But, no, she never asked what we wanted; she just told us.

The issue here is not whether Gretchen's program was appropriate. The issue is that for professionals to deal effectively with parents, they must match or fit their services to the needs of the child *and* family, *and* they must communicate with the family. Hans and Berta were upset because they saw no value in the therapy. If they had had the opportunity to help set the goals of therapy and had been informed or educated about why the therapist was "just playing, all the time playing," they no doubt would have been more satisfied. It is even possible that if communication had been better, therapy might have followed the same course, but with much higher satisfaction and support from Hans and Berta.

Just as we would have recommended, Hans and Berta expressed their doubts about the therapy and tried to become more involved. Unfortunately, their efforts were thwarted. They then reported their dissatisfaction to the therapist's supervisor and finally to the county, but no changes were made. Their final decision was to discontinue all services. We believe that this final step should only be taken if other therapy providers are available or if the therapy is doing damage to a child, neither of which was the case here. We would have recommended that Hans and Berta continue the therapy and work on slowly forming a more positive relationship with the PT, incorporating their goals and objectives into Gretchen's program.

This preferred "slow change" method is well exemplified by the mother of a 2½-year-old boy who is legally blind yet has enough vision to see dark and light, recognize faces, and identify large pictures up close. In the following passage his mother describes her first interactions with a young, "fresh out of college" home trainer (a specialist whose job it is to travel to the homes of children with disabilities and provide direct services to children as well as consultation to parents):

Mother: We had suspected for quite a while that he had problems with his eyes, and he had been through all the testing, but we just got the formal diagnosis about eight months ago. Before then, I had talked to a lot of doctors and read quite a bit. I mean, I wasn't formally trained or anything, but I knew what was going on. By the time the diagnosis came in, it was no surprise.

Well, then they [the local agency responsible for providing services for young children with exceptional needs] sent out this girl, and she starts telling me stuff about Jason. I mean, she's never met him before, and she's lecturing me about him. The whole time she's talking about some kid who's not my son. She's, like, telling me what it's like to be "blind," and she thinks "blind" means nothing coming in, no vision, pure darkness. So I stop her and tell her that Jason can see this and that, and she just says, "Oh."

Next thing she starts is telling me how we've got to work on getting him out, getting him to explore more and not stay in a corner, like, not be afraid. I'm thinking, "This gal is not in touch; she's from outer space." Because, you see, this doesn't describe Jason at all. I've looked at the books, and I know that a lot of blind kids are supposed to be like that, but it doesn't describe him at all.

I thought right then and there that she wasn't going to be much help, and for awhile I was right. She came out for the next few months, and I felt like I should have been paid for educating her, because she sure didn't help us much. I felt like I had to watch her every minute because I knew she didn't know what she was doing, and I didn't want her to use Jason for a guinea pig.

I decided then and there that it was up to me to make it work. We live way out in the boonies, so there was no way I could change services or get anyone else to come out. So I just was real straight with her and told her what I liked and didn't like about her style, and what we needed and didn't need. Well, she came around slowly, but she came around. She started listening more and really communicating with me.

Things are going really well now. This gal still doesn't know as much as me about visual impairments, but we're learning together. I think that if you give most people a chance and communicate with them, they'll come around and do their best. I almost threw this gal out, but I'm glad I didn't.

Parents in a spot like this need to evaluate their choices real carefully. If I'd had more choices, I wouldn't have put so much into trying to work with this teacher, but the choices weren't there, so I had to.

The message here for professionals is to listen, watch, find out what the needs are, and assist in developing a program around the child and family's unique patterns of strengths and needs. Professionals with limited experience can earn the respect of parents who have "been around." They *can* help, but they must do this as coinvestigators *with,* and support personnel *for,* parents, not as dictators or bosses.

The message for parents is to communicate your desire to participate. Let the professionals know that you want to be a part of the program. Tell them you want to know what they are doing and why and to be asked for your ideas.

Question:

Some people are so rude and insensitive. I tend to get mad or just hold it inside. Is there a better way to deal with my feelings?

Answer:

Getting mad and holding it inside are two techniques that many parents use; however, most parents recommend another, initially more difficult, but in the long run healthier and more productive technique: honest confrontation.

Many individuals respond to rudeness and insensitivity by either holding in their feelings or getting mad and upset. But these reactions rarely improve situations or alter the behavior of offending individuals and often end up creating even more physical and emotional stress. Rather than holding in or bursting forth with emotions, parents should experiment with expressing their thoughts and feelings to the offending parties. Although this technique takes time and courage, it often leaves the parent less distressed and more satisfied and can also have the advantage of educating the individuals who have been confronted and perhaps heightening their sensitivity to others.

The mother of a 4-year-old boy with hydrocephalus and profound mental retardation reveals the futility of holding in her anger:

Mother: Sometimes I feel like walking up to people and just shaking them. I want to shake them and yell, "Stop staring at us!" I mean, yes, my son has a large head; yes, he drools; yes, he makes unusual faces; yes, he pulls on his ears; yes, he rocks back and forth; yes, he stares at people — but I can't help it!

The older he gets the harder it is to take him out — physically and especially emotionally. It used to be, when he was younger, that they wouldn't stare so much. He was younger, and I guess he blended in better, he wasn't so noticeable. But the older he gets the worse it seems to get.

You'd think people would be more sensitive. You'd think they'd have learned that it's rude to stare. I don't know, I guess it shouldn't bother me so much, but it does. Sometimes I just feel like hiding. I feel like staying home and never leaving.

When I go to the mall or someplace out in public like that, it's a real drain. I'm never, we're never just part of the crowd.

Sometimes you just want to go somewhere and not be noticed. You want to just sort of be inconspicuous, sort of blend in. That never happens to us.

The questions people ask, the things they say, can be pretty weird, too. Sometimes I like it when they come up and talk, but some people are really off the wall. "Can't you make him stop drooling? Why don't you keep him at home? If you can't control him you shouldn't take him out." There have been lots of times I've come close to grabbing someone. Sometimes I get these real violent pictures in my mind, like I'd like to hurt them, hurt them like their stares and the things they say hurt me. I never have, but it really makes me angry! I mean, people can be so hurtful, so thoughtless sometimes.

It's not only strangers in the mall who at times demonstrate insensitivity to how their actions might affect others. Professionals have also been known to exhibit similar behavior. Bev, the mother of a girl with CP (described in Chapter 2), was disappointed and hurt by the insensitivity of her daughter's preschool director. Rather than holding her feelings in, she expressed herself and ended up feeling better about the situation and about having a positive impact on the attitudes of another person.

Bev: To begin with, it's not all that easy to find day care or a preschool for a child with special needs. I guess people figure, "Why bother? They're more trouble." Anyway, Polly was going to this preschool, and we were happy to have her in, so we ignored some little things that bugged us and just tried to make the best of it.

Well, it was getting close to Christmas, and they were preparing for the big holiday program, but they wouldn't let Polly in it because she couldn't walk, with the CP and all. I tried to explain that it wasn't fair and that she would feel hurt, but this lady wouldn't listen. Polly was the only child not in the program. Try explaining that to a kid! It just broke my heart. I couldn't believe it. Talk about making a kid feel different, feel out of it. You think you're not in the dark ages anymore, but you are.

Well, the bad news is that Polly wasn't in the program, and we pulled her out of the school. But the good news is that a few weeks later, that same director called me and said, "I thought about the things you told me, and I feel terrible. You're right. I should have let her be in the program. I just wanted you to know that nothing like that will ever happen again, not in this center."

It's impossible to know the true motivation underlying this preschool director's not allowing Polly in the Christmas program. Perhaps she only wanted to shield Polly and her family from embarrassment, or maybe she hoped to hide what she regarded as a blemish on her school and its festivities. Regardless of the reason or reasons, what resulted from this demonstration of insensitivity was hurt and the further distancing of a young child from a typical, "normal" preschool experience. If it had not been for Bev's honest communication with this director, it's likely that no behavior or attitude changes would ever have taken place and that Bev would have added one more unresolved stress to an already stress-filled life. However, Bev's frank expression of her feelings and concerns helped educate the director and, most probably, strengthened Bev as a person and a mother.

One of the most certain ways to increase emotional distance is by placing unreasonable demands on individuals who are already barely able to keep their lives together. Ellen, referred to in previous chapters, is single-handedly raising her three young children, all of whom are receiving some type of special services. As you might expect, she was not thrilled when one of her children's teachers made demands of her that she perceived as unreasonable and insensitive.

Ellen: It's not easy raising three kids on your own. I can hardly ever go out. I'm usually [1½-year-old] Sara's mama or [3½-year-old] Jackie's mama or [4½-year-old] Johnnie's mama. I'm not Ellen anymore. I'm everybody's mama. All the teachers come and they just talk about what the kids need. What about me?! I don't count for anything! I have no time for myself, for my needs.

I changed one of them — I mean I had Johnnie changed to a different class at school — because his teacher, she came and she didn't listen; she didn't see the whole picture. Well, she was really something else. She said that I wasn't paying enough attention to Johnnie. She said that I should devote more time to him or he'd never get better. There I am, a single mom on welfare, living in a little dump, sick half the time, giving everything I've got twenty-four hours a day to those kids, and she bops in to tell me I'm selfish and lazy. I just couldn't take that kind of stuff.

People come in, like that teacher, and they have all these great ideas, these big plans, but sometimes they just are out of touch. Like that teacher: she brought all these books and papers and things and said that Johnnie wouldn't make it in school unless I worked with him on this stuff for at least an hour a day. One hour — now where am I suppose to get an hour? I rarely get a whole hour with him one to one now, and that includes talking, dressing, feeding, playing, everything. You add all this stuff on top of that, and, I don't know — where is the time and energy supposed to come from?

I'd like to see them do all those fancy plans, have all that "quality time" stuff, if they was raising three handicapped kids, living in a little apartment, with just enough money to put food on the table and never with any time for themselves, like not even a chance to brush their hair or take a bath in peace and quiet. Some of them just aren't realistic; they aren't sensitive to how things really are.

So I told her how I felt, but nothing changed, so I talked to her supervisor, and finally we had Johnnie changed to a different teacher.

Honest communication doesn't always change the behavior of the offending parties, but it almost always benefits the offended and usually leads to a change for the better. In this case Ellen freed herself from the burden of repressed emotions; Johnnie got a new, more sensitive teacher; the teacher got some clear feedback on her performance; and the teacher's supervisor was alerted to a dimension of her school's program that needed attention. One clear communication led to a number of positive results.

What Ellen needed was not someone to come in and tell her what to do, someone to supply solutions without knowing what the real needs were. What she needed was someone to understand the reality of her day-to-day existence and assist her in improving her life situation, starting from where she was.

Question:

Sometimes it seems I spend half my life waiting. Doctors, therapists, and school psychologists so often have little or no respect for our schedules, for our time. Is there anything I can do about it?

Answer:

When the services are being provided by private parties, all you can really do is express yourself. If nothing changes, find a new service provider. But when the services are provided by an agency or school district, under special education laws clear and specific guidelines exist.

Waiting may not be one of the most enjoyable aspects of life, but it is a reality that must be faced; immediate gratification of needs and desires is not always possible. Despite this, within each society acceptable parameters of how long individuals can be expected to wait usually evolve.

The medical profession is most notorious for making individuals wait. Professionals want to serve as many of their clients as possible on the day and at the approximate time the clients wish to be served — even if that goal is unrealistic. In some cases long waits are due to medical emergencies beyond the control of physicians and nurses; unfortunately, delays may also be due to the intentional overbooking of appointments in order to maximize profits.

Therapies of varying types usually require far less waiting time than do medical services. If a pattern of being forced to wait too long becomes evident, the most feasible response is communication with the service provider and, if that doesn't work, seeking services elsewhere.

In public agencies, however, a chain of command with clearly delineated grievance procedures usually exists. In the specific case of special education services, minimum requirements are established by federal law and reinforced by state laws and regulations that are at least as demanding and often more demanding.

The following stories tell how frustration, resentment, and anger can build when individuals are made to wait longer than seems reasonable and what can be done about it. The first example describes the frustrations of the father of a 5-year-old boy, one to two years delayed in most developmental areas, as he tried to follow up on a teacher's recommendation that he contact the school's principal in regard to a concern about the safety of the kindergarten playground (the child's early childhood special education class uses the playground for recess).

Father: I'll tell you, if I ran my business the way that guy [the princi-
            pal of the elementary school] runs his school, I'd be bankrupt
            before you could wink your eye. I must have called him three
            or four times. I left messages, but he never called me back.
            Finally, I just had the secretary schedule me an appointment.

                I go to school to meet the guy, and I sit around waiting for
            him for twenty to twenty-five minutes. His secretary said he
            was in the building somewhere, but she didn't know where.
            Finally, the guy walks in, and I stand up, expecting him to
            walk right up to me to apologize, but he doesn't even notice
            me. He goes to the secretary and spends about three or four
            minutes chatting with her. Then he walks over to me and
            introduces himself and shakes my hand. I'm bubbling over
            inside, like all churned up and angry, and this guy doesn't
            even apologize.

                So we go into his office and I start telling him my concerns
            about the kindergarten playground. It's really a mess — all
            this equipment is on top of old, cracking cement, with splin-
            ters in the wooden play structure, swings just waiting to fall
            down, weeds with sharp stickers, a slide that's so steep I
            wouldn't go down it and so hot that you could fry an egg on
            it, just lots of problems. So I tell him all this stuff, and he says,
            "Thank you for bringing this to my attention. I'll look into it
            and get back to you." Do you think he ever called me back?
            Nope! Two weeks later I called him and went through the
            same rigmarole as before — he was never in and no calls
            returned.

                Finally, I just gave up on him and called both the director of
            special education and the superintendent's office to complain.
            I talked to the superintendent just a couple of weeks ago but
            haven't heard back, and the playground is still the same. I just
            sent a letter to the school board and have been trying to get in
            touch with the state's Department of Education to find out
            how I can proceed if the school board doesn't act.

This father began with a mild concern about playground equipment,
a concern that may have been satisfied by a good listener and a few hours
of maintenance work. He ended up frustrated and angered, thwarted in
his effort to help make his child's school a better place. But if he was
thwarted, he wasn't powerless. He proceeded up the chain of command,

hoping and trying to have his concerns dealt with as close to the source as possible. Frustrated at each level, he is now working beyond the school district level, trying to find a state agency that will lead him to a solution.

Another example of endless delays is given by the parents of 4-year-old Stacey and 5-year-old Jenny. Both girls have a number of exceptional needs, including life-threatening liver diseases and developmental delays.

Al: We've had trouble with the public school system, as far as them making arrangements to get the kids into the programs. Just getting them enrolled has been a real struggle.

Helene: It took us months to get Stacey into school, just because of the paperwork involved. The answer that I got was that she [the director of special education] had so many kids that she had to screen and everything that it took her a long time to get everybody done.

Well, see, Stacey's birthday was in August, so they didn't want to start switching her over [from the Association for Retarded Citizen's birth to 3-year-old program to the local school district's 3- through 5-year-old program] until she turned three. The ARC was sending their therapist here, to the house, until she turned 3. Then she was supposed to switch to the local school district. So the ARC was working with us up until the very end, until she was three. Then the school district made us wait ninety days [the *maximum* allowable by both federal and this state's laws] for the district to process her for special education eligibility. They didn't finish in the ninety days, either. They went a month or two after that, so it wasn't until about the end of January or early February until she started with the public schools. She ended up going almost five months without any therapies or special teachers.

What I can't understand is why they waited, why they didn't get going on it. I mean, they knew she was coming. They knew she was going to qualify for services. I guess it's sort of a game: "Let's see how long we can keep them waiting." They've got to realize that every month is important. You just can't keep a kid out of therapy for four or five months because you're "too busy to get to her." I don't know; it seems like the laws are there, but some people try to stretch them as much as they can.

Although both federal and state laws contain regulations and time-lines that must be adhered to, they are meant to define the lowest level of acceptability, not the expected level. Agencies and school districts that provide only the minimum level of service and wait as long as they possibly can to move through the evaluation and admissions process are doing a disservice to those they are supposed to be helping.

The parents of a toddler who just turned 3 and who is legally deaf experienced a similar roadblock, but handled the situation differently:

Mother: We called the local school district when our daughter was 2½ and told them she'd be enrolling in their program when she was 3, in March. They said that it would be better to start her in the beginning of the year, the following September, and that the program was really full anyway. Well, I just said, "You can't do that. I want her tested, admitted, and starting her new IEP the day she turns 3." They didn't call back or contact me, so I just marked my calendar, and ninety days before her birthday I went to the district office and demanded that they sign the papers for having her tested. They shifted me from office to office and finally had me talk to the director of special education. I just told that lady point-blank, "Listen, don't mess with me. I know my rights, and if we don't start this process today and if my daughter isn't in your program on March 15 [her birthday], we'll be sitting in a fair hearing and I'll be the winner." That really got her attention.

You hate to get to that point, but, gee, I'm not going to wait around for them to meet their own needs or whatever. I know my rights, and I know how some people, some schools can abuse those rights, so I get tough when I have to.

That was the last problem I had with the district. They signed the papers, tested her, and on March 15 she started in her new program. And by the way, the new program's great, and the teacher and therapists are really good and working really hard. They're really caring and concerned people.

When you deal with schools and agencies, your first steps should always be (1) learn your rights and (2) conduct honest and rational discussions with those personnel designated to handle your request or concern. If an acceptable agreement is not reached at that level, parents should move to the next higher level and so forth, up the chain of command. In the case of agencies and schools that provide special education services, the formal processes are delineated in both state and federal laws and regulations. Whenever possible, parents should make every attempt to reach agreements through negotiation rather than forcing issues to formal grievance or legal proceedings.

Tips for Parents

- Read, study, and practice honest communication, including the art of expressing "I" messages; use this skill when someone's pessimism is affecting you.
- Know your rights.
- Make every attempt to deal with issues at the level of your initial concern before moving up the chain of command.

Tips for Professionals

- Be honest but avoid becoming overly pessimistic; hope provides parents with significant amounts of motivation.
- Listen and observe before advising and try to see the whole picture rather than the limited perspective of your specific discipline.
- Be sensitive: parents of children with exceptional needs are often experiencing significant pressure and stress.
- Be prompt: waiting upsets many people and making people wait is a clear sign of disrespect.

Conclusion

A critical factor in the success of early childhood special education is the attitude of parents. When parents don't like an agency, school, or provider of services, for whatever reason, the chances for success are significantly decreased. It is therefore crucial for parents to try to establish positive relationships with the agencies and individuals who work with their children. Developing such attitudes and relationships usually requires a significant amount of openness and honesty. Parents are advised

to make every effort to identify their thoughts, feelings, and concerns —
both positive and negative — and share them. This degree of frankness
may be hard to attain, but the eventual rewards will almost certainly be
worth the effort.

6
Stress

It is difficult for those without children to imagine the added stress that often arises in becoming a parent. Besides the obvious — loss of sleep, decrease in free time, burden of responsibility, added expenses — a dramatically new perspective on life and the future begins to take form. This new perspective forces parents to consider their decisions more carefully (e.g., the house must be baby proofed, daily activities need to take naptime into account, trips and vacations become major undertakings). Despite these adjustments, the love and joy derived from a new baby and the knowledge that life will gradually become more normalized help make the hard times less difficult and the burdens less overwhelming. However, when parents learn that their young child has exceptional needs above and beyond most other children and that those needs may persist for a lifetime, stress and the burden of care are magnified, and the hope and expectation that life will get better and better is clouded by the doubt and fear that it will become worse and worse.

The added stress of parenting a young child who requires more attention and care can take many forms. Lack of sleep; fear of the unknown; less time and energy for yourself, your spouse, and other children; dealing with many and varied professionals; the need to make critical decisions; financial responsibilities; and difficulty in finding child care are only a few among many new challenges confronting these parents.

Question:
All the new stresses and strains of having a child with exceptional needs is tearing my family apart. How can I meet these new challenges while keeping myself and other family members sane?

Answer:

The key ingredients here are watching, listening, and being sensitive to changes in your behavior and emotions and those of other family members. When something starts going wrong, don't wait — act! The action may be as minimal as spending more time together and doing more listening, talking, and sharing or as major as seeking individual or marriage and family counseling.

All parents, all people need to be sensitive to changes in their own behavior and emotions and the behavior and emotions of loved ones. When these changes are positive, it is a time to rejoice, identify what has occurred to bring the changes about, and make efforts to continue and enhance the newfound state. When these changes are negative and unwanted, however, parents need to respond quickly and decisively. The longer a behavior or emotion is allowed to continue, the harder it becomes to modify or get rid of.

Norm and Linda had managed to maintain a well-balanced and fulfilling life during the first few years of raising their family. Providing for the needs of three children, two boys and a girl, hadn't been easy, but the rewards had by far outweighed the problems. It was therefore with excitement and confidence that they brought home their fourth child, Teddy. Their optimism soon began to disappear as his exceptional needs became apparent.

Linda: Life for all of us changed dramatically after Teddy was born. He had so many needs; it was so different than the first three kids. When he was a baby, he almost always threw up an hour or so after he drank. The food would come rolling out of his mouth. He'd also stop breathing sometimes. He'd just stop. That was real scary. It got worse and worse and finally he had to have an operation on his stomach.

Well, after all sorts of doctors, evaluations, and operations — it's been almost five years now since he was born and this all started — we pretty much know what we're dealing with. He's got congenital hypotonia — that's a kind of real low muscle tone where the kid's got real weak, floppy muscle control. He's also mentally retarded and has problems with his eyes and problems with his speech. He's got an inverted high hard palate — the inside of his mouth is shaped differently — and, well, there's lots of things.

Teddy is now 5 years old — five years of searching for a diagnosis, cause(s), and a prognosis; dealing with multiple hospitals, specialists, and surgeries; giving and caring for Teddy's exceptional needs. The past five years have taken their toll on the entire family:

Linda: It has affected all the kids. Samantha [age 11] has had a rough time emotionally and tends to get pretty anxious and stressed out whenever problems arise. Nick [age 9] started seeing a cardiologist because his heart was beating fast and throbbing — that began around the time that Teddy started all his surgeries. And Elliot [age 7] demands a lot of attention — the more that's going on with Teddy, the more Elliot seems to need.

It's like it never lets up. You just barely get a chance to catch your breath and it's something else — someone has a problem about this or that. There's been a lot more stress with all of us. In a family, you know, everyone affects everyone else. When one person is having a bad day or is upset, it ripples over and everyone sort of shares it.

Over the past five years I've had to go in for stress management and counseling, alone and with Norm, a few times. On and off I get severe headaches and nausea — the doctor diagnosed it as anxiety attacks. Right around one of those times, Samantha also started having some emotional problems and started seeing a counselor. She and I tend to be sort of in sync like that — we go up and down together.

You really need to stay on top of things — keep checking up on how you, your marriage, your kids, everyone and everything is doing. We use to wait a lot longer before we'd talk about things or seek some kind of help, like counseling or tutoring or extra therapies. We don't do that anymore. We've found that it's best to act right away when we sense that something isn't going or working right. If you don't act, if you don't try to change something as soon as you see that it's not going right, you're sort of asking for trouble. It's like when you're driving a car and you feel yourself dozing off, falling asleep. That's a sign to pull off the road. If you ignore too many signs like that, you may end up in a ditch and you may even be dead. After all that we've been through, we figure that safe is better than sorry, so we jump on things pretty quick around here.

As Norm and Linda's family story illustrates, stress can arise from a number of sources, manifest itself in many different ways, and involve more than one family member at a time. The strain of having a sibling with exceptional needs can be particularly hard on a child. Parents who watch, listen, and are sensitive to behavioral and emotional changes in themselves and their family members and take action when those changes are not in a desirable direction are doing the most important things they can to minimize the negative effects of the challenges inherent in raising a child with exceptional needs.

Norm summarizes what living with stress has taught him:

Norm: I use to let a lot of things slip by. Linda would look sad or down or make a negative comment, and I'd just brush it aside; one of the kids would start complaining a lot or acting unusual, and I'd tell them to cut it out or go to their room. I don't do that anymore. I've learned that every word, every expression, every sigh means something. If you're not aware, if you aren't sensitive, you're just asking for little things to grow out of control. I've learned that it's a lot better and easier to catch problems early and deal with them. We spend a lot more money on counseling than we used to; go out for meals and shows on the spur of the moment five times more than we used to; and pay to have a lot more things done, like cleaning house, washing the cars, and household maintenance. You need to do that. You need to know when you or the wife or the kids are in trouble, are near the edge, and then you have to do something about it, right then and there. You might not believe it, but I'm sure that we've had a few trips to McDonald's or bowling or the movies that saved one or more of us from getting so low that we'd get sick or start having some real emotional problems. You've just got to jump right on it and not let stuff build up!

Question:
How do you know if your other children are having negative reactions to the exceptional needs and the added challenges or if they're just acting their age?

Answer:
You don't know. But it's usually a better idea to be cautious and take action rather than assume that you're observing "normal" behavior and not act.

Extensive research in the field of child and human development has led to the general conclusion that individuals can vary immensely in their responses to different environments: people aren't always predictable! Having a sibling with a disability may have no noticeable effect on one child, whereas it may lead another to become more passive and withdrawn, another to be angry and unmanageable, and yet another to be outgoing and friendly. All that can be said with certainty is that parents need to be keenly aware of the needs and behaviors of all their children and attempt to structure their environments in a way that maximizes abilities and minimizes disabilities.

In a previous chapter we introduced a 1½-year-old girl named Mandy and described the dramatic effects her constant crying and eventual diagnosis of cerebral palsy had on her parents, Ed and Carrie. Mandy's arrival in the family also affected her brothers, Craig, age 8, and Kurt, age 3.

Carrie: Until recently, I'd let the boys do just about anything they wanted because I just didn't have the energy to do anything. Lots of times I'd just give up, zone out. I just could let everything go and sit in my rocking chair, holding Mandy while she cried and screamed. I didn't have the energy to even talk to the boys, much less discipline them or play with them. It's strange, too, because I think it affected the two of them real differently.

When I'd get in those states, Kurt could do just about anything he wanted to, and he did. He's like a wild animal. He's a "terrible two" — actually he's 3, but he's "terrible" — and he's suffered a lot from all of this, and it shows in his behaviors. I felt like he was crying out for attention and for limits, but I just wasn't there to give him what he needed. The more I'd get depressed and inactive the worse he'd get.

Craig went the opposite way. He's a real good boy, a good helper. He'll pick Mandy up for me and play with her; he helps out in a lot of ways — sort of your basic "good kid." Sometimes it's almost scary how easy he is — I mean compared to Kurt and Mandy. I think he saw what I was going through and sort of helped take up the slack. It's like he put himself, the kid inside him, on hold and became real mature, real fast.

When Ed comes home from work, when he comes in the door, I tend to throw all the kids at him and say, "I can't do this anymore." Then things pull together a lot better for awhile, but when it's the kids and me, it's usually real awful.

Ed: I often worry that Craig keeps too much inside — doesn't let his true feelings or self out. I don't think we're seeing the whole picture with him, but there's so much other stuff around here to deal with that I usually keep those thoughts on the back burner. The other two kids take so much of our energy that we sort of just appreciate Craig's being the "good boy."

Carrie: I really don't know how much of it [Craig's being a quiet, easy-to-manage "good boy"] is normal behavior, just because that's who he is, or because 8 is an easy age, or if it's because he realizes that we're under a lot of strain here already and we can't handle much more.

It's very difficult, or perhaps impossible, to observe a child's personality and behavior and reliably determine what factors or situations created them. Is Craig's being a "good boy" or Kurt's being "terrible" related to Mandy's disability? There's no way to know for sure, and it doesn't really matter. What parents need to do is find a balance between loving and accepting their children for who they are and providing them with an environment and experiences that assist and encourage them to be the most they can be. Parents need to avoid excuses such as, "There's nothing we can do about it; that's just the way she is" and "He's just trying to get some attention because his sister gets it all." Parents need to put aside theories of why their children behave as they do (innate disposition vs. learned behavior) and focus more on the goals of their children's behavior and how to meet those goals in positive ways.

All children go through stages and are at times more difficult or easier to manage. With most children, parents can pretty much sit back and do what comes naturally, and a relatively "normal," intact individual will someday emerge. This approach doesn't work nearly as well in families under significant stress — stress such as having a child with exceptional needs. In these families parents need to begin with the attitude that the environment may be having negative effects on their children's psychosocial development and take steps (seeking counseling, encouraging interaction in peer groups, giving more attention) to ensure that this does not occur.

Question:
How can I help my other children cope with their feelings?

Answer:
Sibling support groups are an excellent outlet for siblings of children with exceptional needs. Even if you don't have any real concerns about your other children, starting them in a support group can be strong preventive medicine.

There is often something very special about being with people who have similar needs or interests. The opportunity to share thoughts and feelings with others who can identify with you because of their own situations can enable you both to open up and to process experiences in new and productive ways. Sibling support groups (see the Resources at the end of this book) allow children to share experiences and feelings with other children who are living through comparable challenges and emotions.

The need for groups such as this is illustrated through the example of Walter, the 15-year-old brother of a toddler, Leon, who has had dozens of surgeries to remove cancers from his skin and has been left with scars all over his face and body:

Walter: Well, you feel like people look at you, and a lot of people look at Leon because he's got so many scars on him. When we take him to the swimming pool or the store or something, it's like they look and they want to ask, but they're afraid to. Why don't they just ask instead of standing there like geeks, with their mouths wide open? I'd rather have them ask than stare. I just sometimes feel that people are so ignorant.

            Sometimes, though, it's almost worse when they do ask. We were in a department store one day, and I was with Leon, and he's in the cart and this is when he had to have the surgery on his face and so he had stitches, you know, a couple here and there, and this one lady said, "What happened to him? Did he get in a fight with a cat?" I looked at her and I said, "No, he's had over 100 tumors removed from his body. You got any more questions?" I mean, I wanted to smash her face. I was really angry.

Most of the time I sort of stay home when they [the family] go out. All those stares and people looking at us — it gets to me. I get into this paranoid trip where I think people blame me for it, or they think it's something they can catch, and they think I've got it too. It's hard, you know.

It's hard having friends over, too. Like, it's embarrassing to have to explain stuff all the time.

The ones who can really understand what's going on are the guys in my sibling group. They all have brothers and sisters with different problems, too, so, like, they can relate. We get together every week and it's pretty cool. We just sort of hang out and rap. We don't *tell* each other what to do — we, like, talk about stuff. It's good to know that you aren't the only one who gets bugged by this stuff.

Walter's embarrassment about being the center of attention in public places is a concern of many siblings. Other common concerns include:

- less attention from parents
- not being provided with information about the disability and its cause or prognosis
- fear that other children or teenagers won't want to be their friends if they "find out"
- not being included in decision making
- feeling guilty about negative thoughts and death wishes (directed toward their sibling)
- resentment for all the time, attention, and money that is devoted to their sibling's disability

Siblings need the opportunity to discuss these feelings with parents, professionals, and others who are going through similar experiences.

Question:
I'm concerned about my relationship with my spouse. It seems we're both giving so much to the kids that we don't have time for ourselves or each other. Where's the right balance?

Answer:
The balancing point varies for different people. The key to remember is that in the long run individuals who don't take care of themselves and their own needs usually don't have that much to give to others.

Unfortunately, the increased needs of all the children in the home place added burdens on parents at just the time in their lives when they are under the most pressure and probably have the least to give, a time when they are trying to reorganize shattered hopes and dreams they had previously shared and work through new strains and difficulties in their own relationship.

Parents need to stay in balance and take care of themselves and each other. Most would agree that it's preferable for parents to give 50 percent or 75 percent or 90 percent of their love, understanding, and attention to their children over a long period of time rather than give 100 percent and burn out after a few weeks, months, or years.

The mother of a 4-year-old girl who has many severe medical difficulties accompanying her cerebral palsy talks about her situation:

Mother: They all — my husband, mom, sisters, friends — they all think I'm sort of selfish because I get out a lot and do a lot of things. I leave the kids [the other daughter is 8, and has no exceptional needs] with sitters or friends quite often. But, hey, what do they want, a martyr? Do they want me to crack up? When I'm with the kids and with my husband, I'm really with them; I'm not one of those neurotic, nervous, on-the-edge housewives who lives for her kids and family and doesn't do or talk about anything else. I figure that if I don't take care for myself, I won't have much to give, so I do take care of myself.

                One of the women in my support group [in this case a group of moms, each of whom has a child with cerebral palsy] let herself really go. She got fat, stopped going out and doing fun stuff and hobbies and the like, didn't try to keep her marriage exciting and alive; she just was a mommy, and gave, gave, gave to her kids. Well, now she has no husband, no money, no life, and no fun. She looks and acts twenty years older than she is and is unhappy and real mean and cranky with her kids.

                If you don't take care of yourself that's what can happen. I mean, it's like a pail of water: if you keep taking out, taking out, taking out, and you don't put anything in, it ends up dry, nothing left.

My husband complains that we spend too much money, especially on baby-sitters and entertainment, but he also admits that our marriage is the strongest it's ever been, and our lives are pretty good. We do things, have fun, spend time together. So as far as I'm concerned, all those people who think I should be and act differently just aren't seeing the big picture. They're just focusing on the parts where I'm taking care of me and not realizing that just maybe that's an important part of the whole show, which is a marriage and a family that's doing pretty darn good, all things considered.

Most parents of children with exceptional needs — at least those parents who are successfully meeting the challenges of their lives and growing and maturing as individuals, spouses, and parents — would tend to agree with this mother. *Take care of yourself!*

The next story reveals how bad things can get if parents don't take care of themselves. For Jenny and Ron, both of whom have learning disabilities and participated in special education programs throughout their schooling, the burdens of life and raising a child with exceptional needs were so overwhelming that during those periods when they most needed to take care of themselves and support one another, they seemed to have the least ability to do so. A month prior to this interview, Jenny gave birth to her third son, David. This — added to an active 6-year-old, Clint; a 2½-year-old, Bart, who is speech and language delayed, mildly hearing impaired, and a bundle of energy difficult to manage; and Ron's being out of work and drinking excessively — created a lot of stress and strain:

Jenny: He [Ron] was working at an auto body shop, but a few weeks after I got pregnant this last time, he got fired for not showing up. I knew he was going to lose it, too, because he kept getting drunk and would have me call in and make excuses for him.

See, he has a drinking problem. Every time we get extra money, he'll take it and buy beer and wine and whatever he can get his hands on. It seems like it gets worse whenever I get pregnant or there's bad news, with stress, you know. He just goes under whenever the stress goes up. I think a lot of my stress is coming from him, too, even more than from the kids

— with his drinking and yelling at me and the kids. Sometimes he seems better for awhile, and things go OK, but it's been pretty much a downhill slide for the past few years. He's just not there when I need him.

I'm on AFDC, and I told them with this third one [child] I needed some help with it because I didn't know if I could cope. I was mostly worried about getting Bart, my little one, situated, with the new baby coming and all, and about Ron and how he'd handle it. Actually, I was worried about everything. I still am.

I was talking to my social worker, and she suggested that because of all the stress, I should go through family training. But they want Ron to go through the training and counseling with me, and I'm scared. I'm afraid that I'm going to lose him if I say anything to him, that he's going to walk out and I'm going to be stuck here with three kids and I'm going to be in a worse boat than I am now.

A number of the mothers interviewed shared this same concern: "I'm afraid that I'm going to lose him [the husband or boyfriend] if I say anything, that he's going to walk out and I'm going to be stuck." The irony here is that in not demanding more from their partners, and more for their own lives, these parents are leaving themselves with a less fulfilling life and less to give to their children. Fearful that her husband, Ron, will leave her if she tries to improve their relationship and home life, Jenny is actually making her life worse. Instead of raising three children on her own, she is raising three children with an alcoholic and sometimes abusive husband — and receiving little assistance (emotional or financial) in return.

Once again, balance is the key. Being a person, a parent, and a spouse is like juggling on a tightrope. You have to divide your attention among a number of challenges, never forgetting to keep your balance. The worst of all possible mishaps is to lose your balance and fall, because then everything falls.

Even with individuals and relationships that are more fully functioning than Jenny and Ron's, raising a child with exceptional needs can create significant tensions and difficulties between partners. The father of a 4-year-old girl with spina bifida (who is unable to walk or control muscular activity below her waist) describes his marital difficulties — which eventually led to separation:

Father: I felt so helpless, like I was watching my marriage slip away,
watching my wife grow further and further from me. Whatever I did wasn't making things any better.

I thought that we had a great marriage and life, but after
our Sara was born, my wife became like a crusader. It was as if
Sara was her whole life. She was always reading about her
condition, going to workshops and trainings, doing therapies.
I felt like I was just in the background.

We went to counseling for awhile, but it didn't help the
main issue: Sara was getting all the love and attention, and
there wasn't much left over for me.

I can sort of relate to people married to workaholics because I was married to a "momaholic." I'm sure it could happen even if your child didn't have spina bifida or another
disability, but I think all of Sara's extra needs had a lot to do
with our marriage problems.

Like the juggler on the tightrope who maintains balance and juggles
simultaneously, parents must find a state of balance in their own lives
and at the same time divide their attention and energy among those
aspects and people in their lives they most value.

Question:
I'm tired most of the time. How can I do my best to meet all the
situations I have to face if I'm always tired?

Answer:
Most people can't. One of the first challenges to maintaining your
balance is to get enough sleep!

Parents who are trying to deal with caring for a young child, especially a young child with complicated medical and personal care needs,
require more sleep and relaxation in order to perform optimally. In most
cases, though, the opposite occurs, and the child's needs are met at the
expense of parents' rest. This paradox leads to a difficult situation, one in
which demands (the child's needs) exceed resources (the parents' ability
competently attend to their child).

Gayle and Dennis understand this dilemma well. Trying to run their
own small business, a tavern, while at the same time caring for baby

Julia's life-threatening medical conditions, proved to be more than they could handle with limited sleep and time for themselves:

Gayle: We had problems with our insurance company. Home nursing was in our policy, but the little fine print said that if mom and dad are capable medically to take care of the child, it voids out your nursing care — the only problem there being that mom and dad couldn't operate twenty-four hours around the clock taking care of a baby that had a bedroom full of hi-tech equipment that had to be monitored all the time.

We had been told all along that we'd have nursing care after we left the hospital. As we were preparing to be discharged, the doctor called the nursing station and said, "Don't discharge her!" He told us, "Don't discharge her. They just told me you can't get nursing care." I said, "It's too late. She's out. She's in the hall in a stroller right now, waiting for me to walk out the door with her."

So my husband and I talked about it and decided that we were going to bring her home anyway and that we would take care of her. Well, that was all fine and noble until after ten days we thought we were going to drop, taking turns staying up around the clock and trying to operate a business that's open eighteen hours a day. So we were working with her twenty-four hours a day and a business eighteen hours a day. Doesn't add up, does it!?

After ten days I called the primary physician and said, "Look, you have to do something and help us. We need something. We cannot keep going like we're going." He said, "I'm sorry; they've refused it." And I said, "Fine, then I'll admit all three of us to the hospital at X hundreds of dollars a day, and you can take care of us all." "Well, no, no, let's don't jump the gun," he said. I said, "I'm going to have to put her back in. I cannot take care of her anymore. I'm run down. I am to the point where I can't keep going; my husband can't keep going. We don't know what else to do, and she has to come first. If I have to take her back to the hospital in order to get the proper help and the care that she needs, that's what I'm going to do. I'm not going to lose her over something so dumb as money and insurance."

As shown in this brief story, it's impossible for anyone to be fully functioning over any period of time without enough rest. What is more, the expenditure of mental energy — thinking, studying, worrying, dealing with critical or emergency situations — intensifies the physical drain, making even more rest necessary. So in effect, the more parents need to draw from their personal energy reserves, the less they have.

Sleep, like nutrition and shelter, is basic to human existence. Parents who find themselves constantly tired must find resources to help them meet this need. Relatives, friends, baby-sitters, respite agencies, insurance companies, church groups, county boards, and day care providers are a few of the many resources parents should turn to when they're suffering from sleep deprivation.

Question:
I need to get away once in a while, but how can I? How can I get more time to do other things?

Answer:
Most cities have a variety of resources that provide respite for parents of children with exceptional needs. Find these resources and utilize them.

Webster's dictionary defines *respite* as "a temporary delay" or "an interval of rest or relief." "Temporary delay" of what? As it applies to our topic, temporary delay in providing service, watching, supervising, caretaking, tutoring, teaching, and more. For parents of children with exceptional needs, *respite* is the term used to describe a variety of different types of care for their children. It may be as basic as dropping a child at a day care center or having a baby-sitter come over; it may also be as involved as an overnight — or even longer — stay at a school, dormitory, or residential or foster home. Whatever it is, and for however long it lasts, the majority of parents raising young children with exceptional needs regard respite as one of their most critical needs.

Several references have already been made to Ellen, the single mother of three young children, all of whom have exceptional needs. Her own words best describe the importance of respite.

Ellen: I don't get to go out very much. With John [age 4½] it's really hard because I've had baby-sitters before, and John goes into fits where he gets violent and nobody wants to take care of him. It gets really hard on me because they're really emotional fits. When he doesn't want to do something, he'll scream, cry, and fight and end up just sitting down, defiantly, sucking his thumb. At home he takes it out on me and the girls. When he doesn't want to eat, he'll throw his plate, whatever's on it, or if I take the plate away, he'll pick up his fork and go towards Jackie [age 3] like he's going to stab her.

He's given Jackie quite a few bruises. When they were little, Jackie and John used to sleep in the same room. One time John had Jackie on the floor. He had taken all her clothes off and was pounding her head into the floor, pulling her hair, and pounding and pounding her, saying, "I'm gonna kill you! I'm gonna kill you! I'm gonna kill you!" I separated them, and they've slept in separate rooms ever since, but you get the idea?! I just can't relax for a minute. Baby-sitters are afraid to be with him, especially if they have other kids to watch — like my girls. They're afraid that he'll go out of control.

The only time I get a real break is when one of the agency gals comes in for respite. I get respite, from the county, for twenty hours a month because of John. It's great because the people are real well trained and used to dealing with handi-capped kids. I can get out and not worry too much. Pretty soon I can sign Sara up for it, too, because of all her needs. That'll get us another ten hours a month.

I have to pay $1.50 an hour, and the county takes care of the rest. The best part is that the sitters are trained to deal with stuff and are pretty well paid — like, I think around $8 or $9 an hour. See, the $1.50 I pay is just a small part of it; the county pays them a lot more. They can really do the job, and I don't have to lie to them or feel guilty because I know what they're going to go through — they're used to it. I could never afford to pay what they get, without the financial help.

My church helps out, too. They sort of got together and started a group that provides things for people in the commu-nity. One thing they do is take kids places. They know about my kids, but they take them anyway. They just make sure they have lots of help those days.

The university here, too, has a program where one week-end a month they'll take your kids and watch them, over a Friday night and most of the day on Saturday, and give you a break. The kids have to be in a special program, and you need to have the financial need and stuff. So that really helps. When they take the kids, I usually will go out with friends and party — you know, blow off some steam and then sleep all day. It's great! So there are some choices, but it's never enough.

Providing for a child's exceptional needs while maintaining a balanced personal and social life can hardly be done without respite. There are only so many hours in a day, and when new jobs and responsibilities begin creeping into your life, you have to make choices. Parents must either take advantage of opportunities to release themselves from caretaking responsibilities or curtail or discontinue some previously valued leisure and personal activities. For many parents, the first activities they drop are those they regard as selfish: personal development and recreation (exercise, hobbies, sleeping in, movies). Realizing the urgency of their child's needs, they put their own needs on hold and give as much of themselves as they possibly can. The problem is that this give-all approach works only for short periods of time. Most parents find that when they attempt to put their own needs on hold for any length of time, the quality of love and attention they have to devote to others diminishes.

Ellen was an extreme example of this — a single parent raising *three* children with exceptional needs — but the same phenomenon also occurs in intact families where only one of the children requires more time and attention. Jan and Chuck are the parents of two little girls. Corrine is almost 4, and her younger sister, Abby, is 18 months old. Mom and dad are both teachers and, with the exception of Corrine's blindness, lead a fairly typical life. "With the exception of Corrine's blindness" — now there's a phrase that carries a lot of significance.

Jan: Corrine is legally blind and classified as ROP, retinopathy of prematurity. She was born almost three and a half months premature. They had to give her oxygen to keep her alive, but the oxygen caused her blindness.

            These days one of our biggest problems is finding someone to watch the kids so we can get a break. We don't have very many people that we feel comfortable leaving the kids with. Corrine is physically normal, but you've got to find people who will be sensitive to her visual needs. It's so easy to overlook things. For instance, when she's walking or running around, if there's a discrepancy in the sidewalk, just the slightest crack or rise, she'll trip on it. She won't see that variance.

It's hard finding sitters who are sensitive to little things like that, so we don't leave the children in the hands of too many people.

Its been pretty hard, pretty confining. In fact this last year, with the addition of Abby, it's just been hell! We haven't gotten out at all. It's hard enough to watch one, but then to watch two — and one that needs extra attention, and Corrine really demands attention from people — it's that much harder.

Chuck: Both the girls are very demanding. They require a lot of attention, and time is a problem, a big problem. From that standpoint, like we mentioned before, we just don't have a lot of time to ourselves. We're always doing more for Corrine and Abby than for ourselves. I guess that's normal for parents, but with Corrine's extra needs and all, it really can be overwhelming.

Jan: I know for me there are a lot of things that I just don't have time to do, like anything outside of the home, outside of work and home. Chuck's gone a lot, about three nights or so a week, officiating high school sports, and I'm stuck home. I really don't have any other outlet, and sometimes that's real hard. I'd like to have a membership at the fitness center, but when would I ever get to go? Sometimes I feel that I just don't have any personal time, like I don't have a life of my own.

Raising children is far more like running a marathon than a 100-meter dash: it goes on and on and on. If a marathoner were to start a race as if it were only a short sprint, without setting a reasonable pace, he or she would never cross the finish line. Those who take part in the marathon of childrearing must go slowly and steadily, particularly when a child has exceptional needs. If the runner (the parent) sets too tiring a pace, the outcome of the race (the growth and development of the child and family) is placed in jeopardy. Jan and Chuck need to do two things: (1) make every effort to find more help to obtain the respite they so desperately need and (2) if they cannot find help that meets their standards, lower those standards. It's better to compromise your standards a bit and complete the marathon of raising a child with exceptional needs rather than face the prospect of dropping out of the race (divorce, mental breakdown, foster care placement, child abuse).

Question:
More, more, more. I'm supposed to get more sleep, pay more attention to things, spend more time caring for my own needs. What gives? With all of this "more," who or what gets "less"?

Answer:
The answer to this question is a lifelong challenge to most individuals but especially to parents of children with exceptional needs. One answer — many answers no doubt exist — is to try to combine goals and activities.

Father: We didn't even want to have another child; I mean, I was ready to go into have a vasectomy, and, boom, we're pregnant again. That was a real shocker. We already had the two boys — they were 2 and 5 years old at the time — and that was fine.

Even before Tina was born, my wife and I didn't have enough time to say hello to each other. It was all work and taking care of the boys. I'd get home late and, boom, the boys would be on me: "Play with me daddy, read to me daddy. . . ." I didn't have time for myself or for my wife.

Then comes Tina, and finding out that she's deaf and that we need to do this with her and that with her and that it needs to be done *now* — I guess you know that when kids are hearing impaired the most critical time is the first two or three years. So the doctors and therapists and teachers are telling us how important it is to take care of Tina's needs, *now*, and I'm wondering, "What about me and my wife and the boys? Where's the time going to come from?" It's like fitting an elephant into a sports car: it just won't fit!

"It just won't fit!" Finding time to do more for your child when there wasn't even enough time before; expending the energy to study and learn about medical conditions, therapies, and disability-specific educational techniques when you're already too busy to read your own mail; and knowing that if something isn't done now, today, the same effort later may not yield as significant a result — all this places a great deal of pressure on parents.

A number of parents meet this challenge with the two-for-one technique. One father describes this philosophy as follows:

Father: You just have to combine things. I found that we were spend-
            ing a lot of time waiting for appointments, so I started bring-
            ing along a book. Rather than resent my daughter or the
            doctors or therapists for making me wait, I got some time in
            on my favorite hobby, reading. When we started having mar-
            riage and family problems and started with the counseling,
            we looked on it as a chance to do some housecleaning inside
            ourselves. We started the counseling because of the new
            stresses and problems, but our attitude was, "Hey, this should
            help us in a lot of ways." Our friends and social life tend to
            revolve around the relationships we've made with other par-
            ents of kids with special needs. You could look at that and be
            depressed because there isn't enough time for this or that, or
            you could do what we do, which is make the best of it and
            combine our social life with having other needs met [learning
            about living with a child with a disability, belonging to a
            support group, social and political action]. It's all a matter of
            attitude. We've decided to make the best of what life's dealt us
            by cutting down on the number of different things we do and
            spending our time involved with things that meet more than
            one of our needs.

    Cindy, the mother of Simon, a 3-year-old with Down's syndrome,
expresses this same attitude:

Cindy: Most parents of 2- or 3-year-olds aren't sitting in ARC meet-
            ings or going to special workshops or therapies; they're not
            doing IFSPs [individual family service plans: specific pro-
            grams, agreed upon between specialists and families, to maxi-
            mize the development of a young child with exceptional
            educational needs]; they're not sending their child off three
            days a week to therapy sessions; and they're not pressured to
            work with and teach their child all those things that kids are
            suppose to just learn, without any special attention, like walk-
            ing and talking.
                Our other children just developed. I don't know how they
            got up and walked. But I had to figure out how to get Simon to
            turn and sit this way and stand up. I had to pay attention to
            every little detail and make sure that he was encouraged to
            learn and develop. The other children just did these things —

no fuss, no special therapies, no fancy positioning or furniture or materials.

I think this is what wears me out the most. It's just you feel like you've always gotta be doing things for him and looking and searching and reading so that you don't miss anything. Kids with Down's can be a lot higher functioning than people used to think, but you have to keep on your toes with them. I mean, they need to be pushed more, to be provided with more experiences. That puts a lot of pressure on a parent, knowing that if they don't do something, I mean if they don't be sure that something is learned or experienced or achieved, it may not happen on its own!

So we're giving a lot more, but it's become more than just dealing with Simon's needs. The reading and studying and groups and educating others is also a big part of how we involve ourselves in the community and also our social life. Reading a new article or going to a conference or observing a therapy is more than just helping Simon; it's developing me as a person and building my knowledge base for a lot of things I do. I'm real involved with the schools and ARC and parent groups. If it weren't for the Down's, who knows, I'd probably be heavily involved in something else, like save the tropical rain forests or women's rights. So I'm meeting his needs, but at the same time I'm meeting my own needs to learn and grow and be involved with something important.

As an individual's life becomes more and more complex, busier and busier, the competition between responsibilities and personal interests intensifies. Most people have priority lists — either written out or in the back of their minds — of jobs or tasks or activities they would like to start or complete when they can find the time. Cleaning the kitchen cabinets, straightening out the garage, writing an old friend, reading a novel they started last summer, learning to play the piano — for some, the list goes on and on, grows longer and longer, and is more of a fantasy than an achievable goal. Others chip away at their lists, eventually accomplishing some entries, altering others, and discarding those that have become less important over time.

Parents often have such lists in regard to their children: start Sally's violin lessons, get Sharon involved in soccer, check on braces for Billie's teeth, buy some wooden building blocks for the twins. Fulfilling the goals on these lists may very well benefit their children, perhaps leading to happier or more balanced or more productive lives for them. But the lists certainly aren't critical for typical developmental progress or the establishment of a "normal" life.

Unfortunately, this is not the case when parents of young children with exceptional needs draw up lists for their children. Early auditory and language stimulation for an infant with a hearing impairment; physical therapy and learning about body positioning for a toddler with cerebral palsy; behavioral interventions and speech and language therapy for a preschooler with autism — these and other such "entries" must be acted upon as soon as possible in order for children to maximize their potential and minimize the handicapping effects of their disabilities.

Reconceptualizing lists of responsibilities and interests so that the two coincide as much as possible is one way that some parents manage to meet the added demands of raising children with exceptional needs.

Question:
The thing that worries us the most is money. What resources are there for parents who have all of these extra expenses but can't afford them?

Answer:
Besides contacting the resources listed in the back of this book, talk to other parents of children with disabilities similar to your child's. Parents often know more about financial resources and options than anyone else.

The majority of Americans are concerned about money and financial stability. Surveys suggest that balancing the budget is one of the most stressful aspects of family life. This concern is often magnified in families with children who have many different types of exceptional needs, in particular physical and health impairments.

The bad news is that there aren't enough resources to meet all the needs, and many parents search in vain for assistance. The good news is that many agencies and groups — not to mention other parents — exist to help individuals find various types of resources, including financial help.

Let's return to Gayle and Dennis, parents of 2-year-old Julia; their story should encourage parents to begin this search early, before bills pile up too high. While trying to keep their own small business afloat, Gayle and Dennis had the added financial burden of Julia's medical needs. Because her parents' insurance program had a high deductible and paid only 80 percent of most bills, Julia's ten weeks' premature birth, at 2 pounds and 8 ounces, proved to be a costly start in life. Added to the costs of the NICU were the ongoing expenses for many different medical conditions.

Gayle: We can't pay all the bills. We're way, way behind. I mean *way* behind.

While I was pregnant, our group insurance program was canceled. After Julia was born, the state declared her totally disabled, and she was granted a one-year extension of partial benefits. This held us until a few months ago. Now we're on another group plan, but it's a basic major medical with high deductibles, and then they only cover certain percentages of this and that. So financially our life is a disaster.

We've had a terrible time getting help. We ended up talking to senators and congressmen, meeting with some of those people to tell them our problems and see if they couldn't get us some help. In the beginning we weren't aware of the financial assistance that's out there. Now that she's getting a little better, I'm just starting to learn that there are mega sources of funding. We just recently applied for SSI [Social Security Income, a federal program] and could have had it from the day she was born. Unfortunately, it's not retroactive. They figure that she could have been collecting around $500 a month, and we've missed two years of that. Meantime I sit on $80,000 of unpaid bills.

I don't even open the bills anymore. I look at the return address and throw them in a box on my desk and about once a month, when I get ambitious, I sort it all out and run through it and pile it up in organized piles. That's about all I can do right now.

If you talk to any parents of really young kids, you tell them to get out there and beat the bushes right away. Apply for everything, and, whatever they do, don't just listen to one person. Get lots of opinions. Sometimes someone will tell you, "No, sorry, you don't qualify" or "No, we don't do that or have that," and it's just not true. The ones who know the most about where the help is and where the money is are the parents who've gone through the process themselves. Contact

one of your parent groups [see Resources] and they'll help
you out.

Few families can afford expenses such as those just described. In
addition to hospital and doctor bills, parents of children with health and
medical needs are faced with the expenses of lost wages, transportation
to services (e.g., doctors, hospitals, and therapists), food and lodging
while their child is in the hospital, and special adaptations of the home
environment. Although these expenses may be partially or fully covered,
they often are not. Even parents with excellent medical insurance face a
significant financial fear, the fear that they will exceed their expense cap,
the maximum amount the insurance company will pay. (Does your policy
have a cap? Check and see!)

Many resources are available; however, parents are forced to search
them out at the exact moment in their lives when they have the least time
and energy to do so. The shock, denial, anger, confusion, hurt, depression, and emptiness of learning that their child is not "normal" is often so
overwhelming that parents don't clearly consider the funding possibilities and are slow to learn about what is available to them.

Tom and Cindy, parents of 3-year-old Simon, an active little boy with
Down's syndrome, summarize this challenge:

Tom: It's so hard to figure out what's out there — like programs and
          funding and things — and how to get them started. It's not
          like you can call one place or talk to one person or read one
          pamphlet and figure it all out — no one's handing it to you on
          a silver platter.

          The paperwork is just too much. I don't see how anyone
          who's working could research it all and do the paperwork. As
          a working person you're really at a disadvantage if you're
          trying to figure out the system. The thing is, there are a lot of
          different agencies, and that's very difficult to weave your way
          through.

Cindy: I just kept reading and reading and talking to everyone and
          asking them questions. I've found out about a lot of things.
          There's a group called DDSI, Developmental Disability Serv-
          ices, Inc., which I found out later on was started by the ARC
          here in town. They have regular support group meetings for
          parents and guest speakers, and so I went and attended one of

those in the fall, right after Simon was born. I joined. Hey, now there's a place to learn about what's available.

Parents who have been through it themselves know more than all the social workers put together. They know all the ins and outs of what's available and how to get it.

Then there's the rehabilitation agency, which offers additional therapy for people who don't get it through our local birth-to-three agency or need more than what they can get there. These agencies don't come out and say, "Here we are! We're ready to serve you." You sort of have to find them and get to meet the people and talk to them. Then, once you *find* them, they seem very helpful and committed to serving the needs of the children.

There is another set of money available for families called family support money — it comes from the state. That's through our comprehensive community services agency. They have funds set aside for families for things that aren't covered by Katie Beckett [another program Tom and Cindy found their way to] or your insurance, things like therapeutic equipment or ramps for the house, fences for the yard, toys, special games, adaptive equipment.

One good thing is that with a lot of these programs, like Katie Beckett and family support services, you don't have to have a low income to get money. Many of the other programs require a low income, while these are based on the needs of the child.

The financial stresses related to parenting a young child with exceptional needs can be diminished through insurance, aggressive research, and assertiveness, but it is the rare family that doesn't suffer to some extent in this area. How it feels to be in the midst of this type of financial crisis is best described by the father of a young boy who spent the first three months of his life in a neonatal intensive care nursery and had a total of eleven surgeries and eighteen hospitalizations prior to his third birthday:

Father: At first I was a wreck. I mean, I was always nervous and anxious about it — the bills and all. Then a while later it got to the point where I was just numb. The numbers were so big — hundreds of thousands of dollars — that it became like a fantasy, almost like a joke. I started living a lot more just day to day. You reach a point when you realize that it just can't get any worse. Of course it really can get worse, if you look at it from the outside, but when you're inside of it, it's so bad that even if the numbers grow, it doesn't feel any different. It was a relief when I hit that bottom.

I live, we live, a lot more for today. We don't look ahead as much as we used to. We realize that all we can do is take it one day at a time.

Even though many parents take this one-day-at-a-time attitude in regards to stress, it does not and cannot work as a total approach to planning and providing for a young child. Being a competent and effective parent requires future planning and organization.

As far as gathering financial resources, parents are advised to begin the research process as soon as possible. If your burdens are too great and you don't think you have the time or energy to conduct a good search, then try to enlist a friend, family member, social worker, teacher, other parent, parent support organization, or anyone you can find to get the information and get the paperwork started.

Tips for Parents

- Act quickly and decisively *as soon as* concerns arise.
- Consider starting your other children in peer support groups.
- Take care of yourself.
- Search out respite services and use them — before you "really" need them.
- Whenever possible, try to involve yourself in activities by which you can reach multiple goals simultaneously.
- Begin your search for financial resources today; if you're too busy, find someone to help you begin the search and application process.

Tips for Professionals

- Don't wait for parents to ask for help or resources; anticipate what might be coming and suggest preventive measures.

- Suggest peer support groups for parents and siblings of children with disabilities.
- Encourage parents to meet their own needs and reinforce their efforts to maintain a balanced life.
- Prepare and share resource directories related to your specialty.

Conclusion

The stress involved in raising a young child with exceptional needs can arise from many different sources. Lack of sleep, need for respite, limited opportunities to pursue other interests, constant demands, the need for spouses to agree on critical issues, fewer opportunities for husbands and wives to develop their relationship through leisure and recreation, less time for other children, strained sibling relationships, and financial crises are but a few of many areas that may require extra attention.

Although the challenges are great, so, too, are the rewards. Each obstacle they overcome helps parents and families to build the confidence and strength to meet their next challenge. Families that appear best able to deal with stress are those that work together and pull in as many outside resources as possible. These resources are most easily discovered and understood when parents of children with exceptional needs share what they have learned with other parents.

7

Parents as Case Managers

Primarily because of parents' efforts to meet the exceptional needs of their children — to serve as "case managers" — America is one of the most advanced countries in caring for children with disabilities. In their role as case managers, parents have assumed the responsibilities of securing services, and when those services were not available, they have pressured, coaxed, and pushed for their formation. Prenatal nutrition and counseling programs, infant assessment and screening procedures, free and appropriate education to the age of 21, and increased access to public facilities are only a few of the many results of their work. Parents have been and are our country's most powerful and effective lobbying group on behalf of children with exceptional needs; they act as constant reminders that a humane society is judged by how it treats its citizens who are most in need.

When a child requires both more and a different type of attention than is typically provided, parents find themselves forced to discover, or perhaps invent, ways in which to meet those needs. This is often quite challenging in a system designed for "normal," "average" children. In order to ensure that their children receive appropriate services, parents of children with exceptional needs must be more aware and more involved than if their children had been born with more typical developmental profiles.

Question:
Even though there are lots of services out there for children with special needs, it's often hard to figure out how everything works. Do parents everywhere have to scavenge and fight and act like detectives?

Answer:
The systems vary a bit from state to state and town to town, but in general parents of kids with special needs must do this everywhere. The technical term that describes this is *case management.*

Most states, counties, cities, and towns are attempting to improve the delivery of services to children with exceptional needs and their families, yet many inconsistencies and inadequacies still exist. It is often difficult to know what's available in certain areas and to coordinate the many services that some children and families require. In general, children who are identified as mentally retarded (often referred to as developmentally delayed or developmentally disabled) are provided with professional case managers who help the family identify and apply for a variety of services. Parents of children with other disabilities, however, are often required to assume more responsibility in organizing programs for their children and themselves. In almost all cases, parents are ultimately responsible for protecting the rights of their children and seeing to it that they receive what they need to make their childhoods as positive and productive as possible.

The father of a 5-year-old boy with a visual impairment summarizes a parent's role as case manager and expresses both his appreciation of those parents who have led the way and his perceptions of himself and his wife as pioneers, blazing new trails for parents who have yet to learn of their children's exceptional needs:

Father: I sort of have mixed emotions when I look back at all we've been through and all we have ahead of us. Sometimes I feel like we're the only ones who have ever had a blind child — like no one else could possibly imagine what it's like. It seems that everywhere we go, everything we do, we have to educate people about visual impairments. I'm not just talking about friends and neighbors, I'm talking about pediatricians, teachers, therapists — just about everyone.

Then I think, "Yeah, well, at least the programs are there. At least you weren't the first one to go through this!" I may have had to push his teachers to give him this or that, to get materials or something, but at least the materials were there. They are there. Special materials in all subjects and free phone numbers you can call for help and specialists that will come to the school and assist the teachers. They're all there. We may have to watchdog and push people to use all that's out there, but I'm real thankful that parents before us got all these programs going.

When I think of all the roadblocks and prejudice we've faced in the last five years, and then I think about the parents who pushed through all those programs, I take my hat off to them.

It's a challenge for anyone to provide for all of a young child's needs; however, when a child has needs above and beyond those of most other children, parents are required to devote extra amounts of time, effort, research, and study to see to it that their child's potential is fully actualized.

Cindy and Tom, parents of a toddler with Down's syndrome, are doing everything in their power to see to it that their son makes the most of what he has.

Cindy: I feel so responsible for whatever Simon does or becomes. I feel that what I get for him and what I do for him is going to make the difference. Whenever I kind of sit back and relax for a minute and try and go about normal activities, I start feeling guilty. I say to myself, "Oh no, I haven't done this today. I'd better look at my list and get to work with him."

Every once in a while I go through a period where I just say, "That's enough!" I just let go. I do all the normal activities and play with him and things, but I don't concentrate all the time doing this and that for this purpose and that purpose.

When I play with the other children, I play with them because I love them and I want to play with them. Usually when I play with Simon, it's got to have a purpose. It's got to be effective. You know, that kind of gets difficult sometimes. It's hard to feel like you always have to be pushing, teaching, watching. So sometimes I'll take a short break and try to forget how important it is that I keep on top of everything, that I manage his programs the best I can.

Tom: The information about Down's syndrome seems to be very hard to get hold of, and once you get hold of it, it's either so technical or so long that you need a week's vacation to figure it out.

Between all the doctors and therapists and teachers there's so much terminology — the jargon and the legal ramifications of what the state's doing and the statutes and your legal rights and everything that's associated with. It's just overwhelming.

Cindy quit working so she could have the time to start digging, knowing that your best chance is between birth and 5 years old. That's when the most potential is.

I didn't get caught up with the reading and such myself. For the first couple of years the paperwork was just too much. You're out working at a job all day, and then you're doing stuff afterwards, and, well, it's hard. The time's just not there. So that's where Cindy was just all the time beating the bush for more information, more programs. Finding out what this means and what that means. She just beat it to death, and now she's so knowledgeable that . . .

Cindy: Oh, I'm not there yet, but the more I learn the more I learn. It sounds funny, but it's true. The more I learn, the more I pick up or understand when I see or read other stuff. You get to the point where it all starts fitting together. You're sort of like putting all the therapies together, mixing them up, and coming up with a total life program or system. It has been a lot of work — it *is* a lot of work — but it's worth it.

The thing is, there are a lot of different agencies and therapies and things to learn about, and they're very difficult to weave your way through. You've got to coordinate yourself or you're lost. Once you get coordinated, once you get rolling, it gets easier.

Cindy and Tom have managed, through intelligence, collaboration, and hard work, to provide their son with an environment in which he can grow and learn and come closer to becoming the most he can be.

Question:
I can't imagine how I could be a good case manager for my child. I'm barely able to keep my own life together. What if I need help?

Answer:
Most schools and agencies are committed to an approach called empowerment, the goal of which is to help parents to help themselves.

Empowerment: assisting individuals to identify and utilize the strengths and skills they possess so that they may better direct their own lives. One of the keys to helping parents become better case managers for their children is to help them identify what they can do well and encourage them to continue doing that and build upon it. This goal of empowerment is perhaps most important for parents who find it difficult to identify their own strengths or see themselves as capable and competent.

Many people at times feel unable to meet the barrage of problems and challenges that make up everyday existence — unable to cope successfully. Yet most have experienced enough successes to realize that they can take charge of situations and have a significant impact on their lives. For individuals who have suffered a lifetime of failures and disappointments, the birth of a child — a healthy, intelligent, well-behaved child — can force an extremely difficult adjustment. The birth of a child with exceptional needs can be overwhelming and place both the child and family at risk of failure.

The mother of an 18-month-old recently identified as bilaterally hearing impaired summarizes how the diagnosis of her daughter's condition and the resulting professional interactions have changed her:

Mother: After our daughter was born, it seemed like all these problems came up that we hadn't imagined: no free time for ourselves or time for each other [husband and wife], not enough money, our apartment was too small, we weren't getting enough sleep, we were arguing a lot about little things — just all sorts of hassles. There were just a bunch of problems. We separated a couple of times that first year or so, too. Then when we sort of started pulling our acts together a bit, like thinking, "Maybe this will work out; maybe we can do it." Bam! We find out that Tiffany is deaf. We were in shock, absolute shock — had no idea of what to do or where to go or what.

Well, this social worker from the county board for developmental disabilities started working with us, and everything changed. I'm not sure how she did it, but this lady got us making lists and calling around for this and that. She got us thinking about how we could get a bigger place — we moved into this place [a three-bedroom, rented house] just a few weeks ago. She got us, well, she didn't really get things for us, she sort of guided us so that we could get stuff. Anyway, she

showed us how to get this assistance here and into this program there.

As it turns out, our lives, all of our lives, are better now than
before we found out about her being deaf. It's like we were
being carried away, out of control, falling off a cliff that first
year or so after Tif was born. Then once the diagnosis came in
and we started working with this lady, we realized that we
had to take charge of our lives — it was up to us to do
something. So we did it. Our marriage isn't perfect, but it's a
lot better now, and I know a lot of it has to do with that lady,
the social worker, showing us that if we wanted to, if we'd try,
we could change our lives.

Empowerment: helping individuals to help themselves and develop
competencies that previously had been hidden or dormant.

Fred and Claudia are the proud parents of two children. Amy, a quiet,
sandy-haired 16-month-old who seems to enjoy observing others rather
than getting actively involved herself, is mildly delayed in most areas of
development. Her 3½-year-old brother, Mike, is also delayed, has club
feet and a seizure disorder, and has an abundance of energy and curiosity
(so much so that his behavior is very difficult to manage). In order to
meet with success in life — to complete their schooling, find meaningful
employment, and establish a rewarding personal and social life — these
two children may require more than their parents have to give. Why?

Fred was born with epilepsy and diplegic cerebral palsy (affecting
both sides below the waist). He has spent most of his 57 years on crutches,
and for the past eight years, he has been restricted to a wheelchair. He
can't remember how many jobs he's had, but "there's been a whole bunch
of 'em." Alternating between different types of minimum-wage positions
and welfare programs has been difficult. Although not an excuse for
Fred's alcoholism, his difficulty finding and maintaining employment
and caring for himself have not made for an easy life.

Claudia, a friendly, smiling 27-year-old who loves "to be a mommy
and to have an apartment and stuff," dropped out of a special education
program for the mentally retarded at the age of 11 and has been out on
her own ever since. Before marrying Fred, she had spent years drifting
from town to town, living as she could. Unable to read or write above the
second-grade level, she wants her children to "have it better than me, to
make something of themselves."

How can these two people provide for their children in a satisfactory manner? With help, lots of help! Fred and Claudia can, and are, acting as their children's case managers, but they are doing so under the watchful eye of a number of different service agencies and with the help of a number of different assistance programs.

Claudia: When we first got married, me and Fred was living in this other apartment. We wasn't there but two or three months when we got pregnant with Michael. When he was born we had to move out of the apartment. They told us that there was no children allowed there because there was only one bed-room, and so I said, "Oh, great. Now where will we move to?" So we got hold of a lady I know at the ARC, and she told us that we could move to one of their buildings that they manage. They told us in this here meeting, before we moved, they said all these here rules and that, and they told us what we could do and what we couldn't do, and then they said that the only reason why they were letting us in is only if we would put Michael through their infant stimulation program.

They wanted to come into our home when he was a month old and help us work with him with his fine motors and his gross motors [coordination of small and large muscles], and they wanted to teach us how to be parents. They helped us a lot. They didn't, like, boss us around. They was always telling us when we did stuff right and telling us how they could see we was trying our best. It wasn't like, "Do this, do that." They got us to figure stuff out ourselves lots of times. It was hard, but it sure made us think and work, and it was good for us to be better parents.

Fred: A teacher comes here to teach us how to help him with his colors and how to teach him to cut straight lines on paper. We got to make a red line and then he cuts it; make a blue line and cut it. Carol [the "teacher," the early interventionist] says we're doin' a real good job, and we're good parents. She says we put in lots of time and we're helping the kids.

Claudia: She even told us that we might be able to get a three-bedroom place. She told us who to call.

We get lots of help, like last year, when Michael had these here seizures, the school told us to do lots of things; they gave us lots of suggestions. Then we had these parenting teachers coming in September last year and helping us put him to bed. We learned putting him to bed real good. Some nights he goes to bed real good. But then the last couple nights again, he doesn't want to go to bed.

Fred: He tossed and turned. The parenting teachers told us to read to him at night and rub his back and get him ready for bed. Check if he has to go to the toilet or anything, potty him, and tell him to go to bed. Tell him, "We'll read to you when you're in bed." I bet you I read that ABCs book about 500 times already. I know that book by heart.

Claudia: We were having troubles with him going to bed and we were spanking him a lot and they tell us not to spank him at all 'cause that's abuse. We only give him love taps; we don't go wham, wham!

They taught us how to talk to the kids and how not to call them names, because then your kids will talk nicer to you and won't call names or hit so much, and they'll listen to you better and sass back less.

Fred: We were punishing for too long. They said we were doing it much too long. We were punishing them for two or three days without no TV and restrictions, and that was too long.

Fred and Claudia are doing the best they can to raise Michael and Amy; without a number of agencies providing support services, however, their efforts would most certainly be less effective. Fred and Claudia are learning that they can make a difference in their children's lives, that they do have strengths and abilities to help them through the challenges of childrearing. They are becoming more empowered and, through their empowerment, developing the skills they need to participate as their children's case managers.

Question:
Some professionals don't seem to want parents to be empowered, to make their own decisions. How do you deal with them?

Answer:

Make every effort to listen, watch, consider, and learn as much as you can, but remember that you, the parents, are ultimately responsible. You need to take charge and make the final decisions!

In the lives of most parents, times and situations arise when they must choose between following their own intuitions and beliefs or doing what the experts recommend. When parents decide to disregard the advice of professionals, to take charge of a situation, they run the risk of being wrong. This ability to take risks is an important ingredient in case management. Without this factor, without making their own decisions, parents become case custodians rather than managers, passive observers rather than active decision makers. The more actively involved parents are in making decisions, the harder they will work to prove their decisions right.

Helene and Al serve as an excellent example of this point. Having already spent years as their older daughter Jenny's case managers, which included providing around-the-clock nursing (Jenny has a rare liver disease, a seizure disorder, developmental delays, brain bleeds, and brittle bones), they were far better prepared than they might have been when their second daughter, Stacey, was born five weeks prematurely with unknown, life-threatening medical problems.

Al: When we got her [Stacey, their second child] home from County [Hospital], they said everything was fine. She had gained enough weight and seemed OK. We were home for three days and she just wasn't looking right, so we took her back, and they kept her for two or three days. They looked her over, you know, gave her lots of tests and observations. They could tell that some things weren't quite right, but they weren't able to diagnose the problem or give any prescription of what to do. So they said we could bring her home for a couple of days and keep our eyes on her. A few hours after we got home, things took a turn for the worse, so we brought her back. She was there another four or five days, and then the doctor — despite what I'm going to say, he's really a very good doctor — he spotted a lot of stuff, a lot of symptoms of different things. He wanted her to go down to University [Hospital], but we didn't want that.

Helene: We told him from the start that if anything serious came up, we were going up to the clinic in Minnesota, where Jenny [the older daughter] had been treated, no matter what. He kept saying that we should take her down to University, that our best bet was University.

Al: He was real definite about it and didn't want to discuss Minnesota. Well, we had already dealt with Minnesota for a year and a half with Jenny and knew how good and caring they were and how everything worked up there. If things got worse with Stacey, we didn't want to get a whole new set of doctors involved. We didn't want to have to go to another hospital. But the doctor from County just didn't want to hear about Minnesota. His mind was made up. On Friday he called us and said that he had it all set up. They were expecting Stacey at University on Monday.

            So on Saturday we checked her out of County and Sunday morning Helene and Stacey were on the plane for Minnesota. By Wednesday they knew everything that was wrong with her and had her stabilized on medications.

            I didn't even call the doctor from County Hospital until after Helene and Stacey were all situated in Minnesota. I was all through talking about what we *should* do. Like I say, we told them, we told them ahead of time that we weren't going to go.

Helene: You know, experience really is the best teacher. Now when we hear or see something we don't like or we know is wrong, we don't sit quietly. We jump right in. I think we learned a lot of this from talking with other parents.

Al: [laughs] I'll say! When you spend as much time waiting around intensive care wards as we do, you get to talk to a lot of different people. Usually when we're at hospitals, we're in with a lot of other very sick children and their families. After you've been through what they've been through, what we've been through, it makes you less patient when you're getting BSed. You want to cut through it faster. You want to hear it straight. You [parents of chronically ill, hospitalized children] talk a lot among yourselves. You spend a lot of time talking. They tell you what's happening and ask you how you're doing emotionally and financially and with the doctors. You talk and ask about lots of things. You just compare notes about everything. It's a real education.

Helene: One thing it teaches you is that you have to check and double-check all your information. Most doctors, hospitals, social workers, clinics — all of them — you don't necessarily get the right answers all the time. You have to be like a hawk, watching every little thing, listening, comparing, analyzing. Nobody is going to watch out for you and your kids as well as you are yourself!

Al: The nurses down here at our local hospital know us real well. The last two times we've been there, when she's had brain bleeds, we've taken our own medication. We take all our own stuff rather than try to get it through their pharmacy. We just take our own medicine up there and we do it ourselves. The nurses just stand back and watch. They're amazed, but the hell if we're going to sit there and watch them try and figure out what to do. We've got everything she needs, and we know what to do with it. We don't need to have some rookie nurse try and figure out a complicated procedure and take the chance of having her screw it up when we're right there. I was standing there one night and I was crushing pills and preparing medications, and one nurse that we like real well was there and she said, "I feel absolutely useless. I don't know what I'm even standing here for."

Helene and Al are an extreme example of taking charge, but the message is clear: be an active, fully functioning member of the intervention team and don't allow your lack of degrees or credentials to get in the way of your participation!

Parents sometimes forget that despite their lack of formal education or training in a given discipline, their specific knowledge about their own child and their child's condition is of critical importance. Norm and Linda, the parents of 5-year-old Teddy (who was introduced in the last chapter, where the stress experienced by other members of his family was discussed), attempted to share with the nursing staff at the hospital their expertise as case managers. Initially, they failed:

Norm: After his first surgery, they were going to give him morphine.
            I asked them why, because he had difficulty in the past with
            medications and he was already on the heart monitor and
            respiration monitor. I asked them, "Why are you giving him
            morphine?" The doctor said, "For the pain." I said, "Is he in
            pain?" And he said, "Yes, well, he should be." So I said, "Well,
            how do you tell if he's in pain? How can you tell if a little
            guy's in pain if he doesn't cry?" The doctor said, "His respira-
            tion and heart rate will go up." I said, "Is it up?" I looked. His
            respiration was at about 100, and his heart rate was about 120.
            I said, "Well, what's normal for a baby his age?" And he says,
            "Oh, respiration about 100, heart about 120 or 125." So I said,
            "Well, he's not in pain then. Don't give it to him!"

            We were real concerned about an overdose because he has
            very low muscle tone; he's very loose and everything sort of
            stays in him. He doesn't work it out fast. A normal child's
            muscles move a lot more; they burn it off sort of. Well, in
            Teddy you put it in, and it takes so long to get in his blood-
            stream. And if it takes that long to get into it, it's going to take
            that long to get out. That was my understanding.

            Well, I think it was after the third day, a different nurse shift
            came on. That was the first morning we didn't come up to the
            hospital before the doctors got there. Anyway, the night shift
            nurse came in. On his chart they didn't write down anything
            about the morphine or monitoring him before giving any
            medications. I guess we shouldn't have left it with just telling
            the doctor. We probably should of insisted he write it down.

Linda: It's hard being too bossy, too pushy. I mean, telling doctors
            and nurses what to do isn't that easy.

Norm: Well, on his chart it says every four hours a shot of morphine.
            She gave him a shot at midnight and again at four o'clock in
            the morning. At about 6:30 or 7:00 a.m., he quit breathing on
            her. Overdose.

            Fortunately, he came out of it OK, but on his second surgery
            — he's now had eight operations altogether — they were
            going to do that again, and I told them, "I don't want him to
            get any morphine. If he has any pain, he's going to be on the
            monitor, right? And if he has any pain, you should be able to
            tell that." They agreed with me, but they wanted to know why,

> so I told them about the first experience. They said, "Very
> good, sure, OK." Then they made sure they wrote it down on
> his chart. They had to make sure, because I told them I wanted
> to watch them write it, and I did!

This story clearly demonstrates that parents need to both share their
knowledge and desires with professionals and assert themselves to ensure that their decisions are not reversed. It also demonstrates that some
professionals need a good kick in the pants: they need to be reminded to
listen to and respect parents.

Question:

My child has a low-incidence (uncommon) disability, and it seems
that with all the reading and studying we've been doing about it, we
know more than most of the professionals we're dealing with. How can
we get them to listen to us and respect what we know?

Answer:

Unless you're in a very large city or near a research university or
institute this may well occur. Make every effort to share your knowledge
with professionals. Explain your positions, provide them with readings
and resource materials, and reinforce them when they try to listen and
learn. If they don't progress in their abilities to deal with your child's
needs, you may need to look elsewhere for services.

Listening to and respecting the knowledge and experiences of parents is always important, but it's critical when dealing with low-incidence, seldom-seen disabilities. Few professionals have had experience
with all exceptional needs, all types of cases, or all syndromes. When a
child's condition is uncommon, it is of utmost importance that parents
share all the knowledge they have and that professionals listen and learn.

Parents of children with low-incidence disabilities are advised to
focus on two qualities in professionals who will work with their children:
experience working with other children with similar conditions and the
desire to learn more about the condition — both to gather information
and then keep up-to-date on new findings. It is virtually impossible for
professionals to learn all there is to know in their field, stay abreast of all
developments, and be aware of all research that is in progress. The less
specialized a professional is, the more unrealistic these goals become.
Parents must therefore share information, to set up their own little

information exchange network centered on their child's specific condition and needs. It is also of critical importance that the professionals involved be open to this new information and allow parents the opportunity to share what they know.

Neither Robert nor Mary has ever received any formal education or training in medicine, nor do they have a theoretical understanding of the biochemical functioning of cancer; however, they are more knowledgeable than most medical practitioners on the topic of one type of cancer, neuroblastoma. They have read and studied everything they could find on the subject, interviewed and questioned America's leading experts, and lived the reality of the disease for the past four years. Why? Mary explains:

Mary: My son, Roger, was born with neuroblastoma. When he was a few hours old, they discovered small nodules on his back. When they biopsied they found that the cells were abnormal. At 5 days old he went to University [Hospital], and they performed all kinds of tests on him. It was really shocking, totally unexpected. It progressed to the point where when he was 10 months old they admitted him and removed a primary tumor from his stomach and took out his left kidney. He's got tumors all over. He's covered with thousands of them. Most people who have this have it in one specific spot, just one tumor. They have one tumor that can be removed. The doctors have never seen it so widespread over a person's body before.

He's undergone several different types of chemotherapy, total body radiation, just everything you can imagine, and he was in the hospital for eleven months straight. The type of tumor that he has secretes extra amounts of a certain hormone, a hormone that everyone has. It's a hormone that makes you have bowel movements. Normal levels are anywhere between 50 and 150. His was up to over 2,000. They told us that that's one of the highest in history. They couldn't believe it. I mean, for months, how many months did he have diarrhea?

Robert: Eleven months. Try to imagine that?! Diarrhea for eleven months!

Mary: My mom and I kind of put our heads together and reasoned that if you don't eat solids, how can you stool solids? You see, they wouldn't give him any solids to eat. They were pumping in all these different medications and balancing his entire intake with liquids. So we came up with this theory — it was just common sense to us — that he needed to eat solids. It was just logic. The doctors said that it didn't make any difference. They basically ignored our idea. Well, it did make sense to us, so one night we talked to one of the other doctors, not Roger's regular physician, but one of the specialists. We were just trying to put the pieces together. I said, "Can't you try to take him off of it [some of the medications mixed with an all-liquid diet] and just see what happens?" He bought into the idea and got the others to follow. So anyway, I suggested that, so they tried it. Wouldn't you know it? He started to have a lot less diarrhea, almost immediately.

He didn't know what food was. When he started eating, he didn't know what it was, so we had to train him how to eat.

I feel pretty good about it, because my suggestion really worked; it helped. Now our doctor's philosophy is "Mother knows best." He thoroughly believes that. I told him that I don't know where he'd be if it hadn't been for us saying, "Please try this, please try this. This makes sense, this is what's happening."

Robert: One time he was in the hospital, and we had decided to take a break — just take a couple of days off, away from the hospital. Mary's mom was there, keeping an eye on things, and Roger started acting very different. Mom [the grandmother] tried to tell the doctors that something was wrong, but they didn't believe her. See, nothing had changed medically, like pulse or temperature, but Mom knew something was wrong, just because he was different, not himself.

Mary: They thought he was just cranky because his mother was away. So my mom called us. I left right away and I walked into that room and that kid was hardly breathing. I went out in the hall and I just started screaming and yelling. I mean, I was on the warpath. Of course the doctors came out of the woodwork, but within a half an hour the kid was up in ICU [intensive care unit], and within two hours after that they were coming to us saying, "We've got to put him on a ventilator. He's struggling for his life." What if my mother hadn't been there? What if we hadn't come down? Would they have just let him sit there?

We had to make most of the decisions. I guess that's why I say that sometimes it makes you feel like you're God. You're the one who's there and you're the one who sees him going through this hell, and you've got to decide, "OK, do we go with this chemo [chemotherapy], or do we try this total body radiation, knowing the side effects, knowing that someday in his life later on, it's going to kill him?" When you think about it, he should glow in the dark. Nobody, I don't care how trained they are, nobody can tell me that they know the side effects of all those drugs, all that radiation.

Robert: Medicine is a learning field; they learn everyday. Believe me, there's a lot those doctors don't know. We're helping to educate them. But most of them don't like to be told. They don't like your opinion, even if it's right. They don't even like the nurses' suggestions. Man, they get mad at them. We've seen that.

Mary: Just the other day I said to Robert, "It was our suggestion to take Roger off of certain medications, to stop the fluids at night, and to try the surgeries. For the bills that we get, they should be paying us. We're the ones who saved our kid's life."

Often the knowledge, confidence, and fulfillment of becoming more and more capable as a case manager is accompanied by feelings of frustration and impatience. As parents learn more about their child's specific needs, they more clearly perceive both excellence and inadequacy in service providers. Those who do not give up, who do not relinquish power and authority to the "experts," become very demanding consumers.

Such is the case of Jan and Chuck, parents of 4-year-old Corrine. Although Corrine's blindness is not as rare as Roger's neuroblastoma, it still qualifies as a low-incidence impairment. As teachers, both Jan and Chuck were trained in techniques to meet the unique, individual needs of children, and both were experienced in the utilization of resources (libraries, consultation, and so on) to learn about new areas of interest.

Soon after Corrine's birth and her diagnosis of retinopathy of prematurity, Jan and Chuck began reading about visual impairments, talking with professionals and other parents, and adapting their home and parenting behaviors to best meet their daughter's exceptional needs. Before Corrine was old enough to roll over, her parents had begun building and purchasing materials that would both stimulate the use of her limited visual potential and maximize the development of her other senses. Although they were not formally trained as teachers of the visually impaired, their love and concern drove them to become experts.

It was therefore from a position of strength and knowledge that they began their relationship with Corrine's first teacher, a home trainer from the local infant stimulation program. Jan and Chuck describe how those initial hopes soon gave way to disappointment and anger:

Jan: We had expected or hoped for someone who would give us ideas, bring materials, and share responsibility for Corrine's education, but it just didn't happen that way.

Chuck: It was not very worthwhile because we were already doing more things with Corrine than this gal had ever seen.

Jan: She was amazed that we knew so much and had so much going on our own!

Chuck: She would come only once a week, but it was more like us teaching her than her teaching Corrine or us.

Jan: We finally started just telling her what to do — sort of treating her like an aide. She didn't really know what to do because Corrine wasn't multiply handicapped or delayed in anything except her vision. This was the first blind child she had ever worked with.

Chuck: What we needed was to have some high-input, visual-type things to do, and she just didn't have the knowledge or the materials.

Jan: I don't need people coming out here, taking up my time, just so they can compliment me on the great job I'm doing and ask to borrow all the materials I've made. It was like having a student teacher, like I was training her. I would prefer not to have the inconvenience.

Positive reinforcement and encouragement are important components for professionals to incorporate into their interactions with parents, but they must do more. Most parents want to be provided with guidance, alternatives, activities, intervention strategies, and materials to help them learn and grow in their relationship with their child. Professionals must help bring a freshness or new life to remediation efforts — efforts that are seldom rewarded with rapid change. After *giving and sacrificing* for their children, parents appreciate *taking and receiving* from professionals.

Question:
How do you know if you've got the best services available or if you could find something better? I'm concerned that if I change, it may be even worse.

Answer:
Look before you leap. Talk to other parents; get referrals; interview professionals. You may not find anything better, but the least you can do is try.

It's not at all uncommon in our society for individuals to continue utilizing services that they know are less than ideal. Whether the reason is habit, laziness, finances, difficulty being assertive, or fear of hurting someone's feelings, many people don't make a change even when they know they aren't receiving the best that's available. "I've been bringing my car to him for five years, and he's never once fixed it right on the first try"; "She always cuts my hair too short"; "I wish just once I could get in to see that woman without waiting for over an hour" — all familiar complaints, but complaints that often are not acted upon.

Protests such as these take on far greater significance when they concern the development of children, yet even when critical aspects of a child's development are at stake, many parents don't intervene or force a change: "She's got the worst teacher in the school"; "All that pediatrician knows is antibiotics. I'll bet she'd recommend antibiotics to cure a bloody nose"; "That day care center is a battleground. It's so noisy and wild." Comments such as these are often accompanied by a shrug of the shoulders, as if to say, "Life isn't perfect, and people are too small and insignificant to affect their own destinies."

This is a very dangerous attitude for a case manager to have. If the case manager, the overseer of a child's development, does not see to it that less than adequate services are discontinued and the best that is available is provided, then who will assume this responsibility? Chance? Is adequacy of services to be left to the luck of the draw? Hopefully not!

The parents of 4-year-old Jessica, a bright, cheerful little girl, believe that it is their responsibility to see to it that their daughter receives the best available services. Brent and Julie realize that even though their daughter's cerebral palsy is mild and only affects her legs, the earlier she receives therapy and the higher the quality of that therapy, the better the outcome will be:

Brent: Our insurance company said that physical therapy was no longer needed. I told them it was. They said, "Well the school provides it." I pointed out to them that the school's services were only consultive [a therapist tells the teacher what to do but doesn't necessarily work directly with the child] and that it isn't provided in the summer. So we went around and around, but I wouldn't let up. We've now negotiated that insurance will cover any therapy that the school doesn't provide. If therapy is provided by the school, they won't cover it, but when not provided by the school, like in the summer, they will pay.

Julie: We had the school's therapist write a letter saying that if Jessica didn't get therapy her hamstrings would tighten — which they would — and that could prove detrimental to her walking.

Brent: I feel sorry for parents who don't know their rights and aren't aggressive. I mean, we really had to pound on some doors to get this therapy issue settled. If we hadn't made it happen, then what? Then Jessica's walking and motor skills wouldn't develop as much. For the rest of her life she'd walk a little less well and control her body a little less well. I don't think that would have been fair.

Julie: Parents need to get the help and services their children need, no matter what it is, and really look around and find professionals who know what they're doing. If it's speech and language therapy or physical therapy or counseling — whatever — get the best for your child and get it early. *Early,* that's important! So much progress can be made then. We had a heck of a time finding a physical therapist who had any training or background with real young kids. We heard about and met a lot of therapists, but most of them worked with the elderly or brain-damaged adults or sports injuries — those sort of things. That's a lot different than working with a teeny little girl with mild cerebral palsy.

One great idea is to seek out other parents and find someone to talk to. At first the parents are ashamed and they don't know what to do, but as they learn more about it and meet the other parents, then they start working on their kid's problems and finding out where to go and what to look for.

Brent: You need to keep your eyes and ears open for other things, for other programs, other ideas. I know with us, when we get into a certain program we kind of get channeled in it — like that's the one and only way. That's a mistake. It's best to stay open for new possibilities. There's so much out there, so many good and caring people, that it's really a shame when someone gets stuck in something that's not best for them. We just switched one of the programs that Jessica goes to, and we're very pleased. It's much better. If you're in one program and you're really not satisfied, keep your eyes and ears open for something else that might be better, because most everybody that you go to feels that their way is the right way or else they wouldn't be doing it. But you have to kind of play educator or doctor yourself.

The message is clear: parents need to monitor both programs and progress to be certain that their child's needs are being met and that professionals are competently exercising the practices generally accepted as best in the field.

Tips for Parents

- Read, study, and learn as much as you can about your child's disability.
- Be assertive: express yourself and see to it that your needs and wants are listened to and met.
- Share with professionals the knowledge you have about your child.
- Keep an open mind to new therapies, procedures, and individuals who may be able to help you, your family, and child.

Tips for Professionals

- Empower parents: provide them with information and guidance but let them make their own decisions.
- Listen to parents; they know more about their child than anyone else.
- Be honest with prospective patients and clients: if you aren't up-to-date or trained in the area of their specific need, either don't take on the case or learn as much as you can as quickly as possible to help them.

Conclusion

Although helping professionals may share the responsibility for children with exceptional needs, parents are ultimately responsible. As long as they retain custody, parents are their children's case managers. Teachers, therapists, psychologists, social workers, counselors, doctors, and nurses may enter a child's or family's life and provide a dramatic and wonderful influence; in most cases, however, they do not remain involved for more than a few months or years. Effective case management requires a commitment to a child's total well-being over a long period of time. A child's parents are usually in the best position to provide a service such as this. It is the duty of professionals to assist parents in this role, to provide all possible resources so that parents may succeed with the lifelong task of assisting their children to maximize their potential.

Critical ingredients required to meet with success in the role of case manager are knowledge — obtaining as much information from as many resources as possible — confidence in one's own abilities to make decisions, and assertiveness. Parents, through a combination of their own hard work and support from professionals, can develop these skills and serve as capable directors — case managers — of their children's educations and lives.

8

Support Networks

I never could have made it without all the help I got. Without my husband and sister; without my mom and friends; even the baby-sitters, all those young girls from the neighborhood and the church who'd come over and watch the kids for me once in a while — I couldn't have made it without them!

— Mother of a 6-year-old boy who is deaf and blind

People need people. The degree or type of need may vary and may intensify or diminish during certain periods or times in life. The assistance provided may meet one specific need or many different and overlapping needs. A variety of family, friends, acquaintances, professionals, and agencies may be involved or just one person or agency. The critical factor is people helping people.

Support networks differ from person to person, with no two people, not even spouses, sharing the exact same network. Helene may rely on her husband, Al, for emotional support, whereas Al may rely on his buddies; Leah and John may seek assistance from their church in times of crisis, whereas Berta and Hans may turn to a counselor or social worker; Claire and Daniel may have their parents watch the kids when they need a break, whereas Patty and Ben may hire a baby-sitter.

Support networks are also dynamic, undergoing constant evolution and transformation. Rarely the same from one point in a person's life to another, they expand and retract, intensify and fade as needs and circumstances change. Ted's parents distanced themselves after Ted and Mara adopted Donna, but in a few years they may become more actively involve. Dennis and Gayle had little financial support during Julia's first two years of life and amassed $80,000 in debt, but they are now enrolled in a program that covers many of their expenses. Until Cindy was 5 years old, her parents, Jim and Rene, attempted to share as much of her care as they could; they have recently separated, however, and Rene has been left to find other supports to help her manage Cindy's exceptional needs.

Support networks play a unique role in families of young children with exceptional needs. The burden of responsibility for a child who may forever require extra services; the emotional stress of dealing with the reality that a child is not like most other children, not like the child that was expected; the added expense of medical and educational interventions; the guilt and doubt related to self-blame for the child's condition — all of these factors lead parents to the point where their support networks take on a special importance. As any architect or builder knows, in order for a structure to remain standing, supports must be stronger than burdens.

Parents of young children with exceptional needs find their support in many different ways and places; however, certain sources are quite common. Spouses, older children, other family members, friends, families of other children with similar needs, schools, agencies, churches, and religious beliefs are some of the more common ingredients that can be blended to form a support network.

Question:
What role do spouses or partners play in support networks?

Answer:
Ideally, spouses or partners are the central ingredients in a support network, each being the other's primary source of nurturance and advice.

Tom and Cindy, the parents of four children, including a 3-year-old with Down's syndrome, are an excellent example of supportive partners:

Tom: We learned early on in raising the kids that we had to share responsibility. Neither of us could do it all. I try to do my part, but I rely on Cindy a lot. She shares everything with me, keeps me informed, and we make decisions together.

Cindy: I do most of the legwork, but I always know that he's there to help. He does a lot, too. When it gets to be too much for me, I know he'll give me a break, take over for awhile, while I catch my breath. I don't know how some people do it without partners who help out. I don't think I could.

Cindy and Tom have worked out a system of responsibility sharing in which they regularly analyze what needs to be done, discuss who will do what, and then share the results of their efforts. Each is aware of what the other is doing to help the family, and, at the same time, they are each aware that their system is flexible enough to deal with new situations as they arise. They have built their family and relationship on a foundation of negotiation and mutual agreements in which all members participate and feel both a degree of ownership in the system and a commitment to success. Two of the many agreements they have worked out in this relationship are scheduling and "homework."

Cindy and Tom admit that even if their son Simon had been born without Down's syndrome, life would still have been a challenge. Both Tom and Cindy have career objectives, both have outside hobbies and interests, and they share four children, each of whom has a unique set of strengths and needs and requires love and attention. Added to this is Cindy and Tom's desire to have a close, supportive, and growth-enhancing relationship with one another. Simon's Down's syndrome is not the reason or cause of Cindy and Tom's perceived need to schedule their lives, but it certainly is a contributing factor.

Cindy: This house works on a schedule. We figured early on that if we were going to have enough time for ourselves — for our personal interests and hobbies and things — and still have time to share with each other and be there for the kids, we needed to chart things out. What works for us is family meetings: we do it every other Sunday. We all sit down and go over our schedules and plan out who's going to drive who where and when and who's going to do what around the house, and when Tom and I are going to do our own things and when we'll have time to be together. When we don't do this, it seems that Tom and I — our own needs and our time together — always get left out, and then we end up being grouchy or hard to be around. So our way, the way that works for us, is those meetings and that schedule.

Many parents who lead busy lives find that scheduling times to be together, as well as times to pursue personal interests, is critical in order to achieve a balanced and rewarding life. Those for whom this system works also say that a key element in the scheduling process is cooperative planning. Through the process of sitting down together and discussing schedules, needs, and desires, family members accomplish a number of objectives. They share who they are and what they value in their own lives, learn about each other, practice the art of compromise, and, perhaps most importantly, increase the chances of having their needs met in a way that is compatible with meeting the needs of their loved ones rather than at their expense.

Cindy and Tom have developed another system of organizing their lives that facilitates communication. They call the system "homework." Cindy attends most of the meetings involving Simon, does most of the reading and studying, and is the more active in organizations and school, but she keeps Tom up-to-date with "homework."

Cindy: Tom works pretty long hours, and then when he gets home it's dinner time and he's got all the kids coming at him with all the things that are going on in their lives, and then I sit and try to explain to him something new that's going on in therapy or some kind of program. . . . It's just too much; it's frustrating. We can't keep it all straight, so he gets his homework. I put a folder together for him, and when he has the time or when he takes a business trip, he studies it. I put in current articles or reports on Simon or on the other kids — a lot of things come up when you have four children! There are so many details that you sometimes can't remember them all, so I got organized. I keep the information that I think he'll want to see together, so that when he has time he can have it all there, ready for him.

Tom: I'm like Simon. I get the material, but I just get it a little bit later than everybody else does, a little bit slower.

Partners, husbands and wives, helping and supporting one another: that's how most people hope and anticipate their relationships will be.

Question:
What if your spouse isn't supporting your needs and won't listen to your pleas?

Answer:
The first step is to be honest and open about your feelings and needs. The next steps are counseling — hopefully together — and finding other supports: family members, friends, counselors, agencies.

You need to start here with some clear messages, clear communications that your needs aren't being met. If that's not working or you have difficulty expressing yourself, consider marriage counseling. If neither of these approaches works, you need to look carefully at your total marriage and determine what you want to do with it. If you decide that you wish to continue the marriage and accept the limited support level you're receiving, you'll probably need to look elsewhere — to other family members, friends, personal counselors, or agencies — for support.

Like Tom and Cindy, Norm and Linda have four children; unlike Cindy, though, Linda was unable derive the support she required from her husband. Linda turned to Norm to help her deal with their youngest son's medical difficulties (Teddy, now 5, has been diagnosed as having mental retardation, visual impairments, low muscle tone, and speech defects), but his denial of the severity of Teddy's condition, along with a lifelong habit of not discussing problems or feelings, made it difficult for him to meet the emotional and support needs of his wife.

Linda tried in a variety of ways to confront Norm with her frustrations but constantly felt as if she were pounding her head against a brick wall; neither he nor their relationship changed much. Rather than pursue attempts to change her relationship with Norm, to get more emotion and feeling from him, she suffered within and tried to have her emotional needs met through friends and other family members. After three years of failure with this technique, she confronted her husband and, after weeks of tears and torment, finally got him to agree to join her in marriage and family counseling. Even if Norm is not yet Linda's picture of "the ideal communicator and partner," she is pleased that the counseling is bringing them to a deeper understanding of each other's needs and a sensitivity about ways to meet those needs.

One critical understanding that Norm and Linda have reached is their different use of language — how each of them uses or doesn't use language to talk out problems and concerns. Norm doesn't like to talk about "problems" that much and previously thought that it was just a waste of time when Linda used this technique. He didn't like "wasting time" talking about his fears or feelings, nor did he have much patience listening to Linda talk things out.

Norm: When I'm at work and I'm there sitting and drinking a cup of coffee with the boss or the guys, and they ask me "How's Teddy doing?" I just say, "Fine." That's about it. I don't go into it. I figure, what's the use going into all the details? I don't, but

> Linda would go into incredible detail if it was her. She'd go into every tiny thing with anyone who would listen.

Linda: It sort of makes me feel alone, like I'm going through it alone. I mean, yes, he's there to help out, and I know that he must be having thoughts and feelings inside, but I just don't feel the support or the sharing. I don't feel like we're in it together that much because it's just me showing all the emotions, having all the feelings. I've wished so many times that he would just break down and let it out, like open up his feelings. I need that from him or with him, but he just doesn't.

Over the past few months, Norm and Linda have been attending individual, marriage, and family counseling, and through the counseling process, Norm has learned to listen better and share more of himself. The changes have not yet been dramatic, but they have taught Norm that Linda's talking has value and that talking may help him to work out some of his own feelings. The process has also revealed to Linda that her husband does possess an inner world, a world of feelings, hopes, and fears, and that to learn more about his world she must be patient.

Question:
How much can I expect from my partner? I know it's hard on him, too, so I hate to make things worse by depending on him too much.

Answer:
There is no formula here. The most important ingredient is communication: you need to share and discuss what your mutual needs are and what each of you can do to help the other.

There is no formula for how much support a spouse can or should ask for or receive. The key is communication. Partners need to communicate their needs in a way that their companions understand. Once the communication is understood, it is not time to analyze, evaluate, or criticize; it is time to respond. When a wife or husband says, "I need to be held," the appropriate response is to hold them, not ask "Why?" or say, "Later." When loved ones say, "I'm upset because . . . ," the initial response should be to listen and to try to understand and feel what they are expressing, not to convince them that they're wrong or that they shouldn't feel that way.

Providing this support takes time and patience. Norm, for one, had difficulty with this:

Norm: I'm an action kind of guy. I never liked sitting around talking about things much. I'm a doer. This whole thing of being patient and listening and talking things through is pretty new to me.

Norm wasn't the only spouse interviewed who felt overwhelmed by the amount of time it takes to meet a partner's needs, to be a companion's resource. Many parents — fathers and mothers alike — said they found it difficult to give more at a time in their lives when they had less to give. Since the burdens and time constraints of their child's exceptional needs had been added to their lives, these parents felt less able to meet their partners' needs.

Parents of children with disabilities have devised a variety of mechanisms and compensations to help themselves so that they might better meet these needs. Among the techniques recommended most frequently were

- Sleep more (to gain more physical and mental energy).
- Sleep less (to gain more time).
- Hire baby-sitters more frequently.
- Change work schedules.
- Increase children's time in day care.
- Set up specific sharing times (e.g., during meals, before bed, Sunday mornings).
- Set up a more rigid schedule that guarantees time to talk together and go out on dates together.

The mother of a 4-year-old boy with severe emotional, and behavioral difficulties recalls:

Mother: At first I tried to do it all on my own. My husband had enough pressure at work and helping support and care for his parents and with the bills and things, so I didn't want to bother him with my concerns and feelings. Those first three years I just kept it all in and tried to deal with it myself. We just had the one boy, and I wasn't working, so I figured I should be able to handle it. Well, I couldn't. Month by month, year by year, it just got worse and worse. I didn't really see it when it was happening, but now that I look back, it's really obvious to me that I was destroying myself from the inside out. I gained weight, became more and more depressed, went out less, didn't do the fun things with friends or my husband that I used to do. All I did was take care of my son and hide my feelings and fears.

That was a big mistake. If you're in trouble, you need to tell people, tell your husband. You can't just expect them to know and come to the rescue. My husband was shocked when this all came out — that I was holding all this in. He said, "If I only knew. Why didn't you tell me?" You know, like I just expected him to know what I was going through, expected him just to know and volunteer to help.

Since then, since it all came out, it's been a change like night and day. I get a lot more help, and we share things alot more. I feel like it's not just me now, but us. We're in this together, raising our son, and that makes it a whole lot easier, sort of takes some of the pressure off.

Parents who perceive themselves as and are perceived as supportive partners, or as becoming more supportive partners, overwhelmingly agree that it is an aspect of life that requires communication, planning, and constant evaluation. Being or having a supportive spouse or partner may "just happen," but those who are most experienced, those who have been there, recommend that you don't leave this critical variable to chance.

Question:
My child's teacher recommended that I join a parent support group. What are support groups and how can they help me?

Answer:
These groups bring people together who have something in common — in this case children with disabilities. They help by increasing parents' knowledge of resources and ways to deal with situations and also by bringing people in touch with one another.

A special type of friendship or relationship is often experienced by people who share a common interest — book club friends, bowling buddies, mall-walker comrades. When that common interest is a child's exceptional need, organizations that form around that interest are referred to as parent support groups.

Parent support groups come in all sizes (international, national, state, local, one-to-one) and for all types of exceptional needs (Down's syndrome, prematurity, visual impairments, autism). They may be formally or informally organized or have no organization at all. The two key variables are (1) those involved are going through life experiences that are in some way similar and (2) they possess a desire to share with, grow, and learn from one another.

Groups such as this have been formed not only for parents of children with exceptional needs but for many different types of shared interests. La Leche League brings together mothers who are breast-feeding or interested in breast-feeding; parent-teacher associations or organizations (PTAs and PTOs) unite parents and teachers to discuss improving the education of children; Parent Effectiveness Training (PET) groups enroll mothers and fathers who wish to improve their parenting skills. The list goes on and on.

Although many such groups exist, those that deal with exceptional needs can play a special role for parents. These groups connect individuals whose lives are dramatically altered by their child's needs, people who often cannot find answers to their questions in books or from professionals. In order to meet with success, these parents must become problem solvers, inventing new and different ways to deal with situations, feelings, and relationships. Processes such as this are much more efficiently, effectively, and enjoyably achieved when they are shared ventures.

Candy and Steve joined a support group for parents of children with cerebral palsy soon after their daughter, Connie's, condition was identified when she was 1 year old. They have been in the group for over four years, and it now forms the core of both their support network and social life:

Candy: If I needed someone to talk to, I'd call one of the other moms in my support group; her daughter also has CP. She lives nearby, and we're really close, so I would probably call her because we have a common problem and, you know, just to hear what she has to say. See, that's my outlet, I guess. I always call everyone else to see how they're doing as opposed to saying, "This is my problem." When I hear what other people go through, then I feel better because a lot of people have it worse than me.

Steve: Not me. If I had a problem, I'd probably just keep it to myself and turn my hair gray.

Candy: Yeah, he's grayed a lot in the last five years.

But, really, we have this whole group of friends that we count on. We sort of got linked together through the hospital. It's a group of parents, parents and whole families actually, with kids who have cerebral palsy.

It's really a CP support group, but we have a couple of kids with hydrocephalus and spina bifida. See, they don't have their own group, not one that's nearby, anyway, and the kids and parents have a lot of the same needs and concerns as we do, so we sort of let them merge into us.

Steve: It's a great group of people! We party, have picnics, field trips, all kinds of get-togethers.

Candy: The moms meet once a month, at UCP [United Cerebral Palsy], and have a rap group. We talk about things that are on our minds and share a lot of stuff. It's great! See, most people don't understand what it's like. They try to listen, try to be concerned and help, but it's really hard to relate if you haven't been there. When we're in group, I might say something like, I mean I have said stuff like, "I hate going shopping. I hate the looks and the rubbernecking and the stupid questions. I especially hate it when they sneak the looks, like when they want to watch you, but they don't want you to see. It's like a spy game." Then everyone will go, "Uh-huh, uh-huh." You know that they know, they understand. Then everyone will jump in with their stories and ideas of how to handle it. It doesn't make the problem go away or anything, but it feels better just to say it or hear someone else say it. Sometimes you do get good ideas on things to do or ways to handle it, but just saying it and hearing them say it, it helps.

Steve: I don't go to the groups, but I know what she means. We, the guys, talk more about other stuff, like finances and wheelchairs and lifts — to get the wheelchair into the van. We talk more about stuff like that.

Candy: They play is what they do.

Steve: Yeah, we do play, but you have to. I have to. I'd say my two best friends, well, at least my best friend, he's got a little girl with CP. We met through the group and struck it off real well. We have so much in common that it works out real well.

Candy: And my best friend is his wife, Shelly, the woman I said I'd call first if I needed to talk to someone. We spend so much time together that people get us confused. We both have baby girls — we both have 5-year-old girls with CP in wheelchairs, we both drive white vans, and we look a little alike. It really confuses some people. Shelly and I are closer than I ever was with my sisters. Even if we didn't have the girls, we could be good friends, but the girls make it even better, even more meaningful.

Steve: Oh, I want to say one more thing about our group. We have some really good speakers sometimes. I do go to those, when I can make it. We have people come and talk about specific issues, issues that concern us and our kids. Sometimes the speakers really get us going and a lot of stuff comes up.

Candy: A lot of the speakers are good, but most of them don't know as much as we do. I don't mean Steve and me; I mean our group, all of us together. The speakers are interesting and all, some of them are great, but when it comes right down to what to do when you get home, it's us, all the parents, who know what's really going on. Most of the best ideas come out in the discussions. The sharing together works best for me.

"The sharing together works best for me." Candy's statement beautifully summarizes why many parents value their parent support groups. The significance of working through ideas and approaches with others who have been or are presently going through a similar situation cannot be overemphasized.

Question:
What can extended family members do to help?

Answer:
Many things. If you're honest and open about how things are going, chances are that somehow, in some way, extended family members will become more involved in your lives.

As the saying goes, blood is thicker than water. A special bond exists between individuals who share the same family tree. For many, the bond is one of more than just blood but also of love. Friends may come and go, but family remains forever family.

Although our society is becoming more mobile and families are often spread around the country, or perhaps the world, for many, the importance of sharing their lives with relatives has not diminished. Parents often regard their own siblings, parents, aunts, uncles, and cousins among the most critical elements of their ongoing support network — critical elements that help bring understanding, stability, and joy to their lives.

Ken and Judy are two such people. Family has always been important to them, and it became even more important as life's responsibilities and pressures began to build. Now that they have three daughters under 5 years old, the eldest of whom, Michelle, has Down's syndrome, and Ken spends sixty to seventy hours per week working, much of that time on the road, the importance of their families has become greater than ever before.

Judy: Our families were both very supportive. All through we never had any negative feedback from anyone on either side. Everybody accepted Michelle and the way things were going to be, and they're all very loving and giving and supportive. I think just knowing that made it easier for us — just knowing that it was OK, that they still loved us, and loved her, anyway.

We both have pretty big families, and most of them live close by. Everybody wants to learn the signs [sign language] so they can work on them with her and communicate a little more. We're always running off copies of the new signs that we learn. We have to make a bunch of copies, too, because they all really love her and want to learn them. There's never been any negative feedback from anyone in the families, really. We see each other a lot, and the phone is always ringing. There are cousins all over the place, and the kids spend a lot of time together; they do a lot of things together. She's just one of the guys, fits right in. Everybody wants to be with the girls. If we need a sitter, everybody wants to do it. It's like, "Why didn't you call me last time?"

Sometimes families that were not that close prior to the birth of a child with exceptional needs pull together to meet the new challenge. Bethanie, the unwed, teenage mother of 3-year-old Melissa, born blind and with facial deformities, describes her relationship with her own mother and how it changed when Melissa was born:

Bethanie: My mom and me was never really close. She, like, threw me out when I was 16. I got in some trouble — it wasn't the first time — and she just had it. We fought all the time and couldn't agree on nothin', not the time of day, not nothin'.

It all changed when Melissa got born. I said I was thinking of giving her up [for adoption or foster placement], but Mom, she says, "No way. She's blood. You guys come live with me, and we'll raise her together." She gives me this great big hug, starts crying and all and telling me how much she loves me and Melissa. I'm crying and bawling, too. What a sight we was. I think that was the first time ever we hugged like that — at least since I was a little kid — and for sure the first time we cried together since I can remember.

That was three years ago, and Lord knows we done a good job of it since. I couldn't done it without Mom. She was right there the whole time. She and me's the closest we ever been. I guess when something like this happens, you either give up, go under, or make it work. Well, we're makin' it work.

Before we leave the topic of family support, we turn to one more story, the story of two sisters. Readers may remember the difficult time Ed and Carrie had dealing with their daughter, Mandy, who is now 1½ and has been diagnosed as having cerebral palsy. Mandy's constant crying, along with the behavioral problems that arose in one of her two older brothers, made life in their home almost unbearable. Well, as storms are often accompanied by rainbows, so, too, do crises often bring out heroes or heroines. In this case the heroine is a sister:

Ed: It was kind of like Carrie and I were the rocks of the family. We were the strong ones, the stable ones, the ones others could count on in both our families. For years everyone would come to us if there was a problem. This was before Mandy was born, for years before. I guess we were pretty stable and didn't have too many crises in our lives. Now it's coming back; now we're the ones who need the help. People are helping us now when we need it.

Carrie: Like my sister; she's my best support. Yeah, I'd say my sister and brother-in-law have become the rocks of the family since Mandy was born. I know we count on them a lot. They're always there for us. We have the most in common with them because we both have young kids and they live pretty close by, about an hour and a half drive from here. When we go down to University [Hospital], we stay at their house and she's helped a lot with the kids when things have gotten really bad. She's taken them for days at a time.

          Just today I got something in the mail from my sister. She went out shopping and bought me two outfits because I was sitting there one day complaining about how I never get to go shopping. I've got the same clothes this summer that I had last summer, and I got this package in the mail today with two outfits in it. She's always sending me funny little cards, like, "Keep your chin up," that kind of stuff. She's been a good friend.

          Sometimes I'll be home with the kids, and Ed will be gone — he works long hours — and I'll feel like I'm stranded on an island. I'll feel like it's just me, and I'm the only one to watch over them or care for them. Then the phone will ring and my sister will be on the other end, and I'll remember I'm not alone. It's a little thing, but it can mean so much. It's like she knows just the right time to call, just at the points when I really need someone or something.

Ed: I had a week off over Easter, and Carrie's sister said, "Hey, we'd love to have the kids stay with us. Bring 'em by." They really wanted them, all three of them, so we did. We took all three kids down to her sister's.

Carrie: She took all three of them. We came home. We thought, "Hey, why not? We don't have to pay for a hotel or eat out. Pay all those high prices — what for?" We could just come home and be in our own house where it's quiet for once. It was wonderful!

Ed: Quiet! Restful! It was perfect!

Carrie: It was a wonderful week, and we did some things that we had wanted to do for a long time but just never were able to. It was real fun! The timing was just right, too. I mean, we really needed that break. I can't think of anyone else in the world we would have left the kids with either, and I don't think we ever would have asked for them to do it, so it was just the perfect setup.

Family, when it works right, is hard to beat. How often do friends or acquaintances volunteer to watch three kids, one of whom has cerebral palsy and another who is quite active and difficult to manage? Family has always been and remains one of the keys to an effective support network.

Question:
Since we started having all the problems with my child, my friends have grown more distant. Those friendships used to be so important to me. What can I do to keep them going?

Answer:
The maintenance of friendships usually requires at least two critical ingredients: (1) sharing enjoyable experiences and (2) mutual giving. Check to see if you've neglected either of these, and, if so, bring them back into your relationship.

The identification of exceptional needs in a child sometimes places families into such a state of turmoil that everyday patterns of life are temporarily upset. During this period it is not uncommon for parents to focus more intently on their personal and family needs, directing increased amounts of time, attention, and caring in these directions and less to other activities and people. Although most friends and extended family members will probably be understanding of this change in priorities, some may not. Individuals can become less caring and giving when they think they are receiving less, or they might feel rejected or not cared for. In order for most friendships to continue and grow, all involved parties need to continue sharing positive experiences and need to establish a mutually rewarding balance between giving and receiving.

Two stories, two very different stories, illustrate the importance of friends and the ingredients necessary to keep these relationships alive and well. The first friendship dates back to school days B.C. — before children — whereas the second is more recent, between an employer and an employee. The friendships began differently and play somewhat different roles in the lives of each family, but they share the critical elements of people caring about and helping one another and sharing both good times and bad.

Mark is not yet 3 years old and may very well develop quite normally; however, his background and present speech and language delays place him at risk of having difficulties in school and life. His mother, Sandra, explains:

Sandra: Well, I was seventeen and living with one guy, but another guy raped me, and I got pregnant with twins. The guy I was living with went from mean to worse. He talked real bad to me and beat me and stuff, and when I was three months pregnant I miscarried one of the twins. I miscarried the one, but the other one, Mark, was OK. My boyfriend and I split up after that, and then a few months later I married this other guy, but he started abusing Mark and me both. We split up a few months ago. Things are a lot better now. My new boyfriend treats me good, and Mark and I are both doing OK.

I think most of the problems with Mark [speech and language delays, acting very shy and withdrawn] are from my ex-husband abusing him, and him and his mother making me leave him in the crib all day. See, I was not allowed to even pick Mark up or otherwise I was spoiling him. The only time he was out of the crib was to be changed or fed.

He didn't do much, didn't make many sounds. I was the only one that would talk to him. That's the way that my ex-husband thought a family should be run — you were not allowed to talk to kids that much. The child was there to be seen and not heard. His mother is the one that told him that.

I could hardly ever get out of the house. My ex-husband almost kept me like a prisoner, and when he wasn't home his mother was almost always there. She lived under us. His mother had told him that as soon as a woman's married, she's not allowed to have any friends, so I was not allowed friends — well, I kept my friends, but I had to hide it and not let them know about it. I was not allowed to use the phone except for business purposes. I was not allowed to go out and leave Mark with a baby-sitter for any reason at all. I was not allowed to do anything. He had his mother doing my grocery shopping for me and the whole bit.

Sandra was abused and isolated for over two years. Her own parents and siblings were scattered all over the country and showed little interest in her or her child. The only contact she had with the outside world was with a group of high school friends, and the few communications with them had to be hidden.

Sandra: I got no help from family — zero, zilch, nothing. From friends I get a lot of help; as a matter of fact, it was friends helped me get away from my husband and his mom. They planned it all out, some of my old buddies from high school. One day, when I was home alone with Mark — and that didn't happen a lot, believe me — they crashed into the place and like swooped me and Mark and all our stuff out of there and took us to a shelter, like for battered women. They planned it all out, and I mean it was fast! Like the Green Berets in Vietnam or something.

Yeah, without my friends I don't know what would've happened — what I would've of done. We're real tight, real close, my friends and me. Every single one of them have kids of their own. So for baby-sitters, none of us ever have to spend money. We all baby-sit for each other, which is real helpful. Most of my friendships go back to high school. We met in a class for school-age mothers.

All my friends count on friends; they don't count on their families for nothin'. Most of us were thrown out of the house or left on our own before we graduated. A lot of our families don't approve of us having kids. They figure, "You made your bed, now lie in it. You stay with the kids twenty-four hours a day and don't you dare get a babysitter for not even one minute."

There's like fifteen of us that all hang around together. We're like a little community, like a commune, but we don't live together. We meet downtown or at the park or one of our apartments. We have a ball together.

There's over 50 of us who were in the program together, and that group gets together at the hospital once a month. My little group — the fifteen of us — like to see each other more, about once a week. When I was married I'd only get to see them every few weeks, and just for a short time, but they were there for me. They were there planning my escape, and I didn't even know it.

They're my family. If I need help, money, or advice, or someone to watch the kids — whatever — I go to them; we go to each other. Yeah, they're my family.

Lacking family or other supports, Sandra has friends who have taken on added meaning, added importance in her life. In effect, they are her family. As Sandra perceives life, they are the only people who really care about her and her children.

The second story describes the contributions that an employee/friend made to better the lives of a mom and dad, Gayle and Dennis, and their 2-year-old daughter, Julia, who suffered from a number of life-threatening medical impairments. Barney wasn't the only person to assist Gayle and Dennis. Penny (the NICU nurse who came to the rescue in Chapter 4), Gayle and Dennis's parents, friends, their church, and excellent teachers and therapists all were part of a very substantial support network. No, Barney wasn't alone in his desire to be a part of their lives — not alone, but still very special:

Gayle: Barney helped us I can't tell you how much. He's the man you hear rattling around downstairs [this interview took place in Gayle and Dennis's apartment, which is above the bar they own and operate], getting the place ready to open up. He's our full-time bartender and the only help we have in the bar. He'll be with us three years next month, and he's been like a blessing from heaven from day one.

Before Julia was born I had a bunch of knee surgeries done in less than two years and ended up almost losing a leg. The clinic here sent me to University [Hospital] to see if they could save the leg. We knew that Dennis couldn't maintain the place alone, so we hired Barney to help him out while I was in the hospital. We knew I was going to be there at least three months, and Barney's been a lifesaver ever since.

We all hit it off right away. We spend a lot of time together — you know, sharing and doing things. We love him like family, and he loves us. He's another person we can call twenty-four hours around the clock. He lives just a few blocks away. We can call him anytime, and we did, when Julia was first born. We'd say, "Barney, the ambulance is on the way. We've got a full house. Can you come?" He'd usually beat the ambulance. He drops everything and runs. There isn't a day or night that we've said, "Barney, we need you" and he hasn't been there for us. It doesn't matter what he's doing or where he is. He drops everything and runs. He has worked many, many, many, many overtime hours. He calls them "Julia hours." One time I had to leave home quickly in an ambulance with Julia. It was during a time when our finances were real bad — worse than usual. He knew that. The next day I said, "What time did you come in and what time did you leave? You didn't record it?" He said, "Forget it. Those were Julia hours."

He and Penny have saved our lives, literally. They help make it bearable, make it seem like it's worth going on. "Uncle Barney and Auntie Penny," that's what we tell Julia their names are. That's what she's going to call them.

All families in need should be fortunate enough to have friends such as Sandra's high school buddies and Barney: friends who give of themselves, who love and care, and who are there when needed. But to find and maintain relationships such as these requires an investment of time and giving of yourself. Those who receive the most almost always are those who give the most; individuals who are cared for and loved are those who care for and love others.

Question:
How can I include my other children in my support network?

Answer:
Help them to understand the issues of the exceptional need. Include them in decision making. Encourage them to share their fears and personal problems. Give them attention and love for who they are. Do these things, and the chances are good that they will become critical members of your support network.

The siblings of a child with exceptional needs can be and often are among the most significant ingredients in a well-functioning support network. However, in order to be a part of that network, to participate as significant players in the challenge of building a healthy family life, they must first have their own needs met. These may include the needs to understand issues, to be included in decision making, to share fears and personal problems, and to receive attention and love.

Holly is seven years older than her younger sister, Kris, but it was not until Kris turned 3 that Holly learned anything about why her little sister had Down's syndrome or what it meant. Holly spent three years in fear of "catching" Down's syndrome, three years hating her sister for always making mommy leave home and spend time at the hospital, and three years developing a repertoire of inappropriate behaviors in an effort to pull attention from Kris's needs to her own. It was not until Holly's behavior became unmanageable and her parents, Barb and Paul, sought the services of a marriage and family counselor that a concerted effort was made to meet her needs and to include her in the family's support network.

Now 11, Holly recalls her experiences as the older sister of a young child with Down's syndrome:

Holly: I remember that I hated Kris. I hated her because she got everything, and I got nothing. I thought it was going to be neat to have a little sister. I could dress her up, push her in the stroller, play with her. It was going to be fun. Then she was born, and she was so sick that Mom and Dad were always going to the hospital. All I knew was that Kris needed them more than I did, and I was a "big girl." I never knew what was wrong or what all the operations were about. I just knew that Kris needed Mom and Dad more than me, and I had to be a "big girl." I remember having dreams that she would die, and I could have my mommy and daddy back. If she would just die, everything would be like it was, things would be OK. Sometimes I'd even pray that God would take her. I would cry and cry, and wish God would take her away.

Every day I would look in the mirror to see if my face had changed, to see if my ears looked like hers or if my tongue was pointy. See, I thought I was going to catch it. I really did. Sometimes I was afraid it would happen to me at school, and the other kids would start laughing at me, and I wouldn't

> know why. They'd start laughing, and I'd run to find a mirror, and I'd see my face had changed. I'd think about this all the time, like I'd really see my face all changed. Sometimes I'd wake up in the night and go look to see if it had happened. I was real scared!

Holly's parents had been so busy dealing with the shock of Kris's Down's syndrome, so busy trying to meet all of her medical and educational needs, that they didn't notice Holly's transformation from a happy, well-behaved, academically able first grader to a third grader who was constantly being reprimanded for cheating, lying, and fighting and had fallen more than a year behind her classmates in academics.

It was not until Holly's elementary school counselor contacted Paul and Barb and the family became involved in counseling that the tremendous impact Kris's exceptional needs were having on Holly were identified and understood:

Barb: The whole realization with Holly just floored me. I mean, I had no idea, no inkling. Now that it's all out in the open and we've dealt with it — I mean we're dealing with it — I can't believe we missed it. It's so obvious that we were pushing Holly away, that we were forcing her to act up. We just missed it totally.

Paul: We were so into Kris and all of her stuff that we just didn't see. I think we just figured that Holly was a strong, healthy, smart kid, and we could sort of put her on hold for awhile. We figured everything would be OK. We didn't think or talk much about her, but if we had, I think we would have figured that she understood, and everything would be OK with her. Boy, were we wrong!

As a result of Holly's not being included in the family's support network but instead being pushed off to the side to take care of herself, she developed her own exceptional needs and became another stress or burden on the family rather than the partner and helper she might have been.

Barb explains how the process was reversed and how Holly has become one of her parents' most dependable resources, a critical component in the family structure and mutual support network:

Barb: When we got into counseling, we realized what we had been
            doing. We saw how we had never shared things with Holly
            and sort of forced her to invent her own understanding of the
            truth — like with thinking you could "catch" Down's syn-
            drome. First session, wham, like a brick in the head, we both
            saw it.

            We right away started explaining to her what was going on.
            We started having family meetings to discuss issues and make
            decisions. It was like day and night. We were real lucky be-
            cause Holly turned around real fast. She stopped the cheating
            and lying and fighting and did much better in school.

            Now, looking back, I can't see how we ever made it without
            her help. She has great ideas for figuring out stuff like car
            pools and getting places — all the arrangements that need to
            be made for Kris's therapies and for Holly's clubs and lessons
            and things. She helps with caring for Kris, and — oh yeah, best
            of all, we talk. We talk all the time. I share more with her than
            with anyone else.

            I use to not want to burden her with the problems, but
            now I see that by sharing with her, she feels better about it,
            and so do I. I can't imagine this family without Holly being
            there to help make decisions and share things. It's made
            such a difference.

Whether siblings are 4, 14, or 44 years old, they still possess their
own wants and needs. Parents cannot expect or demand that brothers
and sisters of children with disabilities place their siblings before themselves. As anyone who has ever been injured knows, damage to one part
of the body is often followed by strains, sprains, and soreness in other
parts. When one part of a whole becomes impaired, the disequilibrium
that results places other parts at risk.

Question:
Can the professionals you work with be part of your support
network?

Answer:
Most definitely! At the very least the services that professionals provide is a "support," but many go far beyond that.

Professionals can be critical elements in a family's support network. Knowledgeable, sensitive, caring, and sharing helping professionals can and should play a significant role.

Chapter 4 discussed what parents appreciate in professionals and examined how helping professionals can create feelings of support and caring. The following story reveals how their effective behavior can highlight professionals' roles in support networks.

Earlier in this chapter, Bethanie described the critical part her mother has played in assisting her to raise Melissa, her 3-year-old daughter born blind and with facial deformities. Thanks to the efforts of a team of interventionists who specialize in assisting parents of infants and toddlers with disabilities, Bethanie's support network stretches far beyond the walls of her small apartment:

Bethanie: Those ladies gave us so much help it was unreal. We never would've known about what to do if they hadn't shown us. Like they was the ones who gave us the names of different doctors and stuff. They didn't just give us the names, but a couple a times they even went with us for appointments — took us all the way down to University [Hospital], spent most of the day, helped us figure out what was goin' on.

They didn't, like, push or boss; they more, like, explained and was there to sorta walk us through it. Mom was there, too, but she and me wouldn't have asked the questions they did; we wouldn't have got so much information without them.

One was a teacher, but the other she's a — I think she's a nurse or somethin'. She does the parenting project at the center. She teaches the parents stuff. We call them first. When something comes up, we know them the best, and we know that they love Melissa almost like we do. They ain't always asking for forms, like to fill out, papers and such, or looking at us like we're some kind of trash. You know, some people do that. They treat you like you don't know nothing, like you're trash. They don't do that.

We was real upset when Melissa had to leave the program [in Bethanie's town responsibility shifts from the early intervention program to the local school district when a child turns 3], but they did everything they could to get us off on the right foot. They got her into a real good class in the school and made sure that all the therapies kept up. See, the school wanted to

> stop the OT and PT, but they said, "No way. There's no way she can go without." So the school said OK.
>
> Melissa's been out of their program for months now, but they still keep tabs on her; they still care. Just last week, Joy — she's the parenting teacher — she came by and took me out to lunch. She did it 'cause she cares, not 'cause she had to. It makes ya feel good, like they really care, like it's not just a job.

Few job descriptions require helping professionals to prove that they "care" or to follow their clients after they have transitioned to other programs, but in Bethanie's words, "It makes ya feel good." Although it's hard to measure the significance of "feeling good," it seems obvious that if parents feel better about themselves and their competence in caring for their children's exceptional needs, they will do a better job.

Question:
What role do spiritual beliefs play in support networks?

Answer:
The answer to this question was "very little" for about half of the parents interviewed and "quite significant" for the other half.

Roughly half of the parents interviewed never mentioned spiritual beliefs, religion, God, or church. Since this is not a research study and the parents interviewed were by no means chosen randomly or with any desire to have them represent a cross-section of America, all that we can draw from the omission is that *some people* don't consider spiritual beliefs, religion, God, or church as resources to turn to in time of need.

The other half, however, were very positive about the role these resources had played and were playing in their lives. Many parents ranked their belief in God or their church as their number one resource in time of need.

Although many stated that they had strong religious convictions prior to the birth of their child, a large number were led in this direction by a need to make sense of what seemed to be an incomprehensible tragedy. It is safe to say that God and religious beliefs, regardless of origins, provide many parents with a structure or point of view from which to approach their lives.

Kyle, the single mother of a 5-year-old girl who was born prematurely with a number of medical complications, was led to a new belief structure by the love and giving of an entire congregation:

Kyle: I had belonged to a church but never really attended much and wasn't what you'd call a devout believer. But boy oh boy, the congregation sure came to my rescue when I needed them. I didn't know many of the people in the church, but after Mira was born, you'd have thought they were all family. All these folks were visiting me in the hospital and sending me cards and flowers and stuff. When I brought Mira home, they set up a whole system of bringing cooked meals to us and people visiting us and helping out with housework and other chores and things. They even put on a big fund-raiser to help me out with the bills — $6,000: they gave me $6,000! That really floored me. I mean, all these people who didn't really know me from Adam, and they did all that for me, and then to raise all that money. It's unbelievable. Well, as you might guess, that hooked me in real good to those folks and to that church. Ever since then I've been real active. I don't know how I'd ever have made it without all they did for me — and are still doing for me. I don't know if there are other churches like that. I've heard there are, but I'll tell you, they turned me into a believer.

Kyle was brought into her church and a new belief structure by the goodness and kindness of the members. Other parents are very fortunate already to have in place a belief structure that helps them to accept and love their child regardless of disabilities and explain the often-asked question, "Why me?" Jim, the father of a 4-year-old girl who is severely delayed in most areas of development, is one such parent.

Jim: Jane [Jim's wife] and I were ready to accept whatever was to come. We didn't decide to have another baby [their fourth child] so that he or she would be the best athlete in the world or a great scholar or another Rembrandt. We had a child as an expression of our love, as a way to share ourselves and our love, and share our lives and our home. All the problems our daughter has had didn't change any of that. As a matter of fact, we think they've helped bring us closer to God, to our church, to our beliefs, and to each other. The challenges we've faced these last few years have pulled our family together closer than we ever were and provided us the opportunity to give and love from our hearts.

Sure, things were rough at times, and it's put us through a lot of emotions and challenges. But looking at the big picture, it's been more than worth it.

When speaking of support networks, we are tempted to look to others, to family, friends, and institutions. Yet in the end it is to *themselves* that individuals must look. Personal beliefs and perceptions are among the most important ingredients in determining how we function in life. The mother of a 2-year-old who weighed only 4 pounds at birth and is deaf regards his exceptional needs as a blessing.

Mother: Before Jas was born, my life wasn't worth much. I was a crack-head [addicted to cocaine], and did a lot of things to myself and to others that I'm not real proud of.

Jas changed all that. I saw his little face and it was love at first sight. It was like he changed everything; he gave me a reason to become a human being. It was like a chance to do something right. Since he was born I haven't done any drugs, and I've changed my life around, too, like day and night.

When I found out he couldn't hear — that he was deaf — it hurt a lot, but it didn't change anything. I mean, it didn't make me love him less. I take it back: it did change things, because I wanted to give him even more. I looked at it sort of as a test of who I was, you know, like, could I handle this. I thought, "Gal, if you can't even love and raise your own kid, no matter what problems he's got, you're pretty worthless." That really got me going. It got me thinking about who I was and what I was doing to my life. I've known lots of other druggies who've had kids, and I know most of them don't turn around this way when they have a kid, but I've met a few who went through just what I did. It can really make you sit back and take a new look at everything, and I did. I set my mind on what was important to me and what I really believed in, and I've really changed my life around. The way I see it, God brought Jas into my life for a reason. It's like the spirit in me was sleeping, or gone for awhile, and it came back again with Jas.

Many parents' support networks are enhanced by their religious beliefs; religious institutions can also be of assistance. This assistance may be the intangible, internal type, but may also take outwardly visible form, for example, a church fund-raiser that collected over $20,000 for the family of a young boy with cancer; a church-sponsored summer camp that offers weeklong programs free of charge for children with a variety of disabilities; a Bible study group that provides overnight and weekend respite services for parents of children with exceptional needs.

On the one hand, many parents who never mentioned anything about spiritual beliefs, religion, God, or church revealed full, rich, rewarding lives with extensive support networks. On the other hand, many regard spiritual factors as the heart of their support networks.

Tips for Parents

- Set aside regular times to talk and share with your spouse, children, friends, and others. Be open about what you're thinking and feeling and listen carefully to and watch what family members are communicating.
- Make every effort to stay in balance — don't disregard any of the various aspects of your life.
- Don't be afraid to ask for help; search for assistance at the first signs of need.
- Your other children can be critical members of your support group if their own needs are being met.
- To keep and nurture friendships check to be sure that you are sharing enjoyable experiences and that you've struck a balance between receiving and giving.
- Join a parent support group.

Tips for Professionals

- Encourage parents to join groups.
- Provide parents with resources.
- Remember that your role in the family's life may go beyond your position as a professional; be sensitive and caring.

Conclusion

As this chapter has demonstrated, support networks are as diverse and varied as the individuals and families around whom they are built. Although we have limited this discussion to family, friends, parent support groups, professionals, and religion, networks also include resources that have been discussed in previous chapters. Different forms of financial assistance, respite, and community agencies and businesses each have a role to play. When blended together, these varied resources can help make sure that parents faced with the challenge of raising children with exceptional needs will meet with success and can help their children become productive and participating members of society.

9

Personal Growth Through Hardship

Friedrich Nietzsche, a German philosopher of the nineteenth century, wrote, "That which does not kill me makes me stronger." Stated in another way, many parents who are able to manage the extra stresses and burdens inherent in raising a child with exceptional needs will emerge from the ordeal with reorganized values, new skills, clarified perceptions, and enhanced personal characteristics. While all or the vast majority of these parents wish their children did not have disabilities, they are, at the same time, often aware of personal growth derived from dealing with associated hardships.

More patience, a finer appreciation of other aspects of life, greater attunement to feelings, strengthened confidence and maturity in dealing with difficult situations and people, an intensified sense of the importance of relationships, and an increased impetus to succeed in their career or enter a new one are only a few among many qualities that may flourish when individuals face the vast array of responsibilities that accompany raising little children with big needs.

Question:
Some people say that a difficult experience makes a person stronger and more whole. I feel like it's destroying me and my family. Where does the "growth" come from?

Answer:
The growth or strengthening may not occur in everyone and is often hard to discern, especially in the short term. Many individuals and families do, however, learn valuable lessons through the experience of raising a child with exceptional needs.

Some parents are completely overwhelmed by the emotions and demands placed on them by having a young child with exceptional needs. Rather than becoming stronger, they, or at least their abilities to function as parents, are "killed." Of course they do not die in a literal sense, yet these parents lose the ability to effectively raise their children. This may manifest itself as the need for foster home or institutional placement, extended periods of depression, or perhaps some form of chemical dependency.

Those who are not "killed," however, often do become stronger and undergo personal growth. Survivors, parents who weather the storms of shock, denial, loss, frustration, and financial crises and proceed with other aspects of their lives, rarely emerge unchanged from the process and often find that through it some type of personal transformation has occurred.

Such was the case for Rene and Jim. Dealing with 4½-year-old Cindy's cerebral palsy and life-threatening medical needs was the most difficult ordeal either has ever experienced. It has pushed them to their emotional limits and created difficulties and frustrations in almost every aspect of their lives. Yet at the same time, it has helped them to mature and develop. Rene and Jim have each managed to derive personal growth from the great hardships.

Jim: Before Cindy was born, we weren't the most responsible peo-
           ple in the world. I mean, we were good parents [Jim and Rene
           also have a 7-year-old, Betty] and everything like that, but
           we've become a lot more responsible adults. We grew up very
           quickly. People don't grow up at 18 anymore, and they don't
           grow up at 21. They're lucky if they're grown up by 25 or 45 or
           65. Most people are really sort of big kids pretending to be
           adults. Really, this is the way our society is set up. It's more
           fun and games. We grew up very quickly when this happened.
           It was very hard, but the responsibilities were there, and there
           was no choice. I learned a lot that I think made me very
           successful in business.

Rene: Jim's really done incredibly with his job. He's been very, very
           successful in the last three or four years. Since we've had
           Cindy, that has sort of been his outlet. He's really concentrated
           a lot on work and put a lot into it.

Jim: This whole experience [raising a child with disabilities] has
           taught me a lot about dedication. Rene would be at the hospi-
           tal with Cindy, and there was absolutely nothing I could do.

For me to sit there and worry about it twenty-four hours a day didn't help anyone. I couldn't be on the phone all the time, and I couldn't necessarily be there, because if I lost my job the insurance would have canceled and the bills wouldn't get paid. So when I was at work, I learned to direct my thoughts to what I was doing rather than thinking about outside problems. I've learned to focus, to do my job 100 percent while I'm there, to really be on top of it. Because, see, if I let myself think about this and that, if I start drifting off, then I wouldn't help Cindy or Rene, and I wouldn't be able to do my job. So what good would that be? None!

Work at work, home at home: when I get here [home], I handle these problems. When I'm there [work], I handle those problems. Focus — I've learned to do that extremely well.

Rene: For me, the growth came in a different way. The way I feel is that it's brought me closer to myself, to who I am, and to my spiritual beliefs. At first I kind of felt confused as to what had happened, why it had happened, and stuff like that. I couldn't get a real grasp on it — sort of like I was being carried away in a tornado. Then I started really tuning in to how I was feeling and what was going on all around me, and I realized that this was just another scene or act in my life — another challenge. Then it became real clear to me that this was not an accident or bad luck or a real tragedy. It was another part of my life, and it was here and real and, like everything else that happens, an opportunity for me to do my best, to be as in tune and caring and loving as I could be. It was our job to take care of Cindy, our responsibility. It was a real spiritual awakening for me.

For Jim, he was pushed into his work, but for me I was pushed to caring for Cindy, caring for her and loving her.

Actually, it's affected my career or career plans, too. I've decided I want to be a nurse. Taking care of all of Cindy's medical needs has been a real education for me and has taught me or shown me something I'm good at and enjoy. I've started back to school to study nursing.

Jim: Another positive is commitment to prayer. As tired as I am, as much time as I don't have, I pray every morning and every evening.

Rene: It's given us a lot of patience, too — a lot of, like, just accepting things the way they happen. We just realized a few months ago, sort of simultaneously, that we had both changed in this way. Maybe it's from all the waiting in the hospitals and offices, or because weeks and months go by and we see so little as far as growth or change in Cindy. I don't know, but people were telling both of us that we had really changed in that way [in showing greater patience], so we started talking about it and looking at ourselves, and we agreed that we had.

Jim: That one, the patience, sort of sneaked up on us. We didn't see the change until others told us about it, and then it was sort of, "Hey, I guess you're right. OK, good deal." Sort of like getting something free in the mail: "You are hereby notified that you are now a patient person!" I also learned an awful lot from Cindy about what's important in life and what's not. She's helped me focus in, slow down a bit, and just enjoy the moment. We don't go out as much. We try to enjoy quiet times family times, at home more.

Rene: Before this happened, I use to look at life from a pretty narrow perspective. I used to be very self-centered. If we had had any other type of major problems of this magnitude, I don't think I would have handled them so well. I would have just thought about how hard it was on *me,* and I probably would have walked: good-bye; I'm finished. I would have quit. But I'm not that way anymore, not as much as I used to be. It's really helped me be less self-centered.

Jim: I think it's helped our marriage, too. It was very weak for a long time — very, very weak. So it couldn't have gotten much weaker. It had to grow. Rather than calling it quits, it became a commitment. I think we found a way to do it without making ourselves into martyrs; it wasn't like "we can't leave each other because of Cindy." Instead, we worked together, teamed together, and grew together. Rather than running away from problems, we faced them; rather than trying to create more problems, we tried to solve them. We didn't do it because we had to; we did it because the situation just sort of swept us all up together. We found that to survive we had to pull together.

Rene and Jim's story provides an overview of many different aspects of personal growth that can rise from the ashes of hardship and suffering. It also illustrates that some of those changes are subtle and require individuals to pay close attention to how they're feeling and behaving.

Question:

The more frustrations I experience, the less patience I seem to have. Why are some parents able to go through similar experiences but become more patient?

Answer:

Many believe that a key element here is focusing on the positives, the pluses, rather than the minuses.

The typical child matures and develops so quickly that parents are in a constant state of awe. From cooing to babbling to the first word to phrases to sentences; from rolling over to crawling to standing to walking to running: young children seem to be in a continual state of change. No sooner have parents become aware of a new skill or behavior than all of a sudden it's replaced by a more advanced one.

Such is not always the case, especially when a disability exists. Growth and development may be slowed to a snail's pace. When this occurs, parents have two basic choices: (1) become frustrated and anxious or (2) learn to become more patient, more accepting of smaller and less frequent signs of change.

This ability to accept smaller and less frequent signs of change is often accompanied by a deeper appreciation of or satisfaction with life. Progress, when it does occur, is more valued. Little things, things that so many people take for granted, like the ability to stand, swallow, and communicate with words, take on an aura of wonder. Good things are worth waiting for, and the longer you have to wait for those good things, the more you value them.

When their first child, Karen, was born, Bill and Marge didn't have to wait long for the emergence of new skills and behaviors. Karen passed rapidly through the developmental stages, with each new day revealing different and more refined aspects of her blossoming intelligence and curiosity. This did not happen with their second child, Ken.

Ken's brainstem disorder was accompanied by a number of sensory impairments as well as mental retardation and obvious facial deformities. During his first few weeks of life, it became evident that he would require intensive medical and educational interventions in order to stay alive and to function in society someday. The past three and a half years have taught Bill and Marge the meaning and importance of patience and led them to an enriched appreciation of life.

Bill: He's delayed in most things, especially language and muscle coordination. Very delayed. He's around a year and a half behind in just about everything. The lower extremities of his body are weaker than the upper.

Marge: It was this way with his crawling. It took him forever to crawl, and it took him forever to sit up. It took him forever to do, I mean to learn, just about everything. We always set these goals — like, if only he would start crawling by Christmas, if only he would learn this by his birthday. We still do that, but now we set little goals, more reasonable ones. We've been disappointed enough that now we know not to expect too much too fast.

Bill: Then we look at Jenny, our littlest one [1 year old], and we see her learn things and pick up things automatically that just didn't come with Ken.

Marge: We sort of took it for granted with Karen, our older one. She did everything, you know. Well, then Ken came along, and we learned that you can't take everything for granted. All kids don't walk at 1 year or do things at a certain age. We learned to wait and wait and wait. We're still waiting for him to do some things you'd have thought he'd been doing two years ago. Now when the baby [Jenny] does it, we really appreciate it. It's like, "Oh boy, she can lift her head. Isn't that incredible!" Or, "She can put a spoon in her mouth. Amazing! Isn't it amazing!" Things that we just sort of noticed happening in Karen and didn't make a big deal about seem like miracles now. I guess it's from watching Ken and seeing that all this stuff doesn't always happen, so now it seems like a big deal. It really helps you appreciate.

Bill: I'm a farmer, and you've got to be sort of patient in my work. You've got to learn to wait for things to happen on their own because you can't rush them. But you know, with the kids I wasn't nearly so patient before. But Ken has helped me with

that because there ain't no rushing him. He does stuff, he
learns stuff, when he's good and ready.

We sometimes look at each other and smile at each other
because, boy . . .

Marge: His accomplishments are so special. [Marge begins to cry.]
            Right? When he does do something it makes it so much better
            because he's done it. You want to have a party or something
            when he learns something or picks up something new. Little
            things, things that most parents may not even notice in their
            kids, seem so big. You see him crawl or roll over or look at
            something and pick it up, and you remember all the work that
            went into teaching him to do it. You think about all the hours
            of therapy.

Bill: Yeah, right; that's true. You don't take things so much for
            granted. It teaches you to wait better, too. Like, "What's the
            rush?" Just hope it happens and worry a little less about how
            soon it happens.

Marge: We've learned to accept Ken for who and what he is. We have
            hopes and dreams for him, but all we can do is our best. All he
            can do is his best. We just have to wait and see how he does.

How many parents take things for granted?! "The school bus will
pick the kids up at 7:27"; "I'll use the Christmas bonus to buy the kids
their presents"; "Our son will enter college after graduating high school."
When it's 7:43, past the time to leave for work, and the school bus still
isn't there; or it's January 3, and the expected bonus is already spent but
hasn't yet been announced; or when the son decides a career as a heavy-
metal rock musician is a better choice than college do most parents
serenely and casually observe the unexpected turn of events. Or do they
react with impatience and negative thoughts, feelings, and words? Imagine replacing some of the upset and anxiety of delays and unexpected
disappointments with the peace and serenity of accepting events as they
occur. Although not a guaranteed by-product of raising a child with
disabilities, many parents report growth in this direction among the
many rewards that accompany the hardships of their child's exceptional
needs.

Question:
· Sometimes I feel this experience is helping me appreciate some parts of life more. Do other parents of children with special needs ever mention that?

Answer:
Yes. Parents who observe their children delighting in small, everyday experiences, despite their disabilities, are often shaken into a new state of consciousness — a state where they value and enjoy little things more.

Sometimes it's not until you lose something, or almost lose it, that you learn to fully appreciate it. Joe, the father of 5-year-old Tiffany, who had cancer (she died six months after this interview), expresses how his love for and fear of losing his daughter has taught him to appreciate life:

Joe: I look at Tiffany in that bed, wasting away, dying, and I won-
          der how I could ever dare to complain about anything ever
          again. She lies there, slowly withering away, day after day,
          and yet she can laugh when the nurse makes a funny face and
          delight in the sound of a bird outside her window. The kid's
          dying, but she's still excited by the chirping of a bird. You
          know, I'm going to remember that until the day I die. I'm
          going to remember how she was able to find the beauty in
          everything, even though she was being eaten up by cancer.
              If I ever dare to complain about anything, about the
          weather or service at a restaurant or my car being too old —
          about anything — I'll stop myself and say, "Tif would have
          been delighted with it; she wouldn't have complained. This
          would have made her happy." This [Tiffany's illness] is the
          hardest, worst, most draining experience I've ever been
          through or will ever go through, but it's teaching me a lot. It's
          teaching me about love and about appreciating what I've got.
          Because, see, if you don't love and you don't appreciate what
          you've got, you really have nothing.

Perhaps more than any other group, parents of children with Down's syndrome seem frequently to experience this phenomenon of heightened appreciation. This may be related to the commonly held perception that children with Down's syndrome are happier, funnier, and more loving than children of comparable intellectual abilities who do not have

Down's. It may also come about because these children so often achieve higher levels of functioning than parents were first led to believe or feared.

Simon, almost 3 years old, fits both of these explanations: he is a happy, funny, loving little boy and also has progressed further than professionals had expected and his parents, Cindy and Tom, initially feared. Cindy and Tom explain how life with Simon has contributed to their personal growth:

Tom: We appreciate the little things in life more. Simon gets such joy out of little things. He's delighted by a rock or a feather, by any little thing. It's sort of infectious. He's so excited and happy and fresh and alive that he brings it out in you. It's not all pomp and ceremony anymore, like, we don't need big things to have a good time. Now you really get down to the nitty-gritty and you can enjoy life. I think it's made us, well, at least for myself, it makes me enjoy life a lot more. The small things make the world go round.

We enjoy watching our girls, too, but it's different with Simon. Maybe it's because we're watching this tiny person struggle through all the little things that we took for granted with the girls, and you see what a joy it is for him just to be able to get up and do this or that. You really focus in on details, details that you wouldn't have noticed if his development wasn't so different, if he didn't have to struggle with everything. I mean, it's like looking at life through a magnifying glass or through slow motion; that's sort of how it has been with Simon. When you see life differently like that, when you sit back and really look at all the little details, it helps you appreciate it more. Things that you never even gave a second thought to stand out, and all of a sudden you feel like you just opened your eyes.

Cindy: I'm right with Tom as far as appreciating things more. Like the other night when Simon and Mary [age 4½] decided to play in the bedroom. Mary said, "We're going to play in the bedroom, just Simon and me." So I said, "OK." I figured there wasn't really anything they could break in there, and it was pretty safe. Well, they got a hold of a Kleenex box, and all the tissue was on the floor. Then they went in the drawer and took out all the underwear and socks, threw that in there, and then they took some books off the bookshelf and put that in the pile, and there they sat, happy as could be. When I walked in and saw them sitting there, with great big smiles on their faces, I could have broken out in tears of joy. To see how far he has come and how well the kids get along, it means so much to me.

The mother of Julia, the 2-year-old who was born prematurely with a number of life-threatening medical conditions, aptly summarizes the topic of appreciation:

Gayle: In the beginning there, when she was real young, I think every day we appreciated her more simply because we didn't know if we were going to have her the next day, if she was going to die, so we tried to love her with all our hearts. I think that's a special relationship that a lot of parents don't have with their kids.

One of many really neat things that we've learned through our experiences at Children's [Hospital] was that we didn't really have it that bad. See, at our hospital here in town, they'd never confronted problems anywhere as severe as Julia's. We were a one of a kind. We sort of got the feeling that we were the least lucky, most unfortunate parents ever, anywhere. Really, it was like this was the worst dilemma in the entire world. Our first trip down to Children's, before we even got out of the car, just looking around, we found out we didn't have it so bad after all. If you just spend two hours and pick any floor at Children's, look and listen, you don't even have to talk to anybody, all you have to do is look around you and listen, you'll find that your shoes aren't so bad, your load isn't so heavy, and that some people live through pure hell. That doesn't make our situation any easier to live with, but it sure made me realize that even with all the problems we have, it could be worse.

We started to look around at the hospital and realized that we should thank God for what we have. We have a precious little girl who now looks like she can make it and live a normal life. We still have rough times, there's no doubt about it, but every time we think we've hit the pits, we'll say, "Want to take a drive?" [to go down to Children's and spend time around the wards] and it really, really brightens my whole day. See, we know that if we took that drive, we'd see and talk with moms and dads that would make our problems look small. It makes me just that much more grateful for Julia.

As the preceding stories illustrate, appreciation comes from a number of sources: enjoyment of everyday activities that might not have seemed possible, thankfulness that a child is developing more fully and quickly than had been feared or than other children with similar conditions, gratefulness that a critically ill child's life has been spared.

This same appreciation can be communicated in many different ways. Some parents may express greater joy in life's everyday experiences, others may become more caring or sharing, and still others may become more deeply aware of and indebted to God or their faith.

Regardless of its source or how they convey it, many parents of children with exceptional needs regard their heightened levels of appreciation as one among many personal rewards that have helped counterbalance the hardships they have had to face.

Question:
Some parents of children with exceptional needs say that the experience has made them more assertive. How does that process come about?

Answer:
This process happens for many but not all parents. To ensure that it occurs parents advise that you first get in touch with what you really think, feel, and want, and then move into action to get those needs met.

"He who has a why to live for can bear almost any how" — words of an unknown poet, long deceased, but a message that still rings true today. The "why" in this case is self-evident: because a child's exceptional needs require early, competent, and coordinated attention. The how is straightforward as well: by whatever means it takes to get the job done.

Parents of children with disabilities often seem assertive, demanding, knowledgeable, powerful, and confident. Many helping professionals who hold this perception often wish more of the children with whom they worked had parents who were less assertive, demanding, knowledgeable, powerful, and confident. Helping professionals new to the field sometimes wonder how or why it is that children with exceptional needs are so often born into homes of parents who possess these personal strengths.

Yet most parents were forced to develop these strengths to help meet their children's needs. Because of the barriers and hardships they had to face, the choice was simple: relinquish power over their child's destiny and let doctors, nurses, secretaries, administrators, social workers, therapists, and teachers tell them what they should or shouldn't do, what they could or couldn't receive, and how their child and family should or shouldn't react; or take charge and become efficient, effective, knowledgeable case managers (see Chapter 7) of their child's life.

Before Kris was born, Paul and Barb had never thought of themselves as powerful, demanding, or assertive people. In their own words, "We were wimps. Just normal people who followed the rules and did what we were told." Their first daughter, Holly (discussed in Chapter 8; the sibling who developed problems related to her younger sister's Down's syndrome), moved rapidly through the developmental milestones and was an "easy, bright, wonderful little kid." Kris, however, required more. Unfortunately, the county in which they lived was relatively poor and provided few services for children like Kris. Paul and Barb felt this was unfair and, for the first time in their lives, became politically and socially active.

Barb: After Kris was born, we both got a lot tougher and learned to cut through the crap and get what we needed. You see, we knew Kris had Down's as soon as she was born. There was never any question about us keeping her, so we started reading and talking to people to figure out how to handle it. All the books and all the professionals said that it was important to do as much as possible as early as possible. Because, you see, with Down's, they have a real wide range as to how they can turn out, maybe even more than with regular kids. They really need a lot of stimulation or they can be pretty low. With most other kids you don't have to pay nearly so much attention to things, and they'll just soak it up. But Down's kids, well, they sort of need it pounded in.

Paul: Wham, wham, wham [makes hammering gestures]! Just kidding. But really, you do need to focus and teach things that you'd think they'd learn on their own.

Barb: OK, so we leave the hospital, and I've already read like a million articles and books about it and talked to doctors and therapists and stuff. So as soon as we get home, I call the local early intervention program, and they tell me they're full and they have a waiting list and I should either wait a few months or call this other agency that's about 60 miles from where we live. I say OK and hang up the phone, and my heart starts pounding. I start getting really angry.

Paul: And she never gets angry — or, I mean, never used to get angry or show that she was angry before this.

Barb: I call Paul at work, and I'm like wild, crazy. I'm screaming, yelling, crying, banging the table; I'm going nuts. I'm really out of control. While I'm doing this, feeling this way, I'm also sort of watching myself and wondering, "What's going on here? This can't be me!" Well, it was me. It was a part of me that had never come out before, but, boy, it sure came out then.

Paul: I'll tell you! It was the Fourth of July — crack, bam, boom! She was like ready to go to war!

Barb: After I calmed down, I started making phone calls. You name someone, I called them. From the early intervention center to the school district, congressmen, county officers, newspapers, the ARC, CEC [Council for Exceptional Children]. I called everyone, told them my story, and wouldn't let up.

         Guess what? The early intervention agency hired another teacher and another OT. Within three weeks, we had her program [an individualized plan to meet Kris's specific needs] going and people coming to the house to help out. Now, do you think we would have got that if we had just sat back and said OK? No way!

Paul: The squeaky wheel gets greased.

Barb: Sometimes, with some of these agencies, with some of these bureaucrats, you've got to really make waves to get what you deserve. I mean, if you don't challenge them, if you don't stand up for yourself, forget it.

Paul: Like that last meeting at school: they tried a fast one on us, but it didn't work. The school tried to tell us that Kris didn't qualify for occupational therapy because she's developing real well. She's not that far behind. They said that we should continue whatever we were doing at home and that would be enough.

Barb: See, Kris just turned 3, and the early intervention program stops at 3, so we had to meet with the local school district people to set up a new program for her because she's going to be going to the school in town here.

So they come in and tell us how well she's doing. They thought they had it all decided. They had a program all ready and papers for us to sign. I'm sitting their amazed, thinking, "So if you guys have decided, why did you invite us?" I didn't say that, but it really was a railroad job. They just wanted to push us into what they wanted.

I'm thinking, "Whoa, hold on here; this isn't right." After three years of dealing with people like this, I know that if you let them, they'll run all over you, so I took a deep breath and — wham! — I let loose.

Paul: She was great! You know, honey, you should've been a lawyer or something. You should've heard her. She was cool and calm . . .

Barb: You think so?! Inside I wasn't. I was shaking and nervous and angry. What I've learned the last few years is to take those feelings and thoughts from the inside and bring them out. They don't do any good if they stay inside. Who knows? Maybe they even hurt you, like ulcers or cancer or a heart attack. So I watch for and listen to how something makes me feel, and the thoughts that are sneaking around inside me, and I bring them out.

Anyway, I explained how she was doing as well as she was doing because her teachers and therapists and I had worked with her for about a million hours and that if she stopped getting help, then she'd fall behind.

They said they'd keep tabs on her and if she started slipping back we'd meet again and discuss it — this is what I call the old "make 'em wait." You know, it's like the way you treat a 3-year-old who wants some candy. You tell them, "We'll discuss candy after we clean up the toys," and then hope they forget after the toys are cleaned up. I told them flat out that I knew my rights and that if they didn't have the services to meet Kris's needs, I'd be happy to find the services privately and have them billed. You see — I'm sure you already know this — I told them I could go have her tested somewhere else, at their expense, and that I was sure further testing would show that she did need services. If that didn't get her what she needed, I said I'd go all the way to a fair hearing and let them argue with a representative of the state. Because, you see, I could get lots of witnesses to prove that even though she's doing OK in certain things, she still needs help and therapies and such.

Paul: So Barb's lecturing them, and I see the school district representative — the director of special education — lean over to the principal, and the principal nods, like, "Uh-huh, uh-huh." Then the principal talks, and, wham, the whole meeting changes. "Oh yes, you're right, let's add that to the plan . . ."

Barb: Anyway, score one more for little Miss Loudmouth. I'm telling you, that's what you have to do sometimes to get what you deserve!

I'm not the same person I used to be. This experience of having to stand up and fight for Kris has really changed me. I don't hold it in as much anymore, and I definitely don't let people push me around. I spend a lot more time and energy figuring out exactly what it is I want, what I really want, and then I make a plan and go do it or get it.

Question:

Working with my child's physical needs has made me more aware of physical and occupational therapy, and I'm considering one or the other as a career. I'm wondering if other parents like me have started new careers because of their children's special needs and if there's a problem with this — that it's a sign that I'm getting too involved with the therapies.

Answer:

We've spoken with a number of parents, mostly mothers, whose experiences with their child's disabilities have led them to new careers. In and of itself — without other concerns or problems — it is not a sign of being overinvolved or out of balance.

Wilma graduated from high school — barely. She never enjoyed reading or studying but stuck it out because "all my friends were there, so it was the place to go." Since her graduation fourteen years ago, she has worked in "a whole bunch of jobs that I didn't care too much about." Her first job was in a factory, but that only lasted a few months. From there it was a string of short-term, unfulfilling positions in offices, restaurants, and small businesses. In between jobs she has entered, and dropped out of, a total of three training programs, one in cosmetology, one in design, and one in word processing. After all of this, she is just about to complete a program that has trained her to work as a certified occupational therapy assistant (COTA). Wilma has been going to classes part time for the past four years; reading and studying in every spare minute; donating extra hours of volunteer work for more experience; and attending conferences and workshops. She is incredibly excited and motivated by her new career and feels good about herself and her future. What happened? Why, after fourteen years and numerous jobs and training programs, has she finally found her professional niche? Wilma explains:

Wilma: I used to hate school. It seemed so useless and boring. I never was that good a reader either. You know, from the time I graduated high school, for at least, oh, maybe seven or eight years, I didn't read one book, not one magazine article. I was just burned out.

I started three different training programs at the tech [technical college] but dropped out of all of them right away. I couldn't handle the reading and all the work. It was pretty much looking like I was going to spend my life pouring coffee and waiting tables, which I didn't mind but I wasn't crazy about. And then Leslie was born. When we found out she was retarded [Leslie is moderately retarded and has speech and language delays], I started reading the stuff the teachers and therapists gave me. It was the first reading I'd done in years and years, but I had to, and I wanted to, because I needed to know stuff. For the first time in a long time I had a reason to learn.

So that's how it all started. I got real interested in occupational therapy. I wanted to help Leslie learn to use her hands better and to use her body and senses, and I didn't know anything about it. I watched her therapists work with her and thought, "Yeah, that's it, that's what I want to do. I want to help people learn that, help kids." I found a program at the tech and started taking classes.

It's been a slow go, with working part time, taking care of Leslie and the baby [Wilma and Howard also have a 1-year-old boy] and all; but I graduate in a few weeks, and I already have a couple of good job possibilities. It's great, because the job market's real good in OT, the pay's pretty good, and it's easy to get part time, which is what I want — for now, anyway.

I even have a "big plan." I'm going to work part time and take classes at the university part time so that someday I can go to grad school in OT. It will take me years, but I really love it, and after the kids get bigger, I'll have more time.

Once again, the theme of personal growth through hardship emerges. Leslie might have found her way to this career without having suffered through the strain of raising a child with exceptional needs, but, then again, she might not have. The needs that Leslie brought to life helped Wilma fill a need in her own life — the need to find a significant professional role.

Ted and Mara's story is quite different. Both had raised families in previous marriages and now had reached a point in life where they were more interested in finding meaning than money, more concerned about people than possessions. Their search for these goals led them to open their home and lives to short-term, foster child placements. Agencies responsible for caring for neglected, abused, and runaway youngsters placed children in Ted and Mara's home for a day or week or month while searching for more permanent arrangements. This foster parent experience led them to their present "careers," as adoptive parents of two young children (Donna, 4½, and Randy, 10 months) with severe disabilities.

Mara: We've been foster parents for six years, and we've had Donna for four. We had only been in for a year and a half or so when we got her. As soon as Donna moved in with us, we fell in love with her and realized we couldn't send her back. She was just special, knowing she had been hurt, abused.

Ted: Donna was born a perfectly healthy child. At less than 2
            months old she underwent several periods of abuse and as a
            result is cortically blind and has a large amount of brain atro-
            phy [deterioration and decrease in the size of certain areas].
            According to the medical profession, she'll never walk or talk.
            She has failure to thrive, so therefore she is fed through a
            gastrostomy tube. There's lots of other stuff, too.

Mara: Her biological mother is mentally retarded. The father is incar-
            cerated for sexually molesting young children. We decided
            that there was no way we'd let her go back to them. We spent
            so much time trying to help her live and getting all these
            things for her that she needed to survive. You just develop
            such a bond, such love. There was just something about her,
            her history, her heart, her spunk — just something.
                We decided that the joys we have with her are so great that
            we wanted to adopt more special needs children. This is what
            I chose to do for my career. It makes me feel good.

Ted: It makes us feel good, feel like there's meaning in this life. So
            we're now in the process of legally adopting Randy. He's not
            as severe as Donna but has lots of needs, too, with CP, brain
            damage, a seizure disorder, and so on. And it's probably not
            going to stop there; I mean, we're talking about more.

Mara: Like I said, it's my career. I get to have a rewarding job and at
            the same time am blessed with giving and receiving all this
            love. Can't beat it.

Ted: Looking down the road, I see at least one more, probably two.

Ted and Mara feel they have received more from the children than they
have given. They perceive themselves as very fortunate to be blessed
with their new career as parents of children with severely disabling
conditions. The topic of this chapter, personal growth through hardship,
doesn't exactly fit their situation, for they don't perceive the challenges
they face as hardships but as opportunities to share love, caring, and life.
Ted and Mara have not picked their career to become martyrs, to give all
they have to "poor unfortunates," but to do something that has meaning
and through which they receive great rewards. They have chosen their
career because it brings them satisfaction and a sense of purpose derived
from giving and doing a job as well as they can.

Tips for Parents

- Watch yourself carefully and become more aware of any and all personal growth you may be experiencing through the hardships you are suffering.
- Make every effort to focus on positives — the pluses instead of the minuses.
- Don't hold in feelings and thoughts, identify and then share them.

Tips for Professionals

- Identify and reinforce any hints of personal growth you observe in the parents you work with.
- Whenever possible, set up situations for parents to succeed, and encourage them by pointing out that they have succeeded through their own efforts.
- Give parents time to talk and vent thoughts and feelings, then reinforce them to build up their courage.

Conclusion

The personal growth derived from raising children with exceptional needs may take many forms. Among those commonly mentioned are attunement to feelings and emotions, awareness of God or faith, development of a clearer personal belief system, patience, appreciation of life and the things you have, confidence, assertiveness, personal power, and the formation of meaningful career goals.

Not all parents of children with disabilities can identify their own areas of personal growth as well as those who shared their stories in this chapter; however, many parents are aware of the ways in which they have been "rewarded." One law of physics that may well apply to everyday life states, "To every action there is an equal and opposite reaction": the more you give, the more you receive; the more you love, the more you are loved; the more you care, the more you are cared for.

10

The Future: Fears and Anxieties, Goals and Hopes

The future stands before each of us, as close as our next step yet stretching beyond imagination. It dances through thoughts and mental images, most often blurred and changing but sometimes startling in its clarity and regularity.

As long as these visions remain hazy and fleeting, they are mere playthings, serving as distractions from boredom or brief respites from the moment's responsibilities. Tiny pictures of what may someday be, projected on the screen of one's mind, they disappear as quickly as they are formed. Although they may spark a brief smile or deliver a passing chill, they are here and gone, soon forgotten.

Once these thoughts become clear, though, and begin appearing more and more regularly, their innocence disappears, and they are transformed into fears and anxieties, goals and hopes. It is at this point that they begin shaping reality rather than distracting from it. No longer serving as diversions or forms of leisure, they become guiding forces, leading individuals into activities directed either toward fulfilling or blocking their fruition.

All parents allow their minds to drift to their children's futures, but parents of children with exceptional needs often report difficulty freeing themselves from those thoughts: "I'm afraid he'll be stuck in that wheelchair forever"; "I won't be able to control her behavior when she gets bigger"; "I can't stop thinking that he's going to be dependent on us forever!" Fears and anxieties such as these, though they provide motivation for action, also make living in the present and enjoying life more difficult.

Although similar in many ways, goals and hopes such as, "I want him to learn to get around without a wheelchair," "I hope and pray that she learns to control her outbursts,"and, "If we work hard, we can teach her what she needs to know to live independently," function somewhat differently than do fears and anxieties. Goals and hopes are emotionally easier to deal with and much more likely to paint a clearer picture of directions that need to be taken and goals and objectives that need to be achieved.

Part 1: Fears and Anxieties

Question:
I fear that my child's life is going to be like mine, and I'm not pleased with how mine turned out. What can I do?

Answer:
You have to act — do something! The best choice is to work on changing yourself and at the same time find as many resources as you can to help make up for those parts of yourself that you think are lacking.

This is a real concern, particularly for parents who themselves have learning disabilities, emotional disorders, and mild mental retardation. They know how difficult, cruel, and painful life can sometimes be, but in many cases they have not been able to overcome their own disabilities and therefore feel less than capable of helping their children. What's needed for success here is a two-pronged approach: (1) continue working on yourself so that you can be a better model for your child and more capable of meeting his or her needs and (2) find all the resources you can to help your child, especially in those areas in which you perceive yourself to be lacking.

Jenny's greatest fear is that her 2-year-old son, Bart, will have a life like hers, filled with failure, opportunities lost, alcohol, drugs, and dependency on welfare and other government programs. Both Jenny and her husband, Ron, are learning disabled, and Bart is already showing signs of this lifelong disability. Bart's speech and language delays, poor coordination, subtle visual and hearing differences, numerous allergies, and active-aggressive personality all remind Jenny of how she was twenty-five years ago. Although no professional has ever suggested that Bart might be learning disabled (this label is rarely assigned prior to the age of 6 or 7), she can't keep it out of her mind:

Jenny: I don't know if he's [Bart] ever going to get straightened out. I can see he might have a problem in later years because I'm noticing that he's real different from most kids in a lot of ways, and both my husband and me has learning disabilities. Neither of us can read or write too good, and math — I can't even do math. I've got to have a calculator. Bart's young still, but he's got lots of the signs, and I'll just bet ya he's got it.

That scares me because I don't want him going through what I went through. 'Course when I had it, the school didn't realize what LD [learning disabilities] was. Now they got different programs. I was marked as mentally retarded all my life 'cause at the time that's what they considered me, as slow. You were put with these kids and I was getting to the point where, OK, I might as well act like one of them since I'm with them, hanging around them constantly in the same classroom. So I started acting like them.

I can't forget how bad it was, always feeling stupid and never gettin' anything right. I'm not stupid, but not being able to do the stuff the other kids are doing sure makes you feel stupid.

My husband and me can't do all the school stuff, so how are we goin' to help the boys [Bart has two brothers, one is 6 and the other an infant]? We can't. We can't read to them or teach them math. Now tell me, is that how kids should be raised? No! But that's how it's goin'. I wish things could be better for the boys, but what chance do they have? Go try and find a good job if you can't read or write. You can't. It scares me to think about it — Bart, or any of them — growing up and being like me or their dad. It scares me, but I can't see how to change it. How can I change things so they don't live the life I see coming for them?

Jenny is frozen in her fears. She feels that her learning disability has forced her into a life that she doesn't like, and she's afraid that her children, especially her middle one, are destined to the same existence. Although she acknowledges that schools today understand a lot more about learning disabilities than they did when she was a student and that there are many different programs, Jenny has difficulty envisioning her children's lives as any better than her own.

The answer to Jenny's question, "How can I change things so they don't live the life I see coming for them?" is provided by another parent, a father who himself has a learning disability and is also afraid that his child (a 6-year-old boy who has been labeled learning disabled) will experience a life similar to his own, full of failures and frustration:

Father: A couple of years ago I realized that soon my boy would be in school and start reading and stuff, and I decided that I'd better get busy. See, I've had a learning disability my whole life, and I'm still terrible at reading and writing, and I have trouble remembering things, like appointments and things to do, if I don't write them down or set an alarm or something. So when I realized I was going to be a dad, I decided that it was time to push myself a bit, to get to work on some stuff. I enrolled at the local city college in remedial academic skills [reading and writing], I gave up on improving my reading and writing ten years ago, but now I figured, "Hey, what's my boy going to think of me if I can't even read him a story? I don't want him to think his dad is a dummy."

So, I've been working on my reading and writing and also am in a program to help me organize things better. They've taught me to use reminder sheets and an appointment book and check it all the time, and to set alarms on my watch to remind me about important things. I need that, 'cause I forget stuff, like water running in the tub and pots cooking on the stove — stuff like that. My whole life I've forgotten stuff and made a lot of mistakes, you know, a lot of accidents. When he was younger I did some really stupid things, too — like forgetting to check how hot his bottle was and leaving the stroller at the store and not watching him close enough. That's caused problems, and I figured unless I did something to change myself, we could have a bad accident one day. I couldn't live with that. I figured I needed to get my act together.

So I started those programs, and we also got some help from the county. They sent out a social worker, and when she found out about my problems and about our finances, she started getting us into other programs and stuff. So that's been real helpful, and now that he's in school, they've been real helpful, too, real, real helpful.

Ron is taking action. Rather than letting his fears and anxieties dictate the future of his young son, he has determined that it is within his power to change things. By taking his own self-improvement into his own hands along with seeking services from all available agencies, Ron is trying to give his son the best possible chance in life. Through his actions he is converting fears and anxieties into goals and hopes, building a better future for himself and his family.

Question:
I can't get over these thoughts that we're going to lose the services we're getting and then I won't be able to handle the situation anymore. How can I deal with these fears and just live my life?

Answer:
You need to do two things, one personal and one political. On the personal level, you need to talk and work out your fears, either within yourself, with friends or family, or with a counselor or psychologist. On a political level, you need to make both your complaints about and satisfaction with various programs heard: write letters, make phone calls, and support organizations and movements.

Fear and anxiety, like other emotions, are not to be ignored. If something is bothering you, it's a good idea to deal with it. You may want to write down your thoughts and fears and look at them rationally; perhaps discussing them with a friend or relative and asking advice will help; turning to a professional such as a counselor, social worker, or psychologist may be a wise move. What you should not do is try to ignore the fears, try to shove them back inside and hope they don't surface again.

Another often-used approach is to take anxiety and fear and turn them into energy and action. Most of the services available to young children with disabilities exist as a result of the hard work and persistence of parents — usually the result of frustration, fears, and needs they have identified and determined to satisfy. Because of these efforts, a myriad of laws, regulations, and programs exist throughout the country to protect the rights of and guarantee a variety of services for those with disabilities.

Fred and Claudia have lost count of how many programs they have quit or been dropped from. They also claim that every program they've ever been in has changed significantly with each change in personnel — which has been quite frequent. What with Fred's having lived with his own cerebral palsy for fifty-seven years, Claudia's twenty-seven years of programs to help with her mental retardation, and, more recently, all the various types of assistance they've received raising their two children

(3½-year-old Michael and 14-month-old Amy), both of whom have exceptional needs, they estimate the family has been "in a million different programs." Although problems have existed in the services they've received, their greatest fear is that the programs will stop and they will be left to care for their children without help. Fred and Claudia explain:

Fred: I'm always worried that Michael will stop getting all the help. We seen it happen — programs stop. Michael's doing so good now it would be a shame if he didn't get the help. All these agencies and the workers are always nervous about their programs. They're never sure what will be for the next year. I don't know what we'd do if we didn't have the help.

Claudia: Yeah, because they do lots of stuff. They help us learn stuff, and work with the kids, and help with the apartment and school and stuff. They got us this place and showed us how to work with Michael. They help us get to see the doctors and dentists and even plan meals and stuff.

Fred: These are lots of different agencies she's talking about, but really they're all the same — all of them: they worry, worry, worry about next year, next year, next year. They always let you know that you can't be sure, that the program may not last. And sometimes they don't, because we've seen lots of them come and go. Lots of programs, lots of teachers, lots of social workers — whoosh: they're here one day and gone the next.

Claudia: I think we always sit on the edge of our seat wondering what's going to happen, what's around the next corner. We couldn't make it without the help, so I always wonder.

I feel bad because it bothers me so much. I get worried that they'll take the apartment [their housing is subsidized], that the kids will get sick or die [social workers were involved on a number of occasions to insure that the children were properly cared for], that Michael will never walk right [he's receiving physical therapy to help with his club feet]. I get so nervous. Sometimes I can't sleep, can't eat, I'm so nervous.

Though an extreme example, Fred and Claudia are not alone in their anxiety. To many, the fear of losing services and the anticipation of what life would be like without those services are difficult to bear.

In order to combat their fears and make certain that services continue, Fred and Claudia participate in a support group for individuals with developmental disabilities. Their group not only allows a forum for members to talk and share concerns but also serves as a political and social action organization that lobbies politicians and the media to support programs that are needed in the community.

Fred: We belong to this group with other grown-ups with disabilities. We meet and talk about this stuff all the time. Talk about stuff like how hard it is to get by and how we're making it and where to go to get help with this or that. We also write letters to the newspaper and to congressmen and senators and the president. Really, we write to all of them. We figure we got to stand up for ourselves, advocate. We got to be our own advocates and let people know what's going on. We may not get everything we want, but people sure are going to hear from us. Nobody can say we're quiet. We figure that we have to tell what's going on; you know, let people know. If we don't make some noise, then we don't have a chance. Nobody will know which programs are good or bad, or what we need.

It's good, too, because it helps to talk about things that's bothering you. Sometimes you can sort of, like, figure things out just telling it to someone and hearing what they think. So the groups are good for that, too. It does no good to just sit around and worry. Keeping busy like this really helps. You're doing something about it.

Many of the parents who shared their stories discussed the therapeutic value of becoming politically and socially involved through joining organizations, attending meetings, writing letters, and making phone calls. In most cases these parents had never before participated in such groups or activities but now regarded them as critical therapeutic outlets.

Gayle and Dennis (the bar owners who get help from many friends and clients) share Fred and Claudia's fear of what would happen if they lost the assistance they now receive:

Gayle: I think my greatest fear is that I won't be able to handle it without nursing help. You see, we have these nurses coming over at least eight hours every day. They usually come at nighttime, so Dennis and I can both work the bar during the rush, and then we can go to bed. Whether we'll be able to continue these services has kind of been up in the air because of the insurance — they think she doesn't qualify anymore because it's not quite the life-death situation it was before. I sort of carry the fear of losing them around with me all the time. I wonder, "What would life be like if I didn't have the help?" Then a few minutes later, boom, it will pop into my mind again. I'll get away from the thought for awhile, but it always comes back.

I'm concerned that once they are gone, I won't be able to work or sleep at night because I'd be too scared to leave Julia without supervision. We've lived for two years with twenty-four-hour care for her — usually ourselves, but lots of help, too. We struggled and struggled for the first year that she was home trying to get nursing staff, and when we couldn't, I'd stay up. I'm afraid that I won't get much rest for fear of leaving her alone and that I won't be able to keep up with work and her.

difficult life + more burdens = feelings of inability to cope

The above-stated formula represents a commonly held fear: "If things are as hard as they are now, and I can barely handle it, then if anything else is piled on top of that, it just may be too much." This creates a situation that drives many people close to the edge. Some parents of children with exceptional needs perceive themselves as not only being close to the edge but also at the mercy of forces beyond their control. They fear that any one of those forces — their job, other children, marriage, respite, agencies and schools that provide services to their child, financial assistance — has the power to push them over the edge. They often see no real end to the situation, only bends and twists as the years pass by.

Once again, parents should use a two-pronged approach to confront this situation: (1) deal with your emotions and thoughts — don't ignore them — and (2) get involved as an agent of change. Following is a description of how Gayle does this.

Gayle: I couldn't deal with my life if I didn't have lots of caring
          people around to talk to. That's how I deal with what's going
          on inside me: I talk about it. Thank God I've got people to
          listen, because if I didn't, I don't know what I'd do.

          So I take all those worries and fears and talk about them,
          and I also get out there and let everybody know what we need
          and what other parents and families like us need.

          Everyone knows how I feel: doctors, hospital administra-
          tors, insurance companies, the mayor, all the social service
          people, congressmen, everyone. I probably have the biggest
          mouth in town and make more phone calls and write more
          letters than anyone else. That's how I deal with it. If I'm going
          to go down — and I'm not, but if I were — it's going to be
          fighting. My attitude is that I've got nothing to lose. We've
          been at the edge so many times that I've sort of become hard-
          ened. I don't waste time, don't sit around and let others tell me
          what I can or can't do or what I do or don't qualify for. I go for
          it! It took me a while to realize that, to figure out that you
          either express yourself or get led around by the nose. So I'm
          pretty aggressive. That's how I deal with it.

Question:
I worry that we'll be caring for her the rest of our lives and that when
we die she'll be alone, with no one to take care of her or love her. What
should I do to minimize these fears and to ensure that they don't become
reality?

Answer:
1. Establish a will or trust.
2. Your child's journey toward integration into society and independent living should begin as soon as possible, early childhood is the
best time to start.

The first part of this two-part answer is easy. Parents without a will or
trust should make one or have one made immediately. Your will or trust
will specify what you would like to occur in the event of your death or
inability to manage your own affairs. Although the process of specifying
these details may be emotional and difficult, parents often report that
once the task is completed, they achieve a new sense of security and
diminished anxiety.

Sherwyn, the father of 3-month-old Joey, born weighing 1 pound 13 ounces and with a number of life-threatening medical conditions, shares his fears of the future and explains how setting up a trust for his son has made his life a bit easier:

Sherwyn: I know it's crazy, but I couldn't stop wondering about if Fran [Sherwyn's wife] and I were to die, who would care for Joey. The way it looks, he may have medical problems forever, and I've spent a lot of time wondering about who will watch out for him when we're not around. The kid is only 3 months old, and I keep thinking about thirty, forty, fifty years down the road. Sounds crazy, doesn't it?!

It sort of came to a head last month when my brother — he's a lawyer — made me set up a will. Actually, it's called a trust, or living trust. You have to think about everything, like who gets what, who cares for Joey, everything. You have to think of every issue that might come up. So I started thinking, "OK, it's forty years from now, Fran and I have died, and Joey's got this and that and needs a lot of help to get along. Who's going to be there to watch out for him?"

Anyway, the papers are all signed and sealed now; the decisions are all made. I'm still wondering and worrying a little about who's going to really care about him and help him when we get too old or when we die, but the trust answered a lot of our questions and fears, so it's not so bad anymore. Crazy, yeah?! Like we don't have enough to worry about today; we really need to be worrying about forty years from now.

No, it's not really so crazy. Loving, caring, and planning aren't crazy. It would be ideal if you could accomplish all that without the fear and anxiety, but it's not "crazy."

The second part of the answer is more difficult and is the source of much debate among and between parents and professionals. The debate centers on the issue of mainstreaming, sometimes referred to as inclusion. Some believe the best way to ensure that a child will better "fit" into society is by placing increased emphasis on therapies and special instruction; others believe that this is important, but not as important as seeing to it that children with exceptional needs spend as much time, from as early an age as possible, beside children who do not have exceptional needs. The majority of parents interviewed agreed with the authors: both therapies and mainstreamed environments are important, but to increase the chances that children will be more "included" as they grow up, the more important of the two is mainstreaming.

All parents hope, and most expect, that as their children grow older, they will learn to make wise decisions and capably manage friendships, sex, money, living on their own, habits, marriage, career, and all other areas that concern their health and well-being. But when a young child's progress is very slow and it becomes apparent that the child may grow into an adult who has difficulty becoming self-supportive and living independently, adjustments in educational curricula must be made. All too often, however, these "adjustments" or "modifications" pull children further and further away from the mainstream of childhood. Special programs begin replacing day care and preschool; therapies become the focus instead of play, dance, swimming, and other more typical activities; and more and more time is spent learning and socializing with other "exceptional" children and less time with kids who are more "typical."

Parents and professionals must seek an appropriate balance between meeting the exceptional needs of a child and including that child in activities and groups with all types of children. In the past most parents and professionals tended to treat children's differences at the expense of their "normal" parts, and many individuals with exceptional needs have in effect been placed on a track leading them into segregated and dependent adulthood. Parents should consider that the more time special needs children spend in "normal," integrated environments designed for all children, the better prepared they will be to function in the larger society when they enter adulthood.

Despite Karen's not yet having turned 5, her mother, Vera, is concerned about who will care for her when she enters adulthood and how she will fit into society. Many children born with Down's syndrome become capable adults able to make a living, run a household, and marry. Will Karen reach this level? Or will she never really function as an adult? Will her needs be such that Vera and her husband, Jack, will be responsible for their "child" for the next fifty years? Vera explains her concerns:

Vera: She's little now. She's cute and cuddly, and everyone who meets her falls in love with her. She's really a delightful little kid.

I keep wondering, though, what will happen when she gets bigger. I worry that people may take advantage of her or hurt her. I think when you have a child born with a handicap, you have a real strong protective instinct. I sort of vowed that nobody's going to hurt her if I can help it — you know, a real strong maternal-protective thing.

I look into the future and wonder what's going to be. Is she going to learn to read and write, take a bus, work at a job, do her laundry, cook her meals, have a boyfriend or maybe a husband? It can really drive you crazy if you think about it too much, because there's no way to know until it happens. Even still, I think about it.

It's not just me either; this is real typical of Down's parents — wondering, worrying about the future.

With Trev [Vera's second child], he's just 1 now, but with Trev I know he's going to grow up, move out of the house, and do all the stuff that you think of when you think of someone going out on their own. When I'm playing with him, I can enjoy it for what it is. When I think about him grown up, I can see lots of different choices, neat choices. It's like the sky's the limit.

It's not the same with Karen. I worry about making sure that she gets the right programs and learns the right habits — you know, like social stuff, stuff you need to know or do so you don't stand out in a crowd. There's a lot more worry and planning there. I guess the big one is where she'll go someday.

I wonder a lot about where she'll live. When you have kids, you love them and care for them and stuff, but you want it to end someday — I mean, you want them to move out. You don't want to wonder every minute what they're doing and are they OK. You want to think about taking it easy, about them growing up and moving out. You know, the "golden years." With Karen it's harder to look down the line and see what will be.

Think about it. Would you like your child to live with you forever? Of course you wouldn't. But if she couldn't take care of herself, where would she live? See? I don't like to think about it. I wish I could just wash it out of my mind for a few years and then deal with it when the time came. But I can't!

Vera's concerns about whether Karen will fit in and where she will live when she gets older are typical of many parents of children with

Down's syndrome as well as parents of children with other disabilities. What Vera needs to do now is act, do something. There are values in mentally playing with thoughts and fears, recycling ideas through your mind; however, in order to take control, to have an effect on the future, you need to establish goals and objectives, plans and arrangements. You must make decisions and follow up on them.

Another parent, the father of a 6-year-old who has mild to moderate mental retardation and does not yet speak in sentences, has definite opinions on how to do this:

Father: I think — I mean, we [husband and wife] think — that the more time he spends with normal kids, the better he'll be able to live and work and take care of himself when he gets older, and the less we need to worry about his future. I mean, it only makes sense, doesn't it?! If you're raised segregated in special programs all your life, then what are you preparing for? For a segregated life is what. We want him in regular education and the Cub Scouts and all the other stuff the other kids are in. He may be slow and stand out from the group, but at least he'll be in the group; he'll have a feel for how to function, what he can and can't do. We've felt this all along. There's a real tendency for parents of kids with special needs to get them into all these separate programs, a push for therapies and such. We can see the value in all of that, but not when it separates kids. We've never allowed him in a program that wasn't based in regular ed., with regular kids, or put him into social groups or clubs that were just for retarded kids. It just leads you down the wrong road — down the road to being different, to being on the outside looking in.

Parents obviously don't "need" to worry about the degree of competence or societal integration their children will experience as adults or who will be responsible for them in thirty or forty years. But once again, this anxiety is not uncommon. The greater the dependency, the higher the likelihood that parents will look further into the future. That looking into the future ought to involve the establishment of a long-range plan, one that includes a will or trust, as well as numerous opportunities for the person with special needs to work in integrated, typical, classroom and other settings throughout life.

Question:
I'm worried about my other children. How is having a sibling with all these special needs going to affect their personalities?

Answer:
There's no way of knowing how this will affect who they will become. You have some control over the ingredients that go into a child's upbringing but far less control over the results.

Sherwyn, the father who in the previous section described setting up a trust for his 3-month-old son, wonders:

Sherwyn: What would it be like to have a big brother like Joey? The way we see it, he's going to be in and out of hospitals for years. I mean, if you count up all the operations they think he might need, and if he really has to have them all, it will be years in the hospital. What are Fran and I going to have to offer more kids? I can't even imagine it. What kind of a life would they have?

Parental concern about the well-being and feelings of siblings is justified. In far too many families of children with disabilities, siblings suffer from a lack of attention, information, and the opportunity to share their own feelings.

In Chapter 8 Holly (age 11) shared her fears, frustrations, and misconceptions resulting from the birth of her sister, Kris (age 3). No one ever talked to Holly about Kris's Down's syndrome, forcing her to invent her own understanding of it. Holly's parents, Barb and Paul, elaborate on their present concerns about their 11-year-old daughter:

Paul: Sometimes I'm afraid we've gone a little overboard including Holly in helping out and decisions and things. I wonder if we aren't expecting too much from her. She's just a kid, but she knows everything that's going on. Like with Kris's heart condition. Kris has some problems with her heart valves, and we had to decide about this operation. We discussed it all together. Here's this 11-year-old kid sitting with two surgeons, her mom, and her dad, discussing her little sister. We're talking life-and-death stuff. I don't know. Sometimes I'm afraid that we're stealing her childhood away, like making her grow up too soon. It's sort of ironic. First we realized that we hadn't included her enough, and now I'm afraid we've gone too far in the other direction.

Barb: I know what you mean, but I'm not so worried about that as I am about her socially. I've been thinking that she never has friends over and doesn't like it when we go out as a family.

Paul: It's the gawkers; she hates gawkers — the people who look but don't talk. They pretend like they're not looking, but they watch everything you do. She hates that.

Barb: Holly doesn't like it when people stare at us or when Kris's being different makes us the center of attention. She's pretty self-conscious in that way. I'm sure that's why she never wants to go to the mall or out for dinner with the family.

I'm afraid that she's shutting out things because she's embarrassed about Kris. She rarely has friends over, and when she does, she hates it when they pay attention to Kris or ask questions about her.

Paul: The family counseling we're in is like trying to keep a dozen plates spinning. You know, in the circus, the guy who spins plates on sticks? By the time he gets to the end of the line, he has to rush back to the beginning to get the first one going again. Then he's rushing here and there, trying to keep everything spinning. It's like a bunch of little brushfires: get one put out and another one starts. What I mean is that there's always something. You think you're on top of something, that something's settled, and all of a sudden something new comes up, something else to deal with. You focus on that for awhile, and then you realize that an old issue isn't solved or resolved, and you have to go back to it.

Barb: Which reminds me, we've got an appointment tonight to "spin some plates" [attend a family counseling session] after dinner, right?!

Paul: Right. Oh, well. It's hard, frustrating work, but somebody's got to do it. Really, though, there's no choice, because if we don't work on this, if we don't pull together and help each other, there's going to be a lot of pain and suffering. It's up to us to make it work.

Barb and Paul share the fear that having a sister with Down's syndrome is having negative effects on their older daughter. Their fear is real and obviously justified. Fortunately, they are working hard to solve these concerns, to redirect their fears and anxieties. Holly's self-consciousness and "growing up too soon" will no doubt be a topic discussed in future family counseling sessions, in her peer support group, and in the many informal family talks that Barb, Paul, and the children have learned to enjoy. All Barb and Paul can do is their best: spend time loving, caring for, and listening to their children; involving themselves and their kids in peer groups and counseling groups that assist in dealing with feelings and concerns; constantly monitoring themselves and one another to see that concerns and problems are being dealt with. As far as what the long-term effects of having a sibling with Down's syndrome are, no one can say for sure.

Raising a child with exceptional needs does create many challenges in a family, but, as we have seen in Chapter 9, it also provides opportunities for personal growth. Barb and Paul might never have become so sensitive to Holly's needs if Kris's disability had not pushed them to seek professional help. "That which does not kill me makes me stronger": Barb, Paul, Holly, and Kris are becoming stronger as well as more aware of their own and each other's strengths and needs.

These brief sections have barely scratched the surface of fears and anxieties but have only introduced some issues of critical relevance to parents of children with exceptional needs. Fears and anxieties in themselves can be profound drains on attention, enjoyment of life, and energy; however, they can also serve a critical function. Individuals who are able to face their fears and anxieties, analyze them, and find meaning and guidance in their messages are often able to use them as catalysts or motivators for personal growth and development. Fears and anxieties can help inspire parents to action, to the formation of goals and hopes, and, finally, to the establishment of objectives and plans.

Part 2: Goals and Hopes

Question:
Despite all the problems we've had, I still believe everything is going to turn out OK. Am I crazy to hold onto that hope?

Answer:
As long as you're doing all you can to make your goals come true — all the necessary therapies and interventions — there's nothing wrong with holding onto your dreams. Go for it!

The line between optimism and denial is sometimes a fine one. At what point do goals and hopes become unrealistic and their pursuit represent a denial of truth? Should parents of a little girl with Down's syndrome be commended for expecting and working toward sending their daughter to college, or should they be encouraged to see a psychologist to help them become more realistic and stop living in a fantasy world? Are the parents of a preschooler with spina bifida, crippled below the waist, being harsh and cruel when they demand that their son use crutches and refuse to allow a wheelchair in their home? Or should they serve as models and be praised for their attempts to build confidence and independence?

"Everything is going to turn out OK": Is that a goal or hope that can lead to the formation of clear and reasonable objectives and an effective intervention plan? Or is it a denial, a delusion, resulting in the postponement of needed services and the loss of precious remedial time? The answer lies in the actions that accompany the thoughts and in parents' abilities to reshape goals as time goes by.

Brenda believes that "everything is going to turn out OK" for her 2½-year-old son, Jimmy. Despite his having been born three months prematurely, measuring a mere 12 inches and weighing less than 2 pounds; despite his present language, motor, and cognitive delays; despite his small stature, weak muscle strength, eye problems, and bowed legs, Brenda believes that "everything is going to be OK":

Brenda: I don't think of Jimmy as having any "disabilities." I think of him as "delayed." I believe in my head and in my heart that there's going to come one day when he's going to be all caught up. So that means he's just delayed. To me a "disability" is like forever; it stays with you. I don't think that describes Jimmy.

After he was born, the doctors told me that it would take him about a year to catch up for each month he was premature. He was three months premature, so that would mean he'll catch up when he's about 3. When he's 3, he'll be a normal 3-year-old. His surgeries set him back a little bit, so it may be a little bit more than 3, maybe it will be 3½ or 4. That's my goal; that's what I keep working for and planning for.

I expect some of the therapies to continue after that, and he may need a couple of more operations, but he's going to go to a regular preschool when he's 4 and a regular kindergarten when he's 5. Mark my word, this kid is going to make it. He's a fighter. When you're born as small and with as many medical troubles as he's had, and you make it, it shows you're a fighter. We've made it this far, so I know he can do anything.

His doctors don't agree or disagree. They say, "We really have to wait and see." But I know this kid, and I know it's going to work out. I'm telling you, he's a fighter; you can't keep him down.

Brenda has retained most of the expectations she had prior to Jimmy's birth. She is well aware that in order for Jimmy to succeed in school and life, further therapies, operations, and interventions of various sorts will be required, but in her mind, with enough work, any obstacles can be overcome. Brenda should be commended not only for all she has done but for her ability to remain positive and her efforts to make her goals and hopes come true.

Brenda: I'll tell you, his future is sure going to be a lot easier and happier and healthier than his past! I think he'll do good in school, go to college, get married, and have lots of kids. I'd like lots of grandchildren.

He'll probably never be an athlete or real big or have the best coordination in the world. He may not even be the greatest genius who ever lived, but I think he'll be a pretty normal kid. Maybe he'll have some little things, little differences, but, hey, after what he's been through, the future looks real good!

The optimistic outlook Brenda expressed is typical of parents who have weathered the storm of life-and-death medical crises. Compared to where they've been, the obstacles that lie ahead appear like small hurdles on a great horizon full of opportunities. Brenda even acknowledges the possibility of a learning disability (children born prematurely are considered at risk of having learning disabilities) as a minor hurdle:

Brenda: Do you think I'm going to lose sleep over whether or not he's going to have a learning disability? No way. Any kid who can make it through all those surgeries, pneumonias, and therapy sessions; any kid who can smile and want to play when he's got tubes sticking in him all over the place, who's got the spunk to stand up and walk on those twisted, skinny little legs — no, no way I'm worried about him learning to read or do well in school. If he wants to, he'll learn it.

Brenda's optimism is no doubt at least partially a product of previous successes. For a champion fighter who has made it through twenty consecutive title defenses (life-and-death confrontations), an upcoming bout against an unknown and unrated opponent (possible academic difficulties and minor physical problems) creates only minimal fear or anxiety.

Brenda is doing all she can to ensure that Jimmy becomes the most he can be. Although her goals and hopes for his future are optimistic, they are within the realm of possibility. The strength of positive thought, linked with positive action, is unbounded and should be encouraged whenever possible.

Question:

Some of my friends and family members think that I've sort of given up because my expectations are so low for my daughter. But I think I'm just being realistic and am working for something that's really achievable. Am I wrong to focus on goals that are attainable, or should I dream of and go for more?

Answer:

Some individuals prefer setting their goals a little lower to help them focus efforts and assure accomplishment; others prefer the challenge of higher, more demanding goals to help maintain an optimistic outlook and push themselves and their children as much as possible. Neither is right or wrong as long as parents (1) find a level of goals and hopes that allows them to maintain their motivation for success and (2) maintain the flexibility to adapt and change as new information becomes available.

As parents learn more about their child's exceptional needs and begin to form support networks and to accept the situation, fears and anxieties often begin to diminish. Simultaneously, more realistic, basic, and functional goals and hopes usually begin to emerge. Faced with death, a parent sees life in any form as more precious; confronted with the possibility of a child's never walking, a parent lets dreams of sports and medals become overshadowed by fantasies of the child's standing and slowly moving across a room; learning that a child is blind, a parent turns the hope for some perception of light into a cherished possibility. "If only my child could . . .": part plea and part declaration of commitment. "If only my child could . . .": the refrain of parents of children with disabilities.

Adapting goals and hopes in this way is neither right nor wrong. It is a natural psychological phenomenon that helps many individuals maintain their motivation and deal on a day-to-day basis with slow growth and development. If accompanied by flexibility — the capacity to adapt to new information — it allows parents to be more appreciative and accepting of developmental differences and successes.

As the extent of 3½-year-old Polly's cerebral palsy became more evident, her parents, Bev and Ric, slowly began to confront the situation. No longer claiming "everything will be all right," they reshaped their goals and hopes into a different, more modest form:

Bev: What I hope for her future is that she'll be able to walk. Now she can barely take a few steps, like really wobbly and slow ones, and then she'll sit down or fall down. I want her to be able to, with or without a walker, get around better, so that she can function in society. It's too difficult to look ahead to when she's 18 or 21 or whatever, so that's my main goal right now. That's the one I think about the most.

            I look for her to talk, too, to talk and walk. We both work with her, and we send her to therapy, and I think she will walk. I can see now, when the therapists say she'll walk, I see it as possible. It will happen. I believe them. When they say, "Oh, she'll talk," I still don't believe it 100 percent. They keep telling us she will, but I don't know.

Ric: I guess it must be frustrating for you [speaking to the interviewers] because I know you're trying to see what our long-range goals for her are. You want to know what we ideally want to see her doing when she's grown up. But we almost consciously will not think about that. The way we see it is if we set up an unrealistic goal, it's just going to cause problems for us. If she doesn't get any better than what she is right now, yes, we'd be disappointed, but if that's where the plateau is, then we're going to have to work with that. There's a lot of unknown now. A person keeps growing physically and mentally until they're what, say, 18 or 21?! That's a long time. Because Polly's so young, there's something new coming in everyday, and we go with that. When we find out she's reached a plateau and it's definite that she's not going to achieve any better mental or physical development, then at that point we're probably going to have to do some serious thinking about what we're going to do, what she's going to do. Up until that time, we think it's almost like grabbing at clouds, trying to plan for a situation that may never occur.

To be able to walk and to communicate. That's what we want; that's our dream. If she can just do those two things, she'll be able to function on her own a bit, she won't always have to have somebody there. We know that's pretty general and pretty basic, but as far as her future, that's just about all we care about at this point, today, sitting here.

Ric placed a lot of stress on "at this point." Both he and Bev were well aware that other goals and hopes would arise throughout Polly's life, but "today, sitting here," her walking and talking are most important to them. This flexibility or openness to new information as it comes up is critical. Parents need to be keen observers of their children's development so that they are able to make adjustments in expectations. If they don't do this, there is a danger that preconceived limits might hold a child back from higher levels of development or that unrealistic expectations may lead to an intensified perception of failure, which in turn might lead to a crisis in motivation and perhaps cutting back on goals more than is necessary.

As parents of children with exceptional needs learn more and more about their children's conditions and become more and more accepting of who they are and what they can and cannot do, their goals and objectives usually become much more realistic, basic, and functional.

One of the most fundamental activities people perform in a given day is eating. Although the ability to chew and swallow is rarely a concern for parents of children older than a few months, for some it stands first and foremost as a goal in life. Despite her age (almost 5 years), Jenny's poor muscle control, due to cerebral palsy, has left her unable to chew and barely able to swallow. The development of these skills is therefore near the top of her parents' "wish list." Jim and Rene explain:

Jim: I think Rene would agree that one of our major goals is getting her to the point where she can eat on her own or even with minimal help. Just to chew and swallow — that would be great. She's come a long way and has developed a swallow of sorts, but it's not perfect, and only a small part of the food gets down. I just hope that she keeps progressing.

Rene: I agree. We hope and pray that she'll be able to eat normally someday. Even if everything else stayed the same, that would be fantastic. Just that one thing. If she could eat normally and get rid of all those tubes and the hours and hours of our feeding her — wow, that would be something. I'd love to get rid of that tracheostomy tube [placed in an opening cut into the throat to assist with breathing] and her gastrostomy tube [placed in an opening cut into the stomach, through which nutritional liquids are fed]. Then it would be like a breeze. It would be so much easier.

        As it is now, the tubes and feedings make it really hard to be gone from the house for any length of time. It's not like we can just pull into McDonald's and have lunch. We're used to it, but most people would get pretty grossed out watching us feed her, pouring things into a tube in her stomach. How can you have any kind of normal life like that?!

    The last two stories have illustrated how simple and basic parental goals and hopes can be. As Abraham Maslow observed in his *Hierarchy of Basic Skills,* individuals do not seek satisfaction of higher-order drives and needs until those that are more basic are satisfied. Polly is struggling to learn to walk and talk, Jenny to chew and swallow. No doubt once these skills are mastered, they and their parents will move on to new, higher-order learning. These parents have decided first to focus their attention on basic, critical areas of development. If and when their goals in these areas are met, they will reevaluate and progress to new challenges; if future experiences teach them that their goals are not achievable, they will readjust their expectations and form more simple, basic ones. Neither right nor wrong, this is their way.

Question:
My hope is that my child will fit in when she's an adult. Besides helping develop her skills and abilities, I'm trying to consider and deal with all the obstacles that might hold her back. Does that make sense?

Answer:
Yes. For people to "fit in," they must have certain skills and abilities, but it is also critical that as many obstacles as possible be removed from their path.

Although parents may be concerned about the quality of their children's friendships, few worry that their children will have no friends at all; although they may hope that their little ones grow up attractive, with pleasing personalities, it is not common to find parents who fear that their children's looks and behaviors will scare others away; although it is expected that as individuals reach adulthood they may require some time — perhaps even years — to find a place in the world of work and establish a home away from their parents, their children's never finding work and never setting up a separate household is a far less pleasing scenario than most parents ever deal with. In general, parents expect that their children will at very least "fit in," that they will find an acceptable, reasonable niche in life and live out their years struggling through many of the same joys and hardships that they experienced themselves .

In many cases, however, "fitting in," for individuals with disabilities, requires more than having the necessary skills or abilities. Other obstacles may exist, obstacles that require time and attention to overcome.

The mother of a 6-year-old with emotional and behavioral difficulties realized early in her child's life the importance of removing obstacles in order to help her child fit in. Her son is academically very bright, is learning to handle his emotions, and is improving his behavior, but her primary goal is that he stop rocking back and forth:

Mother: If he doesn't stop that rocking back and forth, no one is going to accept him, no matter how smart he is or how well he learns to deal with his emotions and control his behavior. See, he's got this habit — when he's sitting or standing — of moving back and forth. He looks like he's swaying to the music, which would be fine if there was music playing, but he does it almost all the time. We've got him in a behavior modification program to help him cut down on that, and I think it's the number one goal we're working on. It may seem like a little thing, but the way we see it, it just could negate everything else we're working on. He might meet or exceed all our other goals and dreams, but if that rocking continues, his chances of holding a job or getting married and having kids or leading anything like a normal life are going to be slim.

Many would agree with this mother that even if an individual possesses the skills necessary to live in society or do a job, that may not be enough. It can be helpful to identify and modify differences that may prevent your child from being accepted by others.

Ken (3½ years) has a brainstem disorder that has paralyzed the left half of his face, caused him to be deaf and visually impaired on that side, created facial abnormalities, and left him delayed (about two years behind) in most areas of development. When Ken's parents, Marge and Bill, think of his future, one of their greatest hopes is that he'll fit in:

Bill: Our hope is that he'll be as close to normal as he possibly can.

Marge: I'm hoping that he'll be able to make a life for himself out there. You know, just live on his own, have a life of his own — that would be enough. I don't expect college or a fancy job. I just want him to fit in. To be able to walk down the street and look in the store windows or go to Burger King and have a Coke, just simple stuff.

Bill: That's why we had all those surgeries on his face. Only part of the reason was for hearing and vision, most of it was to help him fit in better. If he's going to be slow and have some of those other disabilities, he sure doesn't need to look different, too. If he looks too different, people are never gonna take the time to find out who he is, to get to know him. I figure that he's gonna have enough things different about him, so he better at least look as near normal as he can, or people will never give him a chance to show who he really is and what he knows and can do.

Marge: I just want for him to fit in, to have a life of his own someday. What kind of life would it be for him to stay here forever, not to get out and live? It wouldn't be that great for him.

This same concern is expressed by Cindy, the woman who prepared homework assignments for her husband, Tom, to take along on business trips. Cindy's hope is that her 3-year-old son's Down's syndrome won't stand in the way of his being accepted. She hopes that Simon will someday find a life of his own, away from home, and that he, too, will fit in:

Cindy: With the other children [three older daughters], you just feel that there are no limits. I mean, they can be whatever they want to be. They can go to school and study as much as they want to put into it.

With Simon, right away you think, well, there are going to be limits. When we first had him, I thought right away, "Well, he won't get married; he'll be going to this kind of school. He'll be in special programs, and that's going to be his life." I think I've found that it can be brighter than that and that he will have more opportunities.

There's been a lot more done, like I say: a lot less institutionalization and I think a lot more public awareness. They're [people with Down's syndrome and other developmental disabilities] out and in the community. They are more visible. I think that the more that they are, the easier they are accepted. You know, sometimes it's not just enough to be able to do a job; you have to get past people's prejudice and lack of knowledge or background. There are more obstacles for the person with Down's syndrome than just being a slow learner or looking different. So we not only have to educate Simon, but we have to educate society; we have to expose society to him so they can start getting the truth: that this kid, that most people with Down's, are not weirdos that you have to stay away from, and that they can be kind, loving, sensitive, competent people.

If children with disabilities are to become fully functioning members of society, if they are ever to leave the protective environments of their parents' homes, they must not only develop certain skills and abilities but also overcome a number of obstacles. Parents who help their children around these obstacles not only help their children become more integrated into society but often help society become more accepting of divergence, which in turn helps other individuals challenged by disabilities.

Tips for Parents

- Make every effort to take care of yourself; keep growing and learning and developing even though much of your energy and attention is being focused on your child.
- Find all the services you can and be sure to let those involved in programs and those who decide on the future of programs know when you like or appreciate what they're doing; let those same people know when you're displeased and why.
- Make sure you have a will or trust in effect.
- Whenever possible, have your child involved in non–special education programs and activities.
- Make every effort to meet the needs of your other children, those who don't have exceptional needs.
- Great expectations and dreams are fine as long as you focus your energy on shorter-term objectives and take frequent reality checks to be sure that the current situation fits with your short- and long-term objectives.

Tips for Professionals

- Reinforce parents' optimism: unless you are *certain* that parental dreams and hopes are impossible to realize, make every effort not to steal their motivation.
- Encourage parents to look at both the present and future, monitoring the impact that new data has on long-term plans.
- Reinforce parents' efforts to assist their children through the difficulties of having a sibling with a disability, and if you think more could be done in this area, provide parents with recommendations.

Conclusion

Although the fifty families interviewed for this work varied greatly in describing future fears and anxieties, goals and hopes, they were unanimous in their agreement that these topics consumed much more of their mental energy than they would like. They also shared a number of similar thoughts about the future. These thoughts often came in pairs, with the opposite of a fear or anxiety being mentioned as a goal or hope. Most common among these were:

Everything is just going to get worse and worse.	vs.	Everything will work out.
She will never live a real, involved, rewarding life.	vs.	She will fit in.
He's going to live with me/us forever.	vs.	Someday he'll live in a place of his own.

When parents are faced with great fears and anxieties, their goals and hopes often become very basic and realistic. Yet as each small goal is reached, as progress, no matter how slight or slow, is made, the opportunity for new and greater goals and hopes becomes possible. Unless they notice and appreciate progress, parents find it very difficult to continue believing, giving, and hoping; when positive signs do reveal themselves, however, many parents are encouraged to continue the ongoing quest of working for their child and family's future.

11

Parents' Advice to Parents

When the parents interviewed for this book were asked, "What advice do you have for other parents of children with exceptional needs?" responses flowed quickly and emotionally. As might be expected, many topics were brought up. Some suggested techniques to employ when working with professionals, others shared insights into establishing support networks outside of immediate family members, whereas still others discussed home life and family. They reflected both on what had worked and what had failed, techniques and approaches to be replicated and those to be avoided. At times their advice was contradictory:

"Live in the present."	vs.	"Plan for the future."
"Trust your doctor."	vs.	"Always get a second opinion."
"Be realistic."	vs.	"Shoot for the stars."

More often, however, the opinions expressed were consistent. Despite the wide range of ideas and some differences of perception, a number of topics emerged again and again upon which most agreed. It is those points that we review in this chapter.

Although each of these themes has been touched upon previously, their importance merits a second look. The fifty families whose experiences have been compiled in this book represent a total of over 150 years living with and caring for the needs of children with disabilities — over 150 years; dozens of hospitals, agencies, and schools; hundreds of doctors, teachers, and other helping professionals; and thousands of hours filling out applications, sitting in waiting rooms, visiting and living in hospitals, and observing and providing educational interventions for young children. Experience speaks loudly.

Question:
What advice do you have for other parents of children with exceptional needs?

Answer 1:
Get help early! If in doubt, check it out!

Mother: Some people are afraid they are being overly concerned parents and don't want to rush to the doctor about every little thing. But I think it's important to check out any significant concerns you may have about your child. All you can lose is a little time and money if you're wrong, but if your fears are justified and you don't act, you can lose precious months or years of intervention. It's so important to get help for your child as soon as possible. Don't wait!

My boy wasn't even 2 years old yet, and I just knew that there was something wrong with his speech and language; he just wasn't listening or understanding very well and wasn't talking enough or making enough sounds. Everybody, and I mean *everybody* — my husband, pediatrician, mom, friends — told me not to make a big deal about it. They all said, "Oh, just calm down, you worrywart. He's only 2; give him time." Well, I didn't listen. I took him to a speech and hearing clinic, had him tested, and within a week he had hearing aids in both ears, was in a special education play group, and was seeing a speech and language pathologist.

It's one thing when you don't take yourself to the doctor or when you put off telling someone something that's on your mind — stuff like that. But you can't wait when a little infant or a young child depends on you.

Look, what's six months to you or me? Maybe it's one-fiftieth or one-hundredth of our lives. What is it to a 2-year-old? It's one-fourth of their life. Do you want your child to spend one-fourth of their life not being able to hear or with an earache or having trouble digesting food or in pain? No, you don't. A day or a month isn't the same to a little kid that it is to us. You can't just hang around and wait and hope and pray. You've got to act.

Get help early. Wise words from someone who's been there. How many lives might have been saved from cancer, heart disease, and infection if early warning signs had been heeded and action taken? How many marriages might have eluded divorce if problems had been discussed rather than buried and emotions had been expressed rather than denied? The answers to these questions are obvious. Get help early!

Answer 2:
Develop support systems as soon as possible.

Mother: You really need to seek outside help as soon as possible. Don't stop until you find somebody who has information on how to help you with whatever you need, whether it's nursing care, housework, finances, whatever. If you don't, everything else, your whole life, can break loose, fall apart. I think if we had known that there were so many resources out there, we wouldn't have had to suffer half as much as we did. Go and find anything that can lighten your load as soon as you can. Unless you're very, very lucky, you've got to go out and find it, because it won't just come to you.

   Accepting it was a real hard one for me at first because I blamed myself for my daughter's special needs. I figured I must have done something wrong. After she was born, I was more determined than ever to be a perfect mom, and perfect moms can handle it, can do it all.

   It was like a vendetta. I was going to do everything. I was going to spend every minute at the hospital, keep the home together, keep the business going, be a good wife. I was going to do this; I was going to do that. People offered to help, and I said, "No, no, I'm fine, thanks; I can do it. I can handle it. I can . . ." Don't do that. When there's love or support, accept it, because you're going to need it. When it's not there, go and find it.

Very few people find that help comes to them without their asking. Resources must be searched out. To sit back and wait to be served; to bury your head and expect problems to disappear; to stand alone, proud and independent, not needing anyone or anything is most often a path to failure and disappointment. An overwhelming number of parents who have experienced raising a young child with exceptional needs are appreciative of those who were there to support them and urge other parents to find support systems early.

Answer 3:
Join a parent support group.

Marsha: Find other parents who are in the same boat. All the other stuff will work itself out a lot easier and faster if you get around people who really know what you're going through because, see, if they've been through it, too, they'll help lead you to whatever else you need.

Gordon: For sure! If we had known these people when we started getting worried about Jed, when he was a year or 2 old, we would have known a lot better what to pursue, what we needed.

Marsha: For years I thought that something was wrong with me because I couldn't handle his behaviors. I thought it was my fault, that I must be a terrible parent, and that I was weak. I couldn't handle my own son. I couldn't even take him with me to run errands or shop or just ride in the car. It was awful.

Even after Jed was formally diagnosed as emotionally disturbed and he started his special program and we started getting all the help, I still couldn't handle him, and I still had all the same feelings. It helped a little knowing that he had a specific problem and it probably wasn't my fault, but I still took the blame.

It wasn't until we joined a group and I met the other parents, and we talked and cried and, well, we go through a lot together. When I got into the group, I started believing that it wasn't my fault. I started feeling better about myself and my ability to handle Jed. They gave me lots of ideas and lots of confidence.

Gordon: Really! It was like day and night. She'd come home from being with the group and she'd be all fired up and positive, ready to go. You could really see her gaining strength and support from being with them. It helps me, too, when I go, but Marsha's the one who's gained the most from it.

Marsha: Other people can't imagine what it's like. Even the doctors, they don't really know. The teachers don't even know because they don't have to go home with the kids, and they aren't the parents. They didn't give birth to them, they don't wake up to it every morning and go to sleep with it every night, and they aren't going to be there more than a year or two. So the only ones who can really understand are other parents.

I've learned a lot from them. We're like family; we're there to help each other.

Many other parents agreed with the importance of a parent support group. Some of their comments:

"I never could have made it on my own."

"They really pulled me through."

"I learned so much from them, things I probably never would have figured out myself."

"No one else understands like they do."

Join a parent support group as soon as you can and tap into the vast store of knowledge that other members have accumulated through years of experiencing what you are presently going through and may someday have to face. If your child's specific disability doesn't have a group nearby, either travel to the nearest group, start one yourself, or join an established group that is designed for another, closely related exceptional need. The key variable here is parents sharing with one another — sharing feelings, resources, and caring. Finding the appropriate group or starting one on your own may take some effort, but it's well worth it.

Answer 4:
Treat your child as "normally" as you can.

Cindy: My advice is that parents try to see the "normal" parts of their child and treat them, as much as possible, like they would their other children. If we can't even do that ourselves, how will others accept them?! Starting from the beginning, when they're real young, get them out there, doing stuff, being part of the community. The longer you focus on the special needs and treat them differently, keep them and yourselves locked in, the harder it will be later to come out, to do things.

I think treating Simon just as normal as any of our other children [three older daughters] really helps him. I think it helps other people, too, because we're out and about and he is very visible in our neighborhood and community. I think our being positive about it has helped people accept him. We're out playing with him, and he goes to everything, every function, that we do. We aren't limiting what he can do by anything that we're doing differently. I think it's also helped our extended family — aunts and uncles and cousins and such — feel more comfortable because when we first announced about Simon's having Down's syndrome, they were real concerned that our whole life would turn upside down. By showing that we felt OK, that we could deal with it and our lives could still be good, that made them feel better. Initially, when you tell friends and family, they feel sorry for you, sort of like they think your past life and everything about it has come to an end. When they see that you're handling it and it's OK, then that makes them feel better and then they can accept the situation more easily. I think that helps people accept Simon.

No matter how many exceptional needs a child may have, no matter how many surgeries, anatomical differences, or learning difficulties, a child is, above all else, a child. A 2-year-old is a 2-year-old, and a 5-year-old is a 5-year-old. When parents and professionals become involved with disabilities, there is a tendency to see the disability first and the child second: a *blind* girl, a *retarded* boy, some *crippled* children: labels such as these tell little about individuals. A 3-year-old girl, crippled below the waist from spina bifida, has much more in common with other 3-year-old girls than with the "physically disabled." Knowing that a child is 5 years old and a boy tells us far more about who he is than knowing that he has an emotional disturbance.

Answer 5:
Keep your life in balance.

Mother: At first, after we learned about our son's special needs, our entire life changed. Everything was focused on him and therapies and his future. Our other kids sort of dropped into the background, our marriage and personal needs were kind of put on hold, and the total focus was on "the crisis": dealing with the special needs. After a few months of that and a lot of associated problems, we figured out that you can't just ignore the big picture of your life. You can't ignore your other kids and spouse and personal needs. If you do that, you aren't able to function very well or for very long. We realized that we had to find a better balance.

We started looking at all the aspects of our lives and stopped focusing just on being a family with a special needs child, a family in crisis.

Father: Life works better for us when we remember to take care of ourselves and also keep all the "normal" family things and "normal" kid things, like playing, eating meals together, walking in the park, going on outings — you know, things that everybody else does — going on.

Taking care of our son's special needs is important, real important, but it isn't our whole life. There are a lot of other things that we need to keep going, and we have to keep sight of those things and defend like the dickens our rights to keep our lives in balance.

The more serious a child's condition, the more parents have to remind themselves to pay attention to their own personal needs, spouses, and other children. Therapies and special programs are important, but there is more to life than focusing on one child's disabilities. The more time a family spends enjoying being together and meeting their own and each other's various needs, the higher the likelihood that the family will stay intact and be able to provide a rich, loving, and consistent environment for children to develop both their "normal" and exceptional aspects.

Answer 6:
Don't give up!

Robert: Don't give up! Just hang in there and keep giving it your best.

Mary: You can't let it get you down. We had our days when we were depressed, but if you let it weigh at you, eventually it will eat you up. If you don't get the services you feel your child needs, keep trying until you do. Don't lose your faith because, I mean, that's all you have sometimes.

They're just kids, and if their parents aren't going to have faith, aren't going to fight for them, then who is? I ask you, who's going to fight for a kid if his own parents won't? Nobody! You can't just say, "Well, I did my best, and it didn't work. That's it." You can't do that.

Don't listen to the doubters because it won't get you anywhere. Just have faith in your child and yourself, and do the most you can, as soon as you can, to teach them. Just get right down to it and start giving and giving. The more you expect from them and the more you give, the further they'll go.

The don't-give-up philosophy Robert and Mary expressed is closely related to other, more specific, advice, other parents gave:

"Always get a second opinion, and maybe even a third."

"Know your rights, and make sure the schools know that you know them and you get what you deserve."

"Dig out the answers. Talk to people, read, and study."

"Fight your fears or they'll paralyze you and nothing will get done."

"Be patient. Just keep working at it, minute by minute, day by day, and year by year."

"Keep praying. There are lots of miracles left to happen in this world, and most of those are reserved for people who work hard and pray hard."

Each recommendation is a bit different, yet all are tied together by an underlying message: don't give up.

Answer 7:
Take it one day at a time.

Leah: Just take each day as it comes, each hour as it comes, and try to do your best and try to get the most out of it that you can. There are days I feel 90 years old, believe me. It's so funny. Maybe *funny* is the wrong word. Anyway, one day someone asked me if I ever sat down. I had to really think hard about it. The answer was no.

The only way I can deal with it is by taking each day as it comes. Easier said than done, I know, because you always worry about things, and no matter what you're doing, there's always this long, long list of things that are waiting to be done. It's hard to do, but you have to. If you put too much thought into what lies ahead, like tomorrow or next week or next year, you'd be paralyzed. If I looked ahead, I'd just see work, work, work, and that would be hard to face.

John: Sometimes you have to fight to keep your mind focused, to do what you have to do day to day. You have to block out other things that are trying to sap your attention and energy, things like bills and will this doctor or that doctor be right and will all these hours of therapy make that much difference. If you don't block them out, you can just sit there immobilized, unable to do anything. It's like you're in the middle of a storm or something, and all this stuff is happening around you — or, really, in your head — and you're sort of getting swept away or pulled in or something. You have to experience the moment, appreciate the good things you have and try not to worry about the future. You've just got to put your worries aside and just do what you've got to do, dig in and do the best you can, day to day, and have faith that if you give it your best, things will work themselves out.

The parents quoted in this section, as well as most of the parents interviewed, were well aware of the difficulties that lay ahead of them. Many were aware that their children may not live into adulthood, and others could envision the need someday to place their children in out-of-home, residential, full-time, or partial care. Their philosophies of taking one day at a time and refusing to give up are not based in denial or refusal to accept what is or might be, but rational, well thought-out approaches to dealing with difficult problems.

Answer 8:
Love and faith will give you the strength to succeed.

Candy: As soon as I saw her, I had a feeling going through me like I never felt before. The minute I saw her face and those tiny little hands and feet, the minute I touched her, I thought my heart was going to explode. I couldn't stop crying. Holding her on my chest, feeling her, so little and so helpless. I knew then that we were forever.

She thrived really good when she was little. She was the healthiest baby in the intensive care nursery. She had some breathing problems, but she was happy and grew real fast. They couldn't believe how good she did. She wasn't cranky — a lot of the babies there cry a lot — and she was just a joy.

I have a theory. I think it was our love connection that made her do so good. Most of the babies there spent almost all the time in the isoletes — you know, those little incubator things they keep them in. Not Connie. I was in there all the time, holding her as much as I could and talking with her, loving her up. I never had any doubt that she was going to make it, and I wanted to give her everything I could right away, right from the start.

If you've got a kid with special needs, you've got to love that kid with everything you've got. With all the problems, worry, bills, learning problems, and such, if that kid isn't more important than anything else, then you won't make it. You'll probably make the kid pay back for it in some way, and that gets messy. Because, see, I've seen parents make kids pay for it. I've seen them upset and angry because they thought or felt like they were giving too much and weren't getting it back. When you feel that way, you end up making the kid pay for it, and that's real nasty. So you've got to get your love connection real strong.

Candy's advice is clear and simple: love your child as much as or more than you love yourself. Why? Because if you don't, the burdens involved in raising your child may seem to outweigh the rewards. When this occurs, the parent-child relationship may suffer serious damage.

Claire agrees with Candy's advice but adds another variable that she regards as critical: faith.

Claire: Parents need to have faith. If you don't think what you're doing — all your work and worry and running around and caring — if you don't think it's going to matter, it would be real hard to keep it up. I've seen a lot of people the past couple of years, since Seth was born, people who didn't really think they could do anything to help their kids. They went through the motions, took them to the doctors and therapists and such, but when you'd talk to them, you could tell that they were just doing it to do it. They didn't really think it would make a difference. You won't last long with that attitude. If you don't think it matters, then why do it?

I believe what we're doing will make a difference. I believe that my little boy came to this earth for a reason, that he belongs here. I don't think he's here to take up space or just lie in a bed in some institution somewhere. I think he's somehow here to make the world a better place. It's faith. Faith in him and faith in everything.

A profound yet obvious truth is that no parents, no people could possibly face the vast array of challenges, stresses, and difficulties described in this book without a deep sense of love for their children and faith that their efforts will eventually yield positive results. Without the feelings of attachment and devotion upon which love is based, few could give so much of themselves or dedicate so many years of their life; without the belief and trust that form the heart of faith, that efforts reap rewards, not many would invest so much in such a high-risk venture as raising a young child with exceptional needs.

Conclusion

There are no better guides than those who have traveled the road themselves; those who know the terrain can point out its beauties and warn of upcoming hazards. The families who have shared their experiences in these pages have all traveled the road of raising young children with exceptional needs. We hope their varied perspectives and experiences have pointed out a number of the many beautiful views that may lie along the way and forewarned of some of the more dangerous obstacles that may need to be overcome.

Remember the final words of advice of those who have traveled the road:

- Get help early.
- Develop support systems as soon as possible.
- Join a parent support group.
- Whatever disabilities they might have, children are first and foremost children; treat them as "normally" as you can.
- Keep your life in balance.
- Don't give up.
- Take it one day at a time.
- Love and faith will give you the strength to succeed.

Remember these words of advice, and the journey will be both easier and more joyous.

Organizations Dealing With Disabilities

Adoptive and Foster Parents of Fetal Alcohol Syndrome (FAS) and Drug-affected Children
(201) 261-1450

Aiding Mothers and Fathers Experiencing Neonatal Death (AMEND)
(314) 487-7582

Alexander Graham Bell Association for the Deaf
(202) 337-5220

American Association of Kidney Patients (AAKP)
1-800-749-2257

American Brain Tumor Association (ABTA)
1-800-886-2282

American Cancer Society
(212) 726-3030

American Cleft Palate Education Foundation
1-800-242-5338

American Council of the Blind
1-800-424-8666

American Diabetes Association
1-800-232-3472

American Foundation for the Blind
1-800-232-5463

American Kidney Fund
1-800-638-8299

American Liver Foundation
1-800-223-0179

American Society for Deaf Children
1-800-942-ASDC (voice or TDD)

Association for Children and Adults With Learning Disabilities
(412) 342-1515

Association for Retarded Citizens (ARC)
    1-800-433-5255

Association of Birth Defect Children
    (407) 629-1466

Attention Deficit Disorder Association (ADDA)
    1-800-487-2282

Attention Deficit Information Network, Inc. (AD-IN)
    (508) 747-5180

Autism Network International (ANI)
    P.O. Box 1545
    Lawrence, KS 66044

Autism Society of America
    (301) 565-0834

Beckwith-Wiedemann Support Network
    (313) 973-0263

Better Hearing Institute Hearing Helpline
    1-800-327-9355

Bone Marrow Transplant Family Support Group
    (203) 646-2836

Brain Tumor Society
    (617) 243-4229

Cancer Information Service National Line
    1-800-4-CANCER

Candlelighters Childhood Cancer Foundation
    1-800-366-2223

Center for Special Ed Technology Information Exchange
    1-800-873-8255

Children With Attention Deficit Disorder (CHADD)
    (305) 587-3700

Children's PKU Network
    (619) 587-9421

Cornelia De Lange Syndrome Foundation
    1-800-223-8355

Council for Exceptional Children
    (703) 620-3660

Council of Families With Visual Impairments
   (216) 381-1822

Cri du Chat Society
   (913) 469-8900

Cystic Fibrosis Foundation
   1-800-344-4823

Disability Information and Referral Service (DIRS)
   1-800-255-3477

Dystonia Medical Research Foundation
   (213) 852-1630

Epilepsy Foundation of America
   1-800-332-1000

Exceptional Parent Magazine
   1-800-247-8080

Family Centered HIV Project
   (301) 654-6549

Fetal Alcohol Network
   (215) 384-1133

Fibromyalgia Network
   (805) 631-1950

Foundation for Children With Learning Disabilities
   (212) 687-7211

Fragile X Association of America
   (312) 702-6487

Freeman-Sheldon Parent Support Group
   (801) 364-7060

Graves Disease
   (904) 724-0770

Hemifacial Microsomia/Goldenhar Syndrome Family Support Network
   (215) 677-4787

Hydrocephalus Association
   (415) 776-4713

Hydrocephalus Parent Support Group
(619) 282-1070

Immune Deficiency Foundation
(410) 461-3127

International Association of Parents of Deaf
(202) 337-5200

International Polio Network
(314) 534-0475

International Rett Syndrome Association (IRSA)
(301) 248-7031

International Shriners Headquarters
1-800-237-5055

Juvenile Diabetes Foundation International
1-800-233-1138

Klinefelter Syndrome and Associates
P.O. Box 119
Roseville, CA 95661-0119

Lactic Acidosis Support Group
(303) 287-4953

Learning Disabilities Association of America
(412) 341-1515

Legal Center
1-800-288-1376 (voice or TTY)

Lung Line (lung disorders, allergies)
1-800-222-5864

March of Dimes Birth Defects Foundation
(914) 428-7100

Mental Retardation Association of America
(801) 328-1575

Mothers United for Moral Support (MUMS)
(414) 336-5333

Muscular Dystrophy Association
   (212) 586-0808

National Association for Hearing and Speech Action
   1-800-638-TALK (voice or TDD)

National Association for Parents of Visually Impaired
   1-800-562-6265

National Association for Sickle Cell Disease
   1-800-421-8453

National Association for the Deaf
   (301) 587-1789 (TTY); (301) 587-1788 (voice)

National Association for Ventilator Dependent Individuals
P.O. Box 3666
Erie, PA 16508

National Association of People With AIDS
   (202) 898-0414

National Ataxis Foundation
   (612) 473-7666

National AT&T Special Needs Center
   1-800-233-1222 (voice); 1-800-833-3232 (TDD)
National Captioning Institute
   1-800-533-9673

National Center for Stuttering
   1-800-221-2483

National Cleft Palate Association
   1-800-242-5338

National Committee for Citizens in Education
   1-800-NETWORK

National Down Syndrome Congress
   1-800-232-6372

National Down Syndrome Society
   1-800-221-4602

National Easter Seal Society
   1-800-221-6827

National Foundation for the Chemically Hypersensitive
   (517) 697-3989

National Fragile X Foundation
   1-800-688-8765

National Head Injury Foundation
    1-800-444-NHIF

National Health Information Clearinghouse
    1-800-336-4797

National Hearing Aid Society
    1-800-521-5247

National Hemophilia Foundation
    1-800-42-HANDI

National Hydrocephalus Foundation
    (815) 467-6548

National Information Center for Orphan Drugs and Rare Diseases
    1-800-336-4797

National Information Center on Deafness
    (202) 651-5051 (voice); (202) 651-5052 (TDD)

National Information System for Health Related Services
    1-800-922-9234

National Kidney Foundation
    (212) 889-2210

National Marfan Foundation
    1-800-862-7326

National Organization for Albinism and Hypopigmentation (NOAH)
    1-800-473-2310

National Organization for Rare Disorders (NORD)
    1-800-999-NORD

National Organization on Disability
    1-800-248-2253

National Rehabilitation Information Center
    1-800-346-2742

National Scoliosis Foundation, Inc.
    (617) 489-0888

National Society for the Autistic Child
    (202) 783-0125

National Spinal Cord Injury Association
    1-800-962-9629

National Spinal Cord Injury Hotline
    1-800-526-3456

National Stuttering Project
    (415) 566-5324

National Tuberous Sclerosis Association
     1-800-225-6872

Oley Foundation, Inc. (tube feeding)
     1-800-776-6539

Orofacial Outreach
     (714) 651-6151

Orton Dyslexia Society
     1-800-222-3123

Parent Care (newborn intensive care)
     (317) 872-9913

Parents of Amputee Children Together (PACT)
     1-800-648-0296

Parents of Blind Children (National Federation of the Blind)
     (201) 377-0976

Parents of Galactosemic Children
     (407) 852-0266

Parents of Premature and High Risk Infants International, Inc.
     (212) 869-2818

Parents Without Partners
     1-800-637-7974
Prader-Willi Syndrome Association
     1-800-926-4797

Resource Center for the Handicapped
     1-800-22-SHARE

Retinitis Pigmentosa Association
     1-800-344-4877

Retinitis Pigmentosa Foundation Fighting Blindness
     1-800-683-5555

Retinoblastoma Support Group
     (603) 224-4085

Schizophrenia Society of Canada
     (416) 445-8204

Share: Pregnancy and Infant Loss Support, Inc.
   (314) 947-5000

Sibling Information Network
   (203) 282-7050

SIDS Alliance (sudden infant death syndrome)
   1-800-221-7437

SKIP National (Sick Kids Need Involved People)
   (212) 421-9160

Social Security Administration
   1-800-876-1819

Society for Muscular Dystrophy Information International (SMDI)
   (902) 682-3086

Spina Bifida Association of America
   (312) 663-1562

Spina Bifida Hotline
   1-800-621-3141

Support Organization for Trisomy 18, 13, and Related Disorders
   (716) 594-4621

The Association for Persons With Severe Handicaps (TASH)
   (206) 523-8446

Tourette Syndrome Association
   1-800-237-0717

Tripod-Service for Hearing Impaired
   1-800-352-8888

Turner's Syndrome Society
   (612) 475-9944

United Cerebral Palsy (UCP)
   1-800-USA-1827